RACIAL JUSTICE IN AMERICA

A Reference Handbook

Other Titles in ABC-CLIO's
CONTEMPORARY WORLD ISSUES
Series

Consumer Culture, Douglas J. Goodman and Mirelle Cohen
Courts and Trials, Christopher E. Smith
Dating and Sexuality in America, Jeffrey Scott Turner
Espionage, Glenn Hastedt
Gay and Lesbian Issues, Chuck Stewart
Media and Politics in America, Guido H. Stempel III
Racial and Ethnic Diversity in America, Adalberto Aguirre, Jr.
Reproductive Issues in America, Janna C. Merrick and Robert H. Blank
U.S. Immigration, Michael C. LeMay
Women and Equality in the Workplace, Janet Z. Giele and Leslie F. Stebbins
Women in Prison, Cyndi Banks

Books in the Contemporary World Issues series address vital issues in today's society such as genetic engineering, pollution, and biodiversity. Written by professional writers, scholars, and nonacademic experts, these books are authoritative, clearly written, up-to-date, and objective. They provide a good starting point for research by high school and college students, scholars, and general readers as well as by legislators, businesspeople, activists, and others.

Each book, carefully organized and easy to use, contains an overview of the subject, a detailed chronology, biographical sketches, facts and data and/or documents and other primary-source material, a directory of organizations and agencies, annotated lists of print and nonprint resources, and an index.

Readers of books in the Contemporary World Issues series will find the information they need in order to have a better understanding of the social, political, environmental, and economic issues facing the world today.

RACIAL JUSTICE IN AMERICA

A Reference Handbook

David B. Mustard

A B C CLIO

Santa Barbara, California • Denver, Colorado • Oxford, England

Library of Congress Cataloging-in-Publication Data

Mustard, David B.
Racial justice in America : a reference handbook / David B. Mustard.
p. cm. — (Contemporary world issues)
Includes bibliographical references and index.
ISBN 1-57607-214-2 (acid-free paper) ISBN 1-57607-578-8 (e-book)
1. African Americans—Civil rights—History—Handbooks, manuals, etc. 2. Racism—United States—History—Handbooks, manuals, etc. 3. African Americans—Civil rights—Handbooks, manuals, etc. 4. Race discrimination—United States—Handbooks, manuals, etc. 5. United States—Race relations—Handbooks, manuals, etc. I. Title. II. Series.

E185.M95 2003
305.896'073—dc22

2003015194

07 06 05 04 03 10 9 8 7 6 5 4 3 2 1

This book is also available on the World Wide Web as an e-book. Visit abc-clio.com for details.

ABC-CLIO, Inc.
130 Cremona Drive, P.O. Box 1911
Santa Barbara, California 93116-1911

This book is printed on acid-free paper ♾.
Manufactured in the United States of America

I thank my wife, Elizabeth,
and sons, David Andrew and Stephen Edward,
for their constant encouragement

Contents

Preface and Acknowledgments

> Once upon a time in my younger years and in the dawn of this century I wrote: "The problem of the twentieth century is the problem of the color line." In 1925, as in 1899, I seem to see the problem of the twentieth century as the problem of the color line.
> —W.E.B. DuBois, "Worlds of Color," *Foreign Affairs,* 1925, p. 423

This observation of W. E. B. Du Bois may be even more relevant at the beginning of the twenty-first century than it was at the beginning of the twentieth century. Many contemporary issues are influenced by race, which affects everyday decisions about employment, educational opportunities, and presidential elections. The lead stories on television and radio and in newspapers and magazines often discuss the racial implications of public policies or how members of different races perceive events in markedly different ways.

Because the topic of racial justice is both broad and complex, any book must necessarily limit the scope of topics covered, and this one is no exception. This book's geographic focus is the United States, and it will refer to the broader world context only when the discussion of such material pertains directly to issues in the United States. Although the list of situations affected by racial divisions is lengthy, the book will focus on five areas in which the fight for racial justice has been particularly relevant—criminal justice, education, employment, living accommodations, and political participation. By excluding some issues, the book provides a more detailed and thorough examination of these issues.

Furthermore, this book follows the definition of race used by U.S. government agencies and focuses primarily on black-white differences. Sometimes race and ethnicity are viewed interchangeably. However, agencies such as the U.S. Census Bureau and the Office of Management and Budget (OMB) consider ethnic origin a separate concept from race. For example, people of Hispanic origin may be of any race. The histories of blacks, Latinos, and Asians in the United States are quite different, and to give each the attention it deserves would exceed this book's limits. Therefore, this book addresses ethnic justice as a different dimension only when it pertains directly to the examination of black-white issues.

Because many in the United States refused to recognize the full rights of African American citizens, the courts frequently had to intervene to protect the rights of blacks. Consequently, court cases play an integral role in obtaining racial justice and will be discussed where relevant. The book will discuss racial issues in a historical context, show how they changed over time, and examine the current state of race relations in the United States. A wide variety of sources were used for this book—articles from periodicals such as the *New York Times,* the *Wall Street Journal,* and even *Sports Illustrated,* articles from online and academic research journals, popular and academic books, government documents, and court records. Because technological advances have created many opportunities for people to learn quickly about racial justice issues, the book provides Internet references in addition to the standard textual references.

My academic research is focused on empirical studies of policy-related questions, especially law and economics, crime, sentencing, gambling, lotteries, gun control, labor issues, education, and merit-based aid. My research in crime, sentencing, gun control, and labor issues demonstrates the significant effects race has on public policymaking in this country.

To conclude, the more research I did for this book, the more evident it became that although racial justice is discussed frequently, there is no consensus about what justice means in this context. The word *justice* is used to support widely divergent views and policies. For example, some contend that it would be just to eliminate affirmative action, and others maintain that racial preferences *must* exist to ensure that African Americans can fully participate in our society. This book will not focus on only one view of racial justice. Instead, it will present sharply contrasting accounts of racial justice while documenting the reasons supporters believe such positions. Therefore, no reader will agree with everything in the book; each reader will agree with some arguments although disagreeing with others. It is my hope that by reading the book and seriously considering your own perspectives and those of others, you will sharpen your own views on racial justice.

Acknowledgments

Debts of gratitude are owed to Serdar Akin, Marla Colberg, and Jennifer Hall for their research and efforts to compile information, and to David Robinson for reading critically and providing thoughtful responses on many drafts. I also thank Alicia Merritt and Melanie Stafford at ABC-CLIO, who guided the process from start to finish.

David B. Mustard

1

The Struggle for Freedom

No man can know where he is going unless he knows exactly where he has been and exactly how he arrived at his present place.
—Maya Angelou, *New York Times,* 16 April 1972

This chapter will briefly summarize the history of Africans in America through the 1954 U.S Supreme Court decision in *Brown v. Board of Education,* which prohibited "separate but equal" public facilities for people of different races. This chapter lays the historical foundation for the second chapter, which is a detailed examination of five areas of contemporary society in which racial issues have been particularly relevant—criminal justice, education, employment, living conditions, and political participation. These five issues will also be the focal points of the remaining part of the book. More information about many of the dates, people, laws, and statistics mentioned in this chapter can be found in Chapters 2, 4, and 5.

As Maya Angelou implies above, to truly understand where our country is going, we must understand our historical context. Because so many of our current views about race have been inherently shaped by previous events, we must explore the historical context of the forced migration of Africans and their enslavement in the United States to fully comprehend the current race-related issues in our nation.

The Colonial Slave Trade

Unfortunately, Americans have fundamental misconceptions about even the most basic issues regarding slavery. To illustrate this, consider two questions about the slave trade's size and composition. First, approximately how many Africans were forcibly transported to America during the transatlantic slave trade? Second, what share of the transatlantic slave trade did the United States colonies represent?

The most accurate answer to the first question is 9.9 million (Fogel 1989). Most people significantly underestimate the magnitude of the slave trade. The normal response from my college students to this question is tens of thousands; some say a few hundred thousand. Rarely does anyone say more than a million. For a better understanding of the magnitude of this forced migration, the number is equal to the combined populations of Virginia and Mississippi in 2000 (U.S. Census Bureau 2001). The loss of this many people had devastating social, political, and economic consequences for western Africa. Furthermore, this estimate understates the true loss suffered by the African societies, because many more lives were lost in the acquisition of slaves.

The best answer to the second question is that colonial America represented 6–7 percent of the slave trade (Fogel 1989). Most college students significantly overstate the role of the colonies and estimate that America represented about 60–75 percent of the slave trade. Rarely does anyone answer less than 15 percent. Brazil was the largest single participant in the slave trade and accounted for 41 percent. The British, French, and Spanish West Indies constituted 47 percent of the slave trade; the Dutch, Danish, and Swedish colonies constituted about 5 percent.

The history of Africans in America began with the transatlantic slave trade, which forcibly removed people from their homes, usually in West Africa, and brought them to the Western hemisphere. The beginning of the Atlantic slave trade is usually dated 1451, when the Spanish and Portuguese began taking slaves to the Canary, Madeiras, and Sao Thome Islands off the European and African coasts. The first references to blacks in the documents of Spanish colonial administrators date trafficking in slaves in the New World (North, Central, and South America) to 1502 (Fogel and Engerman 1974). Although the share of slaves going all the way across the Atlantic Ocean to the New World remained fairly small through the mid-sixteenth century, the momentum of the slave trade shifted quickly toward the New World in the late 1500s. The transatlantic trade continued unabated until 1807 when the United States officially terminated its slave trade, and it still existed in other New World nations until the 1860s.

The acquisition of slaves was divided into three stages. Slave traders typically were based in Europe and had a crew of thirty to forty people who spent four to eight weeks going from Europe to the West African coast. The second stage took eight to twelve weeks and consisted of traveling along the coast to purchase slaves. This phase often started in present-day Senegal and continued in areas now known as Angola, Liberia, Ghana, Benin, Nigeria, and Zaire. Slaves were typically captured by African tribes and brought to coastal forts before being turned over to the slave ships. Europeans rarely went inland because diseases for which they had no immunity limited their life expectancy in the heart of Africa to a matter of months. The Europeans competed for slaves with a very active trans-African slave trade. The third and last portion of the trip, from West Africa to the New World, lasted about six to twelve weeks, depending on weather and time of year. Slaves were restrained in the ships' holds. In the 1680s, about 24 percent of slaves died in passage, a rate that dropped to about 13 percent in the 1720s (Galenson 1986). When the ship reached the New World port, the slaves were sold. The captain paid the sailors and then could pursue other employment opportunities. The total trip was between four and eight months long.

Slaves in the New World were used primarily in sugar production. The Spanish and Portuguese initially settled the islands in the eastern Atlantic Ocean, but the rapid increase in the European demand for sugar led these nations to extend production across the Atlantic. As a result, the center of sugar production and thus the destination for slaves shifted in the late 1500s to the New World. Fogel (1989) estimates that between 60 and 70 percent of all the Africans who survived the Atlantic voyages worked in a sugar colony. The Spanish and the Portuguese dominated the transatlantic trade until 1655, when Britain entered the slave trade after it seized Barbados from the Spanish. The French also developed sugar production in the French Caribbean, especially in Haiti.

A very important characteristic of New World slavery was the large scale of the enterprises on which slaves labored. Sugar had significant returns to scale—the cost per unit of production was lower when it was produced in large quantities. As the sugar industry grew, small farms were replaced by more productive large plantations. The greater efficiency of these larger farms was due in large part to the use of gang labor, which divided complex activities during each phase of production (planting, cultivating, and harvesting) into a series of relatively simple group tasks that could be closely monitored. Slaves typically worked in gangs of between ten to twenty people who were supervised by a driver. This intensive form of labor was more productive and easier to monitor than distributing slaves throughout the fields.

In addition to playing a relatively small role in the transatlantic slave trade, the American practice of slavery differed in many other important ways from the slavery practiced in most of the New World (Fogel and Engerman 1974). First, slave labor was used for different crops. Sugar did not grow well in colonial America. Commercial production of sugar in the United States did not start until 1795 in Louisiana, just twelve years before the United States withdrew from the slave trade. At its peak, sugar production involved only 10 percent of slave labor in the United States. Therefore, slaves were initially used for a variety of tasks, such as growing rice and tobacco. After Eli Whitney invented the cotton gin in 1793 and cotton production increased in the United States, the basic style of gang labor used in sugar plantations in the Caribbean was adopted for the cotton industry.

Second, slaves comprised a relatively small fraction of the American population. The pre–Revolutionary War peak in the number of Africans in the population was 22 percent in 1770, compared to more than 90 percent in much of the British and French West Indies. Since 1900, the number of blacks in the U.S. population has remained fairly constant at between 10 and 13 percent (See Chapter 5, Table 5.29). Third, because during most of its use of slavery, the United States did not have a crop that had significant returns to scale (the average cost of production decreased when more was produced), slaves generally worked on relatively small farms in the United States. Fourth, blacks in the United States had much more contact with whites than did their counterparts in other areas of the New World. Similarly, slaves in the United States had less contact with Africa because of the relatively small number of imported Africans. Fifth, the struggle to end slavery in the United States resulted in full-scale warfare when it did not in other New World nations (although the slaves in Haiti gained their independence through a revolt, it did not trigger a civil war). Last, in the United States the natural rate of increase in the slave population was positive—slaves were born at much higher rates than they died. This increase resulted from a variety of conditions, including better food, less intense work, and a better epidemiological environment. In the West Indies, where the work was more intense and the climate more unforgiving, slaves died at a rate that far exceeded the birthrate, and slave owners imported many more slaves to maintain their workforce. In 1800 the black population in the United States was approximately 1 million. If the United States had duplicated the demographic experience of the West Indies, its black population would have been about 186,000.

The New Nation Compromises with Slavery

From the very beginning of the United States, the political tension over slavery was explicit. Many compromises about slavery had to be made before the U.S. Constitution was passed. The southern states generally wanted extremely strong legal protection for slavery to ensure a consistent supply of new slaves, and wanted to count slaves for the purpose of congressional representation. In contrast, the northern representatives argued that because slaves had very minimal rights and could not vote, they should not count toward political representation. The northerners also typically wanted limitations on slave importation and did not want the laws of the southern states to be enforced in their home states. The two sides agreed to four main compromises regarding slavery, which are contained in the U.S. Constitution.

First, each slave was counted as three-fifths of a person for congressional representation (U.S. Constitution, Article 1, Section 2, Chapter 5). Second, the transatlantic slave trade was permitted to continue for twenty years, to end in 1807 (Article 1, Section 9, Chapter 5). Third, owners of imported slaves could be taxed to an amount not exceeding $10 per slave (Article 1, Section 9, Chapter 5). Fourth, each state was legally obligated to recognize other states' laws regarding laborers and slaves (Article 4, Section 2, Chapter 5). This was a necessary component for the South, because it guaranteed that escaped slaves who fled to free states could be legally forced to return to slavery.

Although these compromises were sufficient to ensure the passage of the Constitution, they provided only a short respite from the heated debates about slavery. Both the North and South were very concerned about maintaining an equal number of slave and free states to keep political power balanced in the Senate. However, the nation's rapid westward expansion triggered impassioned arguments about how slavery would be treated in the new territories and states. When the Missouri Territory had grown large enough to meet the population threshold for statehood, many anticipated that Missouri would be a slave state, because most of its settlers were from the South. Consequently, admitting Missouri would have tipped the balance in the Senate toward the slave-holding states. Therefore, the House of Representatives passed a bill to forbid importation of slaves into Missouri and to initiate the emancipation of all slaves born in the state. After a bitterly contested debate, the Senate defeated the bill. The acrimony was temporarily resolved by the Missouri Compromise (1820–1821), which permitted Missouri to enter the Union as a slave state and Maine to enter as a free state, maintaining the balance in the Senate. Also part of this agreement was that slavery was forbidden north of 36 degrees and 30 minutes north latitude, the southern boundary of Missouri.

The Missouri Compromise only temporarily quelled the regional divide. The nation confronted a new crisis in 1849 when California sought to enter the Union as a free state. The problem was complicated by the unresolved question of whether to extend slavery into the Mexican Cession, which the United States had obtained in 1848 at the termination of the Mexican War. Henry Clay, a senator from the border state of Kentucky, was a key facilitator of the Compromise of 1850, a series of measures passed by the U.S. Congress.

To maintain an even balance between free and slave states, a series of five measures was developed by Henry Clay, and strongly supported by Daniel Webster, a senator from New Hampshire. These compromises permitted California to be a free state, allowed the question of slavery to be left to popular sovereignty in New Mexico and Utah, increased the legal provisions for returning escaped slaves under the Fugitive Slave Act, prohibited the slave trade in the District of Columbia, and resolved the border dispute between Texas and New Mexico. The doctrine of popular sovereignty permitted settlers of a region to decide the legal status of slavery rather than having it decided by Congress.

Although the Compromise of 1850 persuaded the South not to secede, it created many new problems. The new Fugitive Slave Act prompted such a strong negative reaction throughout the North that many moderates became determined opponents of extending slavery into the territories. The United States continued to expand, and the area to the north and west of Missouri (which became Kansas) was soon large enough to be declared a territory, a precursor to statehood. The precedent of popular sovereignty led to a demand for a similar provision in the Kansas Territory, which in turn generated tremendous violence as supporters and opponents of slavery fought to provide their respective sides with a numerical and political advantage. Congress's many attempts to organize this area into a single territory failed miserably.

Stephen Douglas, an influential Illinois senator, proposed creating two new territories (Kansas and Nebraska) instead of one. Many understood this to mean that the former state would permit slaves and the latter would prohibit them. In May 1854, after an extended and particularly bitter congressional debate, Congress passed the Kansas-Nebraska Act, which established the territories of Kansas and Nebraska. The Act explicitly contradicted the Missouri Compromise, because Kansas was north of the latitude line that had forbidden slavery. Therefore, an amendment to the Kansas-Nebraska Act repealed the Missouri Compromise, further agitating the antislavery movement.

Although supporters of the Kansas-Nebraska Act hoped its provisions for self-governance would reduce the growing tension about slavery that had been dividing the nation, their hopes were dashed. Following the Kansas-Nebraska Act, small battles were fought between proslavery and antislavery advocates for control of Kansas under the doctrine of popular sovereignty. This period was known as "Bleeding Kansas." The violence was perpetuated with the Sack of Lawrence (21 May 1856), when a proslavery mob swarmed into the town of Lawrence to destroy and burn the hotel and newspaper office to eliminate abolitionist sentiment. Three days later, an antislavery band led by John Brown retaliated. Bloodshed and violence continued as the two factions battled. A political struggle to determine the future state's position on slavery ensued. Although the debate was finally settled when Kansas was admitted as a free state in January 1861, "Bleeding Kansas" had provided the newly formed Republican Party with a much-needed antislavery issue in the national election of 1860.

The Growth of the Antislavery Movement and Antebellum Political Realignment

Given our perspective from the twenty-first century, it is difficult for us to understand how slavery could have been accepted and promoted as a social institution. However, our contemporary view about slavery is a historical anomaly. Slavery existed in many societies for most of the history of the world. Very few philosophers, theologians, or political leaders spoke against it. Slavery was generally viewed as the natural order of society.

It took an unusual coalition of a very small group of idealists on the fringe of society, who were able to grow rapidly into a large and politically powerful group, to challenge this order (Fogel 1999). In both England and the United States, the Quakers were the first to take a strong stand against slavery. In 1688, the Germantown (Pennsylvania) Quakers issued a condemnation of slavery, which is considered the beginning of the antislavery movement in the New World. However, it was not until 1758 at their annual meeting in Philadelphia that the Quakers decided membership was contingent on noninvolvement in the slave trade. These initial critiques of slavery were focused almost solely on the religious beliefs of a small group of people who argued that owning slaves was a direct affront to God. The original abolitionist movement was viewed as a radical fringe group and was quickly dismissed by the general populace.

However, over time the abolitionists broadened their critique of slavery from moral concerns to include social and economic concerns. These broader attacks not only expressed concerns about the high death rates of slaves on the transatlantic passage but also about how slave labor threatened the livelihood of low-skilled white immigrants, and about how slave labor would overwork and destroy the land. Although many of the abolitionists' arguments about the economics of slavery were wrong, they became increasingly persuasive in the political debates after the 1820s (Fogel and Engerman 1974).

As the abolitionist movement grew, so did the commitment to help slaves escape to freedom. The Underground Railroad was an informal secret network of homes during the antebellum period that provided thousands of slaves a means to escape from slave states to free states. Although it was neither underground nor a railroad, it received its name because of the swift and covert manner in which the runaway slaves escaped. Slavery was illegal in the North, but runaway slaves could be returned to the South under the power of the Fugitive Slave Act. Therefore, many former slaves went on to Canada through Buffalo or Detroit. The slaves traveled by night and hid at safe stations during the day. The conductors, the most famous of whom was Harriet Tubman, guided the passengers (slaves) and provided them with food and clothing. The conductors were free blacks and white abolitionists, many of whom were Quakers or Puritans.

The expansion of the abolitionist movement also profoundly affected U.S. politics, especially between the late 1840s and the start of the Civil War in 1861, one of the most tumultuous periods in U.S. history. At the beginning of this period, there were many political parties, and the Republican Party, which won the U.S. presidency in 1860 on an antislavery platform, did not yet exist. The Democrats, one of the two major parties at the beginning of the period, strongly supported states' rights and had strong support in the South. The other major party was the Whigs, which articulated a strong nationalistic agenda. Although the Whigs captured both the White House and Congress in 1840, the party unraveled quickly as it dissolved into factions of "Conscience" (antislavery) and "Cotton" (proslavery) Whigs. As the slavery debate became more polarized, the Whigs were unable to make a broad national appeal, and the party collapsed. The Free Soil Party was a minor, but very influential antebellum party that opposed the extension of slavery into the western territories. The Free-Soilers' famous slogan, "Free soil, free speech, free labor, and free men," was most appealing to small farmers, village merchants, and household and mill workers in the territories who did not want competition from black labor. The American Party, better known as the Know-Nothing Party, strongly opposed immigration. Members were particularly antagonistic toward Irish and German Catholics, who were believed to threaten the economic and political security of native-born Protestant Americans. This party supported a twenty-one-year residency requirement for citizenship, restrictions on immigration, and exclusions of the foreign-born from voting and holding public office. Although the party had forty-three congressional representatives in December 1855, it effectively dissolved the following year along sectional lines.

The controversies over immigration and slavery inexorably altered the new political landscape by breaking apart many of these parties. Disaffected former members of the Whigs,

Democrats, and Free-Soilers formed the Republican Party at a convention in Jackson, Michigan, in July 1854. The Republicans, whose strongest support was in the North, opposed the expansion of slavery into newly created territories. The party's founders placed national interests above states' rights and particularly opposed the Kansas-Nebraska Act of 1854. This new party, which included a longtime Whig named Abraham Lincoln, who opposed the expansion of slavery but not the already existing practice of slavery in the southern states, quickly rose in stature and influence.

One of the most controversial U.S. Supreme Court decisions regarding slavery was made in 1857 in *Dred Scott v. Sandford.* This case concerned a slave, Dred Scott, whose master took him from the slave state of Missouri to the free state of Illinois in 1834. Before returning to Missouri, they lived in the Wisconsin Territory, a free territory under the provisions of the Missouri Compromise. In 1846, after his master died, Scott sued for his freedom on the grounds that his residence in a free state and a free territory made him a free man. The trial court ruled in favor of Scott, but was overturned by the Missouri Supreme Court. Upon appeal, the U.S. Supreme Court upheld the Missouri Supreme Court's decision in a 7–2 vote. Chief Justice Roger B. Taney argued that blacks had "no rights which any white man was bound to respect." Slaves were property, and masters were guaranteed their property rights under the Fifth Amendment. This already controversial ruling became even more so when the Court also declared that the Missouri Compromise of 1820 was unconstitutional because Congress had no power to prohibit slavery in the territories.

In 1860, these unstable political and social circumstances led to one of the most improbable presidencies in our nation's history. The *Dred Scott* decision increased antislavery sentiment in the North, and significantly strengthened the newly formed Republican Party. Abraham Lincoln was the surprise winner of the Republican nomination for president in May 1860, when he upset William H. Seward on the third ballot. The November general election for president was also very close as votes were split between the many candidates. The Democrats, who put up both northern and southern presidential candidates, divided their party's vote. This dispersed vote allowed Lincoln to win the Electoral College even though he received only about 40 percent of the popular vote.

The election of an antislavery Republican president was a strong signal for the southern states. In January 1861, shortly after the election, South Carolina withdrew from the United States.

Some attempts were made to dissuade other states from seceding by proposing a compromise that would ensure slavery could exist indefinitely in the South and that new territories would be divided between slave and free states. Lincoln opposed the expansion of slavery into new territories and therefore rejected such proposals. By 1 February, six more states withdrew from the Union. Mississippi seceded on 9 January, followed by Florida (10 January), Alabama (11 January), Georgia (19 January), Louisiana (26 January), and Texas (1 February). The Confederate States of America (CSA) was formed in February 1861.

President Lincoln was inaugurated on 4 March 1861, and his attention was quickly focused on Fort Sumter, in Charleston Harbor, South Carolina. This fort was defended by U.S. troops when the Confederate States of America claimed it. After weeks of negotiations, the United States refused to evacuate the fort and the CSA refused to relinquish its claim. At dawn on 12 April 1861, the Confederate batteries attacked Fort Sumter and the U.S. Civil War began.

There is some disagreement among scholars about the extent to which slavery, states' rights, or other issues caused the Civil War. However, there is a consensus that as the war progressed, slavery and race became increasingly important issues. As pressure for abolition mounted in Congress and throughout the nation, Lincoln reconsidered his initial position of limiting slavery rather than eliminating it, and announced the Emancipation Proclamation halfway through the war. On 1 January 1863, Lincoln declared that all slaves residing in areas rebelling against the federal government were free. Lincoln's proclamation actually freed few people, because it did not apply to slaves in border states who fought with the Union, or southern slaves in areas already under Union control, and the CSA states disregarded Lincoln's order. However, the proclamation was a very strong statement that the Union was now fighting to end slavery, which was legally accomplished after the Civil War ended with General Robert E. Lee's surrender on 9 April 1865 at Appomattox Courthouse and President Lincoln's assassination on 14 April 1865.

Racial Justice during Reconstruction

Although the Civil War terminated the military battle between North and South, it left many issues regarding race unresolved.

During the period between the Civil War and 1896, when *Plessy v. Ferguson* was decided in the Supreme Court, an active moral battle continued along racial dimensions throughout the nation, and in the South in particular. During this era, many laws were passed to address the plight of Africans in the United States. However, because many people tried to implement legal or extralegal methods to limit the freedmen's opportunities, Republicans and abolitionists questioned whether these legal solutions would be enforced during peacetime, and therefore sought a stronger commitment in the form of a constitutional amendment. The Thirteenth Amendment legally eliminated slavery and involuntary servitude within the United States and gave Congress the power to enforce it (see Chapter 5). It was ratified on 6 December 1865; three-fourths of the states completed ratification just eight months after the end of the Civil War. Although three Union states (Delaware, Kentucky, and New Jersey) did not support the amendment, eight former Confederate states ratified it as a condition of restoration under President Andrew Johnson's Reconstruction program. This amendment concluded a series of Civil War emancipation laws, which included abolition of slavery in the territories and Washington, D.C., along with President Lincoln's Emancipation Proclamation.

In March 1865, Congress created the Freedmen's Bureau (Bureau of Refugees, Freedmen, and Abandoned Lands), a federal civil rights agency. This organization was designed primarily to provide five types of relief activity—work for both blacks and whites in war-stricken areas, regulation of African American labor under conditions of freedom, administration of justice in cases concerning African Americans, management of abandoned and confiscated property, and support of education for blacks. When the congressional plans for Reconstruction were developed, the Freedmen's Bureau was discontinued. However, before it disappeared, the Bureau established many hospitals and schools and provided many forms of assistance to former slaves.

The Civil Rights Act of 1866 was enacted on 9 April 1866, to further strengthen the legal and social standing of freedmen (see Chapter 5). Although President Johnson vetoed the act, there were a sufficient number of congressional votes to override the veto. This act declared that all persons born in the United States were citizens, without regard to race, color, or previous condition. As citizens with full legal standing, African Americans could make and enforce contracts, sue, give evidence in court, and inherit, purchase, lease, sell, hold, and convey real and personal property.

Unfortunately, these legal actions were not always effective, and in the midst of significant social upheaval, the laws failed to protect the rights of many former slaves. Sometimes the laws were not well enforced, and when they were enforced, the offenders were often punished lightly. Furthermore, as laws were passed to protect the freedmen, the ex-Confederate states passed Black Codes that circumscribed the lives of blacks. These codes, which varied across states, generally provided the legal foundation to segregate public facilities and restrict the ability of blacks to work, own real estate, and testify in court. Some interpreted these codes as an attempt to re-enslave the freedmen. Others argued that the codes were attempts "to put the state much in the place of the former master" (Foner 1988) or to keep the free blacks as pseudoprisoners.

During this postwar period, southern states and municipalities enacted Jim Crow laws to legalize segregation between blacks and whites. (The name "Jim Crow" is believed to be derived from a character in a popular minstrel show of the 1830s who did a song and dance routine to a tune called "Jump, Jim Crow.") Jim Crow policies were established both explicitly by law and implicitly by social practices. Woodward (1974) maintained that Jim Crow laws established a practice of discrimination. Whites went to great lengths to devise many ways to separate the races. Blacks had to use different rest rooms, schools, hospitals, drinking fountains, public vehicles, and churches. A deliberate and consistent separation existed in even the most basic aspects of life.

Jim Crow laws became a new means of ensuring whites could maintain their standing in the community and significantly restrict freedmen from participating in society. For example, some states imposed a poll tax or literacy test for people to vote or participate in political affairs. These laws disproportionately affected freedmen, who were poor and had extremely high illiteracy rates, because it had been illegal to teach slaves to read.

The first two sections of the Fourteenth Amendment, ratified in July 1868, tried to redress the discrimination and violence condoned by the Black Codes (see Chapter 5). The amendment used some of the language of the Civil Rights Act to make it unconstitutional for states to make or enforce laws that abridged the privileges of U.S. citizens, or deprived any person of life, liberty, or property without due process of law, or denied any person equal protection of the law. The amendment also punished the former Confederacy by eliminating all debts to those states, guaranteeing the war debt of the United States, and prohibiting prominent Confederates from political participation. It also threatened to reduce state representation in Congress in proportion to the number of male voters denied the right to vote.

The Fifteenth Amendment, ratified in February 1870, was also intended to ensure that the freedmen enjoyed legal protection to vote. This amendment concisely states, "The right of citizens of the United States to vote shall not be denied or abridged by the United States or by any state on account of race, color, or previous condition of servitude. The Congress shall have power to enforce this article by appropriate legislation." The last sentence of the amendment gave Congress the authority to enforce voting laws and provided the legal foundation for future legislative acts regarding voting.

Until this point the history of abolitionists and suffragists had much in common. Many outspoken reformers like Susan B. Anthony, Lucretia Mott, Elizabeth Cady Stanton, and Sojourner Truth had long campaigned for voting rights to be extended to both women and African Americans. However, the political support for extending the suffrage to women was not yet there, and consequently women had to wait for the right to vote for an additional fifty years, when the Nineteenth Amendment was ratified.

The Civil Rights Act of 1875, which became law on March 1, 1875, promised that all persons, regardless of race, color, or previous condition, were entitled to full and equal employment of accommodations in "inns, public conveyances on land or water, theaters, and other places of public amusement" (see Chapter 5). Nor could any citizen be denied the right to serve on juries. One of the most important and contentious issues, equal utilization of public education, was excluded from the law.

Many of the gains in protecting the rights of freedmen that had been made in the ten years immediately following the Civil War were overturned beginning in the late 1870s, when the nation's courts started overturning the civil rights legislation of Reconstruction. In 1883, the Supreme Court struck down the Civil Rights Act of 1875 by declaring that Congress did not have the power to regulate the conduct and transactions of individuals. The decision was one of a long series of Court opinions beginning in the 1870s—the four *Slaughterhouse Cases, United States v. Reese,* and *United States v. Cruikshank*—that eroded the rights and privileges gained by blacks during Reconstruction and guaranteed by the Fourteenth and Fifteenth Amendments. These rulings significantly weakened the Fourteenth Amendment's Equal Protection clause and provided the constitutional basis for many Jim Crow laws.

In 1896, the U.S. Supreme Court, in one of its most controversial decisions, provided the constitutional rationale for legalized segregation. *Plessy v. Ferguson* involved a Louisiana statute of 1890 that required all railroad companies in the state to provide equal but separate accommodations for black and white passengers (see Chapter 5). Homer A. Plessy, an African American who often passed as white, was arrested for refusing to vacate a seat in a white compartment of a Louisiana train. He challenged the law on grounds that it was unconstitutional. After losing in the state courts, he appealed to the U.S. Supreme Court, which maintained that the Louisiana statute did not deprive African Americans of equal protection of the laws. The Fourteenth Amendment "could not have been intended to abolish distinctions based upon color," and laws permitting or even requiring separation of the races did not necessarily imply the inferiority of either race to the other. The Court ruled that such laws were clearly authorized by the Constitution under the police power of the states and there was nothing unreasonable in the Louisiana statute requiring the separation of the two races in public conveyances. In the lone dissent, Justice John Marshall Harlan stated, "Our Constitution is colorblind, and neither knows nor tolerates classes among citizens," and predicted that "the judgment this day rendered will, in time, prove to be quite as pernicious as the decision made by this tribunal in the *Dred Scott* case." With the *Plessy* decision, the "separate but equal" ruling became the new constitutional orthodoxy that prevailed until 1954.

This 1896 Supreme Court case upheld the separate but equal doctrine that constituted a major legal barrier to equal rights for blacks for almost sixty years. The *Plessy v. Ferguson* decision encouraged discriminatory laws that eliminated the gains made by blacks during Reconstruction. Railways, streetcars, public waiting rooms, restaurants, boarding houses, theaters, and public parks were segregated. Separate schools, hospitals, and other public institutions were designated for blacks and typically were of inferior quality. By World War I, even some places of employment were segregated.

Two very influential organizations—the National Association for the Advancement of Colored People (NAACP) and the

National Urban League (NUL)—were formed in the early 1900s in the midst of these segregated times. The NAACP was formally founded in 1910 with Boston attorney Moorfield Storey as the first president. This organization represented a change in emphasis from the more moderate approach in pursuing racial justice, perhaps typified by Booker T. Washington, to the increasingly political use of publicity, protest, and legal cases. The NAACP published *Thirty Years of Lynching in the United States, 1889–1918,* and sponsored many speakers to promote its first major national initiative against lynching. Ida B. Wells-Barnett, a co-founder of the NAACP, was one of the most recognized and passionate opponents of lynching. Her efforts to eliminate lynching began in earnest when some of her friends were lynched in Memphis, Tennessee, in 1892. Her friends were owners of a grocery store and had been criticized for taking business from white-owned establishments. As editor and co-owner *The Free Speech and Headlight,* Wells-Barnett published stringent criticisms of this unjust activity. When her newspaper office was destroyed in response to her writings, she moved to Chicago, Illinois, where she continued to write against lynching (*Southern Horrors: Lynch Law in All Its Phases*) and broader injustices. In Chicago, she mobilized an extensive network of African American women who campaigned for racial justice and women's rights. The significant decrease in the number of lynchings was attributable in part to her efforts and those of the NAACP. Some of the NAACP's most influential work resulted from its commitment to legally challenge many ordinances and laws.

In October 1911, three organizations designed to assist black migrants adjust to urban life merged to create the National Urban League. Founded as primarily a New York–based organization, the NUL quickly grew to have national stature. The first directors, George Haynes and Eugene Kinckle Jones, developed programs and structures applicable to cities throughout the country. One of the NUL's priorities was to end discrimination in organized labor and in federal programs. Lester B. Granger, who became executive director in 1941, worked to integrate the armed forces. After Whitney M. Young, Jr., became executive director in 1961, the league became an active participant in the Civil Rights movement, and league branches were established in many southern cities. In the late 1960s, it concentrated more of its resources on helping the underclass in black communities, aiding high school dropouts, launching voter registration drives, promoting community health, and starting neighborhood improvement programs.

After World War II, the influence of these organizations and of numerous other like-minded people and groups helped mount an effective attack against Jim Crow laws in the South. Blacks in the South used lawsuits, mass sit-ins, and boycotts to hasten desegregation. In 1950 the Supreme Court ruled that the University of Texas law school must admit an African American, Herman Sweatt, because the state could not provide equal education for him. This was followed by the Supreme Court decision in *Brown v. Board of Education of Topeka, Kansas* (1954), declaring separate facilities by race to be unconstitutional.

References

Fogel, Robert W. 1989. *Without Consent or Contract: The Rise and Fall of American Slavery.* New York: W. W. Norton & Company.

———. 1999. *The Fourth Great Awakening and the Future of Egalitarianism.* Chicago: University of Chicago Press.

Fogel, Robert W., and Stanley L. Engerman. 1974. *Time on the Cross: The Economics of American Negro Slavery.* New York: W. W. Norton & Company.

Foner, Eric. 1988. *Reconstruction: America's Unfinished Revolution, 1863–1877.* New York: Harper & Row.

Galenson, David W. 1986. *Traders, Planters, and Slaves: Market Behavior in Early English America.* New York: Cambridge University Press.

U.S. Census Bureau Population Division. 2001. Available at http://www.census.gov/population/www/cen2000/phc-t2.html. Cited April 2, 2002.

Woodward, C. Vann. 1974. *The Strange Career of Jim Crow.* 3d ed. New York: Oxford University Press.

2

Contemporary Racial Issues

Chapter 1 traced the history of enslaved Africans from their arrival in America through *Brown v. Board of Education* in 1954, when they obtained the constitutional right of being treated equally by law, almost a century after obtaining their freedom from slavery. This chapter builds on the first by providing more detailed accounts of the struggle for racial justice in five areas—criminal justice, education, employment, living conditions, and political participation. It concludes by defining discrimination, focusing on policy issues, and evaluating the extent to which potential solutions (like affirmative action and racial preferences) would effectively mitigate discrimination.

Criminal Justice

Many social commentators have argued that crime is the next major area for civil rights action. Although blacks comprise only about 12 percent of the population, they are much more likely to be victims of crime than are whites (see Chapter 5, Tables 5.1 and 5.2). This is particularly true for the most violent offenses like murder, in which the black victimization rate is seven times higher than whites for males and five times higher than whites for females. African Americans are also arrested and convicted for criminal offenses at higher rates than are whites (see Chapter 5, Tables 5.3 and 5.4). Black males are held in prisons at seven times the rate of white males, and black females are incarcerated at five times the rate of white females (see Chapter 5, Table 5.5). The reasons for such differences are complex and long-standing.

Although it is quite obvious that the United States has a long history of unequally enforcing rules and laws against African Americans, it also has a less recognized history of withholding protection from African Americans. Randall Kennedy (1997) contended that this lack of protection is far more egregious than unequal enforcement because it has directly and adversely affected more people than have misjudgments of guilt. Society is less well equipped to address it, because it is less obvious, he says. Withholding protection from African Americans began during slavery when blacks were considered property and did not enjoy the same right of protection as whites. Some acts against whites that were considered punishable offenses were either not defined legally as crimes or were not enforced when the victim was black. For example, white slave owners who killed a slave while trying to subdue or discipline the slave were not held liable (Fede 1992), and frequently the same was true for slaves or whites who raped slave women (Genovese 1974).

Obtaining protection from the government was a very slow and arduous process after the Civil War. During Reconstruction there were rampant beatings and robberies of freedmen, and at times the victims were even tortured before being hanged or burned at the stake. Formally organized groups, such as the Knights of the White Camellia or the Ku Klux Klan, carried out some of these offenses. Former Confederate soldiers initially formed the Ku Klux Klan (whose name was derived from the Greek word *kyklos*, or "circle" in English) near Nashville, Tennessee, shortly after the Civil War. This white supremacist organization protested the social, political, and economic accommodations to freedmen. The Klan's members, who were typically adorned in robes and sheets to frighten their victims and to prevent identification in their nighttime raids, used threats and violence to carry out their agenda. Although the original Klan formally disbanded in 1869, a second Klan started in 1915 near Atlanta, Georgia, and continues to exist today. This version of the Klan initially targeted blacks, but expanded its list of targets to include Catholics, Jews, and immigrants. The Klan experienced a resurgence in southern states during the civil rights movements of the 1960s, when it was allegedly responsible for many beatings, bombings, and other acts of violence.

Physical violence against blacks continued during the twentieth century and accelerated rapidly during the civil rights movement. Michel Belknap (1987) documents 210 acts of racially motivated violence in the five years immediately following the *Brown v. Board of Education* decision in 1954. These incidents included robberies, assaults, beatings, bombings, and murders. Although many of these incidents occurred during public rallies and many were directed at high-profile members of the civil rights movement, neither the federal nor the state governments marshaled strong protection. This violence continued throughout the 1960s, as prominent leaders like Medgar Evers, Martin Luther King, Jr., and Malcolm X were murdered, and many others were beaten and assaulted.

During the 1960s, the racial tension erupted in many cities throughout the United States. The Watts Race Riot occurred in Los Angeles from 11–16 August 1965. The event in Watts began when white law enforcement officers arrested two African Americans for a minor vehicle violation. The police car was quickly surrounded, and additional police were attacked when they arrived. The riot quickly spread through the south-central region of the city as residents fought police, firebombed stores, and looted businesses. The riot eventually ended as law enforcement reinforcements from other state agencies and the National Guard surrounded the area. During the Watts Riot, more than thirty people were killed and there was an estimated $35–40 million worth of property damage. In the late 1960s, racially driven riots occurred throughout the nation in cities like Newark, New Jersey, and Detroit, Michigan.

In the midst of racist aggression and police brutality, some participants in the civil rights movement, which had traditionally been strongly committed to nonviolence, became much more aggressive. In 1966, shortly after the Watts Riot, Huey P. Newton and Bobby Seale formed the Black Panther Party in Oakland, California. The Black Panthers captured media attention with their militant rhetoric and brandishing of automatic weapons as they monitored the Oakland police when the police interacted with African Americans. This controversial organization believed that African Americans were an oppressed black colony within a white mother country. The Black Panthers' objective was to liberate this colony, and they demanded that African Americans be given decent housing and education, be allowed to control their own communities, and be made exempt from military service.

Race riots are not confined to the past, but have occurred in recent years. In March 1991, Rodney King was bludgeoned by a group of Los Angeles police officers. In April 1992, when the four officers (Stacey C. Koon, Laurence M. Powell, Theodore Briseno, and Timothy Wind), who were charged with assault with a deadly weapon and use of excessive force, were acquitted, south-central Los Angeles erupted in another riot. In response to the verdict, thousands of people rioted for several days through Los Angeles. Federal troops and the California National Guard were mobilized to quell the riots. The six days of rioting resulted in an estimated $700 million in property damage in Los Angeles County, 54 people killed, more than 2,300 people injured, and more than 13,212 arrested (Delk 1995). Another incident of rioting occurred in Cincinnati in April 2001, after nineteen-year-old Timothy Thomas, who had fourteen misdemeanor charges against him (two of which were from previous fights with the police), was shot and killed by officer Stephen Roach, who thought the man was reaching for a gun (Pollock 2001). The riots, looting, and assaults lasted four days, and the mayor declared a state of emergency and announced a citywide curfew to subdue the unrest.

In addition to urban unrest, race-related issues are a concern throughout the criminal justice system. Allegations have been made that virtually every aspect of the criminal justice system—policing and apprehension, arrests, prosecution, trial, and sentencing—is racially biased. The rest of this section examines these issues.

Race and Trials: The Ability to Testify and Serve on Juries

The right to testify in court is a basic right that many of us take for granted. However, this right was not afforded to many African Americans until the late 1800s. Prior to the Civil War, blacks were prohibited from testifying against whites in all southern states and in several northern states (Morris 1996). Such laws were justified by the stereotypical notion that blacks had a high propensity to lie and that they could not be trusted. This restriction obviously had significant implications for legal decisions, because whites could often testify without being challenged by black witnesses. In 1866 the U.S. Congress passed a civil rights act known as the Freedmen's Bureau Act, which allowed African Americans to testify in all federal courts.

Justice was also impeded by the inability of blacks to be

members of juries. Prior to the Civil War, Massachusetts was the only state that allowed blacks to serve on juries (Finkelman 1986). However, even freedmen had many limitations on their ability to be jurors. Some states, like West Virginia, explicitly limited jury service to white males over twenty-one years of age (Kennedy 1997). In *Strauder v. West Virginia* (1879) the U.S. Supreme Court first applied the Equal Protection clause of the Fourteenth Amendment to jury selection and ruled that the state's law that limited jury selection to whites was unconstitutional. The response by some to this ruling was to continue excluding blacks through more covert means. For example, Delaware argued that only whites were selected for the trial because "the great body of black men residing in this State are utterly unqualified by want of intelligence, experience, or moral integrity to sit on juries" (*Neal v. Delaware* 1880).

Although excluding African Americans from the jury box was prohibited *de jure,* there was *de facto* exclusion of blacks. This ongoing exclusion was particularly pronounced in the South. Stephenson (1969), originally published in 1910 a survey of every county in the South in which blacks constituted at least 50 percent of the population to determine how frequently African Americans served on juries. The responses were astounding. In one Georgia county, composed of 2,500 whites and 4,000 African Americans, the respondent said, "There has never been a Negro juror to serve in this county nor any other county surrounding this to my knowledge. . . . I am satisfied if one should be put on any jury that the white men on it would flatly refuse to serve at all." Some responses, like one from a South Carolina county that had only a 30 percent white population, stated, "We are careful and painstaking in making our lists; therefore, we never allow a Negro to serve for the reason of the general moral unfitness, and general depravity." Such exclusions were typically justified by arguing that blacks failed to meet vaguely defined criteria, which could be interpreted as court administrators saw fit.

In *Avery v. Georgia* (1953), the U.S. Supreme Court clarified what constituted racial discrimination as proscribed under the Equal Protection clause of the Fourteenth Amendment in a state's jury selection process. In 1952, African American James Avery was tried and convicted of rape in the Superior Court of Fulton County, Georgia. Avery appealed on the ground that racial discrimination in the selection of the trial jury deprived him of equal protection of the law. On 25 May 1953, the U.S. Supreme Court upheld his appeal and ruled that although the petitioner may be unable to identify particular acts of discrimination, the jury selection process, in which prospective white jurors' names were handled on white tickets and prospective black jurors' names were handled on yellow tickets, constituted "*prima facie* evidence of discrimination." The burden of proof in such instances falls upon the state, and in the absence of countervailing evidence of blacks actually serving on juries, convictions obtained before juries selected in this manner had to be reversed.

During the second half of the twentieth century, significant strides were made in opening the jury box to African Americans. However, the U.S. Supreme Court has not invalidated subjective qualifications for jury service. Some areas continue to use subjective and vague requirements of "good character," "integrity," or "sound judgment" that can be interpreted broadly and used to disproportionately exclude certain types of people. Kennedy (1997) also argued that the difficulty in enforcing race-neutral preemptory challenges (attorneys exclude potential jurors without having to justify their reason), the relatively lower likelihood that African Americans are chosen as jury foremen, and jury nullification can also limit the ability of blacks to effectively serve on juries.

Race and Punishment: Arrests, Sentences, and Punishments

Racial profiling has existed and has been criticized for many years. Many African Americans testify that they have been pulled over or arrested largely because of their race, especially when they were in predominantly white neighborhoods. Even well-known African American entrepreneurs and athletes have been detained when they have done no wrong. In 1988, police at the Los Angeles Airport apprehended Hall of Fame second baseman Joe Morgan because they believed he was a drug dealer; police officers stopped former Boston Celtics player Dee Brown at gunpoint outside a Wellesley, Massachusetts, post office; and police handcuffed Olympic gold medallist Al Joyner, whom they believed was driving a stolen vehicle (Most 2000). Recently, however, racial profiling has been attacked with renewed intensity.

One particularly shocking racial profiling incident occurred in New Jersey when four young African American males from New York were traveling to Durham, North Carolina, to try out for a basketball team at North Carolina Central University. On the night of 23 April 1998, Keyshon Moore of the Bronx drove three friends to a basketball camp in North Carolina, and two troopers stopped his van near Exit 7A in Cranbury. Within one minute, the troopers fired eleven times, seriously wounding three of the men (Kocieniewski 2000). The officers said later that they had stopped the van for speeding and fired because it began to move backward and they feared it might run over Trooper Kenna. Because the van's occupants were unarmed, the shooting led to an outcry from minority drivers, who had complained for years that they were routinely pulled over solely because of their skin color.

New Jersey is one of the states most criticized for its history of racial profiling. In November 2000, after an extensive study of its policing techniques, the New Jersey attorney general released a 91,000-page report that showed that a systematic process of racial profiling became a routine part of state police operations (Kocieniewski and Hanley 2000). New Jersey officials maintained that singling out black and Hispanic drivers was a national problem encouraged by the federal government's war on drugs, which started in the mid-1980s and requested that local police forces intercept narcotics traffickers on highways. In response to these reports, Governor Christine Todd Whitman made New Jersey the first state to take sweeping measures to stop racial profiling.

Civil rights activists are mounting new challenges to traffic stops by police. Some groups have established toll-free lines for citizens to report their experiences, others have focused media attention on law enforcement officers who they believe unjustly use race as a factor in arresting people, and some have passed reforms through the legislative process (for example, one bill in Colorado in which police officers have to give their business card to drivers they pull over so that the drivers can file a racial profiling complaint).

Although there are certainly examples of individual police officers who behave inappropriately in making arrests, the most comprehensive study of police behavior in arrests shows that police do not stop cars because of racial prejudice (Knowles, Persico, and Todd 2001). Instead, detailed data from vehicle searches made in Maryland indicate that police arrest behavior is consistent with efforts to maximize drug interdiction.

Another important civil rights concern is differential sentencing by race. Since Sellin (1928) examined sentencing patterns for Detroit offenders, there has been an extensive literature of sentencing studies. Kleck (1981) summarized the results for rape and murder death sentences. Hagan (1974) discussed twenty frequently cited papers written between 1928 and 1973. Many analyses concluded that sentencing exhibits racial discrimination (Overby 1971; Sutherland and Cressey 1970). However, others argue that if the severity of offense and criminal history were controlled for in these studies, there would be little or no evidence for sentencing differences (Kleck 1981).

In the late twentieth century, there was an increased emphasis on changing sentencing laws from indeterminate to determinate sentencing. Determinate sentencing provides a relatively more mechanistic form of sentencing, while indeterminate sentencing permits judges to have much more discretion. The most notable example of this trend is the Sentencing Guidelines and Policy Statements of the Sentencing Reform Act (SRA) of 1984, which applies to all federal offenses committed on or after 1 November 1987. These guidelines generated many new research questions about sentencing and race. McDonald and Carlson (1993) concluded that the disparities between sentences of whites and blacks increased after the guidelines were implemented and that the increase was due primarily to choices made by Congress and the U.S. Sentencing Commission (USSC) in the design of the sentencing policy, rather than unwarranted disparities. In contrast, Hofer, Blackwell, and Ruback (1999) maintained that the guidelines have significantly reduced overall interjudge disparity in sentences imposed. Stith and Cabranes (1998) argued that constraining judicial sentencing discretion through the SRA diminished judges' ability to render just decisions in individual cases with unique circumstances. Thus, they support reforms to provide judges with greater flexibility in guideline departures.

In the largest and most exhaustive study of racial differences in sentencing, David Mustard (2001) examined all the federal offenders sentenced between 1991 and 1994. He concluded that after controlling for extensive criminological, demographic, and socioeconomic variables, blacks, males, and offenders with low education and low income receive substantially longer sentences. Second, disparities are primarily generated by departures from the guidelines, rather than differential sentencing within the guidelines. Departures produce about 55 percent of the black-white difference and 70 percent of the male-female difference. Third, although black-white disparities occur across offenses, the largest differences are for drug trafficking. Similarly, the

Hispanic-white disparity is generated primarily by those convicted of drug trafficking and firearm possession/trafficking. Last, blacks and males are also less likely to get no prison term when that option is available, less likely to receive downward departures, more likely to receive upward adjustments, and when a downward departure does occur, receive smaller reductions than whites and females.

Race and Drugs

The manner in which drug cases are prosecuted has also triggered intense criticism from civil rights groups. After the "War on Drugs," instituted in the mid-1980s to counter the significant growth in crack cocaine use, penalties for violating drug laws became much more punitive. The "War on Drugs" refers to a policy to reduce the supply and distribution of illicit narcotics by increasingly punitive criminal measures. This increase in penalties significantly increased the number of people in prison. This policy figures prominently in discussions about race relations and the administration of criminal law because its enforcement has greatly enlarged the numbers of blacks subjected to arrest, prosecution, and imprisonment. At the heart of the debate is the federal law that punishes users and distributors of crack cocaine much more harshly than their counterparts involved with powdered cocaine. African Americans more frequently use the former drug, while whites disproportionately use the latter narcotic. Although users and small-time dealers of smokeable cocaine face more punitive sanctions, more lenient sentences are imposed on those convicted of trafficking in similar amounts of powdered cocaine. The low-income crack user does the jail time, while the more affluent powder cocaine user is allowed to remain on the streets. More than 90 percent of those convicted of possessing five grams of crack cocaine, a felony offense that carries a five-year minimum sentence, are black. This contrasts sharply with penalties for powdered cocaine users, who are predominantly white. The penalty for possessing five grams of powdered cocaine is a misdemeanor punishable by less than a year in jail (Mustard 2001). Although African Americans constitute only 12 percent of the population, they account for about 35 percent of arrests for drug possession, 55 percent of all convictions, and 74 percent of all prison sentences. Butterfield (2001) reported that there were 44,000 whites in prison for murder, compared with 70,700 blacks, and 50,700 whites in prison for drug offenses, compared with 144,700 blacks.

Although the results of the policy are clear, there is some disagreement about whether the results were deliberate or unintended consequences of a policy designed to address the U.S. drug problem. Many contend that the policies had no racial intent and that the sentencing differential was justified because the social costs of crack were much higher than the social costs of powdered cocaine. Crack is more potent, more addictive, more accessible, and causes more social problems. To date, the allegations of racial discrimination have been insufficiently substantiated to delineate a constitutional violation under governing law. Kennedy (1997) argued that it is relatively unproductive to discuss whether the laws are discriminatory, because in doing so, one glosses over the more important argument that the general policy is not wise.

The response of law enforcement officials to these charges of differential punishment for drug offenses has been varied. The U.S. Sentencing Commission and the Department of Justice have conducted some more detailed studies of the differences, but have yet to endorse a significant change in the laws. However, some states have changed their laws. In January 2001, Governor George Pataki of New York proposed a plan that would reduce sentences for some nonviolent drug offenders.

Death Penalty

Although civil rights activists have been harshly critical of arrest and sentencing processes, they have reserved their most severe criticism for the death penalty. In 1997, 42.2 percent of offenders under the sentence of death in the United States and 36.5 percent of those executed in that year were African American (see Chapter 5, Table 5.6). If there is unjust treatment in punishment, critics are most concerned about it with capital punishment because the stakes are so high.

Baldus, Pulaski, and Woodworth (1983) examined more than 2,000 murder cases in Georgia between 1973 and 1979, and concluded that there was no discrimination on the basis of the race of the offender, that the race of the victim was one of the most important explanatory variables for determining capital sentencing, and that racial differences in capital cases are greatest for those in the middle range of severity of homicides. This pattern occurred because death sentences are typically imposed regardless of other circumstances for the most severe homicides, and death sentences are rarely imposed regardless of other circumstances for the least severe cases. Kennedy (1997), however, documented numerous trials for both rape and murder that showed the decisions to be affected by the race of either the offender or victim or both.

Race and Gun Control

The role of guns has been a hotly contested issue in U.S. society in general, and among African Americans, in particular. Although blacks are perpetrators and victims of gun-related injuries at much higher rates than whites, there are pronounced disagreements about what this means for public policy decisions. Some contend that strong gun control would help blacks. For example, Bogus (1993) argued that gun control measures would have reduced the severity of the Los Angeles riots that occurred after the police officers were acquitted of beating Rodney King. However, believing that stronger gun control laws will reduce crime overlooks the fact that the nation's urban areas, where the majority of African Americans reside, have both the strongest gun control laws and the highest crime rates in the nation.

Historically, many gun control laws were racially motivated. From the beginning of the settlement in colonial America there has been a pronounced disparity between the rights of whites, who owned guns at high rates, and the rights of blacks, who were largely prohibited from owning guns for fear that they would use the weapons to gain their freedom. After obtaining their liberation from slavery, blacks were extended the right to bear arms, along with many other constitutional rights. The Freedmen's Bureau Act of 1865 declared in section 14 that:

> the right to make and enforce contracts, to sue, be parties, and give evidence, to inherit, purchase, lease, sell, hold and convey real and personal property, and to have the full and equal benefit of all laws and proceedings concerning personal liberty, personal security, and the acquisition, enjoyment, and disposition of estate, real and personal, including the constitutional right to bear arms, shall be secured to and enjoyed by all the citizens of such state or district without respect to race or color, or previous condition of slavery.

Although this act guaranteed that blacks could exercise their constitutional right to bear arms, their ability to do so in reality was significantly restricted and sometimes completely eliminated just as their right to vote, hold public office, and own property were circumscribed. For example, Louisiana and Mississippi levied monetary or labor fines on blacks who carried weapons without the special permission of the police, and Alabama completely prohibited freedmen from carrying weapons (Cottrol and Diamond 1991).

Having a high number of armed able-bodied white males was clearly important for many reasons—to hunt and obtain food, repel advances from hostile European powers, and to maintain social control over Native Americans, African American slaves, and white indentured servants. The Uniform Militia Act of 1792 passed by Congress called for the enrollment of every free, able-bodied, white, male citizen between the ages of eighteen and forty-five in the militia (Cottrol and Diamond 1991). Although the act did not explicitly bar blacks from participation in the state organized militia, most states in the antebellum South treated it as a racial ban.

Kennedy (1997) shows that the U.S. government has had an extensive history of withholding protection from African Americans. This lack of protection of African Americans permitted or facilitated physical violence against blacks, which in its extreme form consisted of lynching and murder. Having access to firearms often saved lives by permitting blacks to defend themselves when the state would not. In race riots throughout the North, African Americans frequently used weapons for self-defense. For example, in July 1835 a Philadelphia riot was averted when a rumor indicated that many determined black men had armed themselves (Cottrol and Diamond 1991). Also, extensive acts of physical violence toward blacks followed the confiscation of their firearms (Cottrol and Diamond 1991). In Cincinnati in 1841, a mob of 1,500 whites destroyed black businesses and progressed into the black residential areas to wreak further destruction, only to be repelled by blacks who fired their weapons into the crowd to ward off the mob. After the militia took control, it disarmed the blacks allegedly because they were concerned about the African Americans' safety. Unfortunately, immediately after the disarmament, white rioters assaulted the black residents, resulting in more injury and property damage.

Between 1882 and 1968, at least 3,446 blacks were lynched, the majority of whom were in the South (National Association for the Advancement of Colored People 1969). Brown (1971) estimated that from 1767 to 1951, vigilantes lynched or otherwise killed about 6,000 people. Salter and Kates (1979) showed that firearms in the hands of blacks protected civil rights workers and blacks from white mob and terrorist activity during the zenith of the civil rights movement, when many blacks were being murdered. In summary, Cottrol and Diamond (1991) contended, "The willingness of blacks to use firearms to protect their rights, their lives, and their property . . . renders many gun control statutes, particularly of Southern origin, all the more worthy of condemnation." They further argued that "a society with a dismal record of protecting a people has a dubious claim on the right to disarm them. Perhaps a reexamination of this history can lead us to a modern realization of what the framers of the Second Amendment understood: that it is unwise to place the means of protection totally in the hands of the state, and that self-defense is also a civil right." Today African Americans own firearms at substantially lower rates than whites (Kleck 1997), but both commit crime and are victims of crime at higher rates than whites.

Education

> Discrimination in education is symbolic of all the more drastic discrimination in which Negroes suffer. In the American life, the Equal Protection clause in the Fourteenth Amendment furnishes the key to ending separate schools.
>
> —Charles Hamilton Houston

Throughout U.S. history, education has been a primary determinant of economic and social success. Wages and employment opportunities are significantly affected by both the quality and quantity of education one receives. Therefore, whether people from different races and backgrounds can receive quality education is particularly important. In the United States, African Americans have historically been much less educated than whites. States made it illegal to teach slaves how to read and to give them a formal education. Keeping slaves poorly informed was an essential strategy to maintain control. Although some slaves did learn how to read and received some informal education, the black population in general had very little education and extremely high illiteracy rates, which continued even after slaves received their freedom. Consequently, it was easier for whites to take advantage of freedmen in employment, political, or business situations. This section will discuss different educational opportunities by race at the primary, secondary, and postsecondary levels. It will then analyze possible solutions to these differences such as reducing class size, implementing school vouchers, and changing affirmative action policies for admission to colleges.

Primary and Secondary Education

Although it was generally illegal in the South to educate blacks before the Civil War, African Americans also received inferior education in the North, where public schooling for blacks was generally unavailable or available only at a very low level of quality. In Ohio, blacks were excluded completely from public schools until 1834, when the state supreme court ruled that children of mixed black ancestry who were more than half white might attend. Not until 1848 did the legislature provide for public education for other African American children (U.S. Office of Education 1969). In Boston, the parents of five-year-old Sarah Roberts brought a suit against the city to challenge the system that prohibited black children from attending schools with whites. In *Roberts v. City of Boston* (1850), the Massachusetts Supreme Court concluded that school segregation violated the state constitution's guarantee of equality of persons.

During Reconstruction, Congress included the Equal Protection clause in the Fourteenth Amendment to ensure that blacks and whites would be equal in the eyes of the law. However, as discussed earlier, the states and federal government refused to enforce the Fourteenth Amendment or found ways to circumvent it. In 1896, the Supreme Court held in *Plessy v. Ferguson* that as long as transportation facilities were theoretically equal, separation based on race was lawful under the Equal Protection clause. This ruling was extended from transportation to educational facilities. Although theoretically equal, the white and black educational facilities were in reality starkly different. Schools for African Americans were in disrepair, and some were dangerous.

There was little progress in promoting equality in education between the Civil War and the first half of the twentieth century. Gunnar Myrdal (1944) was the first to document the nearly complete disenfranchisement of southern blacks by large differences in nearly all measures of school quality. For example, in 1911, black teachers were paid less than half of what white teachers earned, the pupil per teacher ratio in black schools was about twenty students higher than in white schools, and term lengths were shorter in black schools by three to four weeks (Donohue, Heckman, and Todd 2001). These authors further found that in 1911 only 16 percent of black teachers (compared with 35 percent of white teachers) had at least two years of postsecondary education, and significantly fewer black teachers had state certification than white teachers. Basic teaching supplies like textbooks, chalkboards, and other educational resources were often very old or missing altogether.

Black levels of education increased between 1910 and 1930, but grew in tandem with white education levels, and the black-white education gap remained large. However, between 1930 and 1960, significant progress was made in narrowing this gap between the races. Donohue, Heckman, and Todd (2001) show that the growth in black education prior to 1930 was largely attributable to significant philanthropic activity by organizations such as the Rosenwald, Jeanes, and Slater Funds. The migration of blacks from rural to urban areas in the South did not affect the racial gap, but the migration from the South to the North narrowed the difference. The study's key finding, however, is that the most significant factor influencing the rapid closing of the racial education chasm between 1930 and 1960 was the commitment of civil rights organizations in filing numerous civil lawsuits—social activism played a substantial role in ameliorating the racial disparities in education. Legal complaints were regularly filed to force states to open their educational institutions to African Americans. One of the central figures in this struggle was Charles Hamilton Houston, the first African American attorney to win a case before the U.S. Supreme Court. Deeply concerned about the stark educational disparities between blacks and whites, Houston mentored many young attorneys to fight for basic rights for African Americans. His quotation at the beginning of this section correctly shows that the key to opening educational opportunities to blacks was ending segregated schools.

The turning point in providing greater educational access to African Americans was the 1954 U.S. Supreme Court case *Brown v. Board of Education of Topeka, Kansas.* In this case, the National Association for the Advancement of Colored People (NAACP) Legal Defense and Educational Fund sought to remove the constitutional obstacles to integrating schools by overturning *Plessy v. Ferguson*. The lead counselor was Thurgood Marshall, one protégés, who would later become the first African American justice on the U.S. Supreme Court. To show that the racial injustice in education was widespread throughout the nation, Marshall and the NAACP initiated suits in Delaware, Kansas, South Carolina, and Virginia. These four cases were consolidated under the Kansas complaint. In one of the most notable legal cases in the history of U.S. jurisprudence, the Supreme Court unanimously reversed *Plessy,* arguing that the doctrine of "separate but equal" has no place in education. Because separate educational facilities based on race were inherently unequal, the Court ruled that African Americans had been deprived of the equal protection guaranteed by the Fourteenth Amendment.

Although this was a critical legal victory for establishing racial justice in education, the job was unfinished. States that integrated their educational institutions often faced passionate protests by whites that sometimes turned violent. The first African American children to integrate schools were often the subject of incessant antagonism and sometimes endured physical threats. Some states responded extremely slowly to the mandate to desegregate schools and maintained the dual systems based on race. Mississippi, which preserved its dual system for many years after *Brown,* was one of the most egregious offenders. In October 1969, the U.S. Supreme Court unanimously declared in *Alexander v. Holmes County Board of Education* that Mississippi's racially distinct school districts had to be eliminated immediately and replaced by integrated systems. *Alexander* marked a significant change in the Court's attitude toward integration by increasing the pace of integration from slow and deliberate to immediate. It also changed federal policy from an emphasis on desegregation to actively promoting integration. States could no longer proceed toward integration slowly, but were compelled to integrate more expeditiously.

In the second half of the twentieth century, some substantial strides were made to reduce the education gap across races. In 1960, 43.2 percent of whites over age twenty-five had completed high school, more than double the rate of 20.1 percent for African Americans (see Chapter 5, Table 5.7). Since then, high school graduation rates increased substantially for all groups, but particularly for African Americans, whose rates increased from 20.1 percent to 77.0 percent in 1999. Therefore, between 1960 and 1999, the white-black graduation gap dropped from 23.2 percent to 7.3 percent.

Although schools throughout the nation have been integrated for a few decades, there is still a remarkable gap between the educational opportunities and achievement of blacks and whites. The National Assessment of Educational Progress, which regularly evaluates the educational performance of children in fourth, eighth, and twelfth grades, shows that the average black seventeen-year-old is four years behind his or her average white counterpart in mathematics and reading, and five years behind in science (National Assessment of Educational Progress 2001).

Standardized test scores consistently show that African American elementary and secondary students score well below their white counterparts (see Chapter 5, Table 5.8). The Standardized Achievement Test (SAT), composed of verbal and mathematical sections, is the examination that most high school seniors take to gain entrance to college. The differences in SAT scores for blacks and whites have closed only slightly since 1975, when white SAT-takers had average verbal and math scores of 451 and 492, respectively, compared to average scores of 332 and 354 for blacks. Therefore, in 1975, whites scored 119 points higher on the verbal section and 138 points higher on the math section. By 1995, the average score for whites was 448 on the verbal section and 498 on the math section, compared to the average scores for African American students of 356 and 388. Consequently, the white-black gap decreased to 92 on the verbal and 110 on the math. Although there has been some narrowing of the differences, the disparities remain sizeable.

One starkly obvious difference between whites and African Americans is that the latter group disproportionately attends resource-poor inner-city schools. Such institutions typically are ranked at the very bottom of the quality continuum and have led one critic to state, "The education, or rather the *un*education, of black children from low-income families is undoubtedly the greatest disaster area in public education and its most devastating failure. This is doubly tragic for it has always been the official ethic of public schooling that it was the poor and oppressed who were its greatest beneficiaries" (Billet 1978).

Scholars have attributed this difference in academic success to many different factors, which can be generally categorized into two groups—internal and external. Internal explanations place greater emphasis on the decisions made by African American individuals and have been articulated more frequently in recent years, especially by blacks. The presence of both a mother and father figure promotes academic success, and whites are much more likely to be married and have a spouse present than are blacks; and black children are more likely to be born and raised out of wedlock (see Chapter 5, Table 5.9). These "internal" decisions about family structure in turn have implications for academic performance. African American scholar John McWhorter (2000) makes the case for another internal factor that hinders black education—blacks have a tendency to claim to be victims and blame failure on an exaggerated concept of racist oppression at odds with the reality of the United States in the twenty-first century. He criticizes separatism that elevates racial solidarity over reason and morality and argues, "Black America is currently caught in certain ideological holding patterns that are today much, much more serious barriers to black well-being than is white racism, and constitute nothing less than a continuous self-sustaining act of self-sabotage." Prominent scholars like Abigail Thernstrom and Dinesh D'Souza have echoed these concerns about cultural attitudes within the African American community that hinder academic performance.

Arguments that stress external factors influencing racial gaps in educational achievement emphasize discrimination and the lack of resources for blacks. Solutions to these problems often involve eliminating or de-emphasizing standardized testing that is allegedly discriminatory, increasing school funding to attract better teachers, decreasing the student-faculty ratio, and providing better and safer infrastructure in schools. During the second half of the twentieth century, citizens and policymakers implemented many of these proposals, the most apparent of which was increased expenditures on education. Inflation-adjusted per-student expenditure increased from $772 in 1940 to $4,622 in 1990, an increase of about 600 percent (Hanushek 1994). Other educational reforms were instituted such as increasing teacher salaries, lowering the student-teacher ratio, and requiring advanced degrees for teachers. In spite of significant increases in funding for primary and secondary education, a growing body of literature shows such reforms have little or no measurable impact on a variety of outcomes (Chubb and Moe 1990; Hanushek 1994).

The continued failure of public education to close the racial gap led a national commission that evaluated elementary and secondary education in the early 1980s to conclude, "If an unfriendly foreign power had attempted to impose on America the mediocre educational performance that exists today, we might well have viewed it as an act of war" (National Commission on Excellence in Education 1983). During the 1990s, after continued frustration with the performance of public schools with regard to their specific inability to consistently provide quality opportunities for low-income African Americans, different types of educational reforms emerged. First, home schooling, in which students are educated at home rather than in school, increased dramatically. A second trend is the use of private for-profit companies to take over schools in districts where public schools have demonstrated poor performance records. Most schools that have been turned over to these educational management organizations are in predominantly urban and black areas. In April 2002, Philadelphia made national headlines when it turned over forty-two public schools to for-profit enterprises and placed another twenty-eight on probation.

There has also been a large increase in the number of alternative programs such as charter schools, which are operated by nonprofit groups and are given considerable regulatory freedom by states and school districts. Charter schools were designed to provide an educational environment that would permit greater innovation and incentives for performance. In 1991, Minnesota became the first state to permit charter schools when it authorized eight schools. The following year, California authorized 100 charter schools. By 1994, Colorado, Georgia, Massachusetts, Michigan, New Mexico, and Wisconsin had extended such educational opportunities to their citizens.

The most prominent of the new school reforms in elementary and secondary education is the rapid increase in the number of voucher programs throughout the nation. Educational vouchers provide grants to parents who can then choose to send their children to private schools rather than the public school nearest them. Some argue that vouchers are especially helpful for low-income families, because without them, these families are restricted to the lowest quality educational institutions in the nation. Wealthy families already have school choice, because they can afford to move to areas with good public schools or send their children to expensive private schools. Because African Americans are disproportionately economically disadvantaged and among those who attend the worst schools in the country, blacks have much to gain from this reform, proponents say.

This concern about the lack of quality educational options for

African Americans was articulated at a debate between Bill Bradley and Al Gore in the 2000 presidential primary. A young black journalist who challenged Gore's decision to send his children to private schools, although Gore opposed giving poor people the freedom to do so through vouchers, asked, "Is there not a public or charter school in D.C. good enough for your child? And, if not, why should the parents here have to keep their kids in public schools because they don't have the financial resources that you do?" ("Blacks v. Teachers" 2001).

Vouchers have a longer history than many people realize. They were espoused in the late 1700s by Thomas Paine, who proposed giving every family £4 for educational purposes for every child less than fourteen years of age (Cohn 1997). Nobel laureate Milton Friedman and his wife Rose (1980) documented how private schools were the primary method of education in the United States until the mid-1800s, when governments influenced not by dissatisfaction with the quality of schools, but by teachers and government officials, successfully campaigned to increase government control over education. This campaign was quite effective, and by the mid-twentieth century, elementary and secondary education came to be viewed as the responsibility of the state.

In the 1990s, Buffalo, Cleveland, Dayton, Milwaukee, New York City, San Antonio, Washington, D.C., and other cities started voucher programs. Some of these vouchers come from public funds and others are from private grants. African Americans with children bear the largest costs of inadequate urban schools and strongly support the implementation of vouchers. Among African Americans under age thirty-five, 75 percent support vouchers; 74 percent of African Americans with children in the household endorse vouchers ("Blacks v. Teachers" 2001). However, seniors within the African American community, who often head many of the civil rights organizations, oppose vouchers. Groups like the NAACP closely follow the teachers' unions, whose members oppose vouchers because they fear such reforms would decrease funding to public schools.

When vouchers were first implemented there were many concerns. Some critics argued that vouchers would not produce any significant gains in academic success; they would worsen the situation for the students left behind in public schools; that private schools would "skim" the best students and leave the worst students in the public schools; and that vouchers would increase racial segregation. Such concerns have led voters to oppose vouchers in more than twenty states and forced President George W. Bush to eliminate the provisions for vouchers included in his initial education reform package in 1999. After just a few years of evaluation of programs throughout the nation, the data seem to show otherwise.

First, the gains for African American students who receive vouchers are significant. One study of the Dayton, New York, and Washington, D.C., voucher programs, shows that the average overall test score performance of African American students who switched from public to private schools increased substantially in all three cities (Howell, Wolf, Peterson, and Campbell 2000). In just two years of the voucher program, the students closed the white-black performance gap by one-third. The performance increase is more than 50 percent greater than the effect of two years of participation by African Americans in a class-size reduction randomized field trial in Tennessee (one of the most optimistic studies of effects of lowering class size).

Second, students who remain in public schools are not made worse off. Instead, the data show that when faced with competition and the threat of losing students and funding, schools are more productive. Caroline Hoxby (2001), who examined voucher and charter institutions and the students who remained in the public schools, showed that when public schools are faced with competition they are induced to raise their achievement. She stated, "The choice reforms that are currently in place do not appear to generate winners and losers, but only winners." Jay Greene (2001), who studied the Florida A-Plus Accountability and School Choice program, shows that schools receiving a failing grade from the state in 1999, in which students would have been offered tuition vouchers if they failed a second time, achieved test score gains more than twice as large as those achieved by other schools. Schools with failing grades that faced the prospect of vouchers exhibited especially large gains. The performance of students on academic tests improves when public schools are faced with the prospect that their students will receive vouchers.

Third, instead of skimming the best students, private schools that participate in voucher programs have enrolled more disadvantaged students. Compared to public schools, private schools in Cleveland use vouchers to enroll more African American students (68.7 percent for private schools compared to 45.9 percent for public schools), students from lower-income families (38.1

percent of its students are from families with incomes of less than $11,000 compared to 24.3 percent for public schools), and students with only a mother present in the household (68.2 percent versus 40 percent; Peterson, Howell, and Greene 1999). Another study confirmed that minorities are much more likely to benefit from school voucher programs. In New York, 42 percent of the students in the second year of the program were African American and 51 percent were Hispanic. In Washington, D.C., 94 percent of the voucher recipients were African American. In Dayton, Ohio, 74 percent of the recipients were African American. White students accounted for only 24 percent of the recipients in Dayton, 5 percent of the recipients in New York, and 1 percent in Washington, D.C. (Howell, Wolf, Peterson, and Campbell 2000).

Fourth, vouchers promote integration rather than segregation. An evaluation of the Cleveland program demonstrates that a voucher program that includes religious schools makes a significant contribution to promoting racial integration in Cleveland schools (Greene 1999). Cleveland metropolitan area public schools were highly segregated along racial and economic lines. The private schools, particularly the religious private schools, transcended resistance to integration in housing to provide schools that are racially and economically integrated. One very important reason why so many private religious schools have accepted the disproportionately black voucher students is that public schools outside of Cleveland discriminated against these students by refusing to allow them to enroll. In 2002, the U.S. Supreme Court narrowly upheld the voucher program in Cleveland.

An interesting and related criticism about the Cleveland voucher system is that 99 percent of the students who receive the vouchers attend religious and not public schools, thus raising concern that the state is violating the First Amendment by merging church and state. However, privately funded vouchers cannot be restricted by constitutional concerns. The publicly funded vouchers are based on the same principle as all other government transfers (unemployment compensation, AFDC payments, Medicaid, etc.), which disburse money to individuals and then allow those individuals to determine how they will spend the money. Vouchers are one of many examples of government payments that allow their recipients to choose whether to attend public or private schools (GI Bill, Pell Grants, state merit and need-based aid for colleges). Recipients of Medicaid can use their money for services at Baptist, Catholic, or Jewish hospitals. Recipients of Pell

Grants for higher education can use their money to attend seminary, a Bible college, or a state-run institution.

In addition to the benefits already discussed, parents who have had children in both public and private schools reported that they were much more satisfied with the academic programs, school discipline, parental involvement, teacher assistance, and teaching of moral values in private voucher schools (Peterson, Howell, and Greene 1999). Also, parents reported less vandalism, absenteeism, fighting, and racial conflict in the voucher schools. The data show that vouchers for low-income urban students have significantly increased the performance of African American students and have provided a safer educational experience that is therefore preferred by parents and students. Because of their fear of public schools losing resources, teachers' unions and the educational establishment are the primary opponents of providing school vouchers for low-income students and have effectively limited the ability of states and the federal government to expand such opportunities.

College and Graduate Education

During the antebellum period there were very few opportunities for African Americans to obtain higher education. Cheyney University of Pennsylvania was founded during the 1830s in response to the general practice of excluding blacks from institutions of higher education. Two other schools designed to teach black students (Lincoln University in Pennsylvania and Wilberforce College in Ohio) were established in the 1850s by blacks (National Center for Education Statistics 1996). These institutions were part of the group of schools that became known as Historically Black Colleges and Universities (HBCUs).

After the Civil War, educational opportunities for African Americans expanded as funds were raised through the federal government's Freedman's Bureau and philanthropic organizations. Some churches stepped into the educational void by establishing schools such as Fisk University in Tennessee and Talladega College in Alabama. The Second Morrill Act, passed by the U.S. Congress in 1890, required all states with segregated systems of higher education to provide land grants for both black and white institutions. As states were required to provide college education for African Americans, many southern states instituted a dual system, similar to what was in place in their primary and secondary schools, which essentially constrained the choices of black students. Although new educational opportunities arose at the postsecondary level, growth was slow for African Americans, who for many years were restricted from full participation. This was particularly true in the South, where African Americans were excluded from many colleges until even after the *Brown* decision. For example, not until the 1961 enrollment of Charlayne Hunter-Gault and Hamilton Holmes did the University of Georgia first permit African American undergraduates. Like their primary and secondary counterparts, the colleges that accepted African Americans were consistently underfunded relative to those that accepted white students. The pressure to dismantle some of these dual systems at the university level did not occur until the passage of the Civil Rights Act of 1964, which stated, "No person in the United States shall, on the ground of race, color, or national origin, be excluded from participation in, or be denied the benefits of, or be subjected to discrimination under any program or activity receiving Federal financial assistance."

Because public institutions provided limited opportunities for young African American scholars, many private schools, such as Howard, Morehouse, and Spelman, were created to fill this gap. These private institutions and the public institutions designed primarily for African Americans became known as HBCUs. In 1965, the U.S. Congress introduced a program to supply HBCUs with financial assistance and stated, "the current state of black colleges and universities is partly attributable to the discriminatory action of the States and the Federal Government" (National Center for Educational Statistics 1996). In the late twentieth century, Presidents Jimmy Carter, Ronald Reagan, George H. W. Bush, and William Clinton signed a series of executive orders that further strengthened the HBCUs. Part of Bush's Executive Order 12677 established within the Department of Education a board of advisors for HBCUs.

For more than a century HBCUs have contributed significantly to the education of African Americans. By the mid-1990s, there were 103 officially designated HBCUs with about 280,000 enrolled students (National Center for Educational Statistics 1996). In 1993–1994, about 28 percent of black bachelor's degree recipients, 15 percent of black master's degree recipients, and 9 percent of black doctoral degree recipients received their degrees from HBCUs (National Center for Educational Statistics 1996). Total enrollment at HBCUs rose by 26 percent between 1976 and

1994, with nearly all of the increase coming between 1986 and 1994. During this same period, the enrollment of black students at HBCUs increased about 21 percent, which is slightly less than the 40 percent increase in black enrollment at that occurred at all higher education institutions (National Center for Educational Statistics 1996). Consequently, the fraction of black students enrolling at HBCUs dropped while more nonblack students enrolled in HBCUs.

Presently, many universities, especially large state institutions, have relatively small numbers of African Americans. Many colleges have explicit objectives to increase minority enrollment and are competing fiercely for minority students, a commitment that has led universities to do some extremely unusual things. For example, in 2000 the University of Wisconsin (whose undergraduate population is less than 4 percent black) inappropriately portrayed itself to be a more attractive place for minorities when it placed a digitally manipulated image of Diallo Shabazz, an African American student, on the cover of an application booklet. The picture showed a group of students in the stands cheering the Wisconsin Badgers football team and tried to create the illusion of diversity by inserting Shabazz into a crowd of white football fans. However, Shabazz never attended a football game. When looking for a publicity photo to demonstrate the university's diversity, officials apparently could not find an authentic one. The altered photo was discovered when a reporter noticed that the sun was shining brightly on Shabazz's face but not on any of the white faces pictured around him. After an investigation, university officials acknowledged that they took Shabazz's image from a layout of Welcome Week activities and digitally inserted it into the admissions booklet cover in a misguided effort to illustrate the university's diversity.

The role of race in the college admissions process has changed substantially over time. In the late 1960s and 1970s, many institutions implemented a quota that reserved a minimum number of places for African American students. These policies were designed to address concerns about past discrimination by ensuring that blacks were no longer excluded from higher education. The number of spaces guaranteed for minorities was typically a relatively small percentage of the total student body. This quota policy was challenged in 1978 in *University of California Regents v. Bakke.* Alan Bakke was a NASA engineer who had been rejected by the University of California at Davis medical school in both 1973 and 1974. Bakke argued that because his test scores were higher than those of many minority applicants the school admitted, the school's affirmative action policy denied him admission because he was white, and in doing so, violated his constitutional right to equal protection of the law. The medical school's admission office had mandated that sixteen seats in each class of one hundred students be reserved for minority applicants to ensure a diverse medical student body. Bakke contended that had this affirmative action policy not been in operation he would have gained admission to the school, because several minority applicants who were admitted had inferior qualifications. The U.S. Supreme Court ruled that state universities could not establish a quota that set aside a specific number of spots for minorities, because that policy would deny nonminorities fair access. However, the Court added in its 5–4 opinion that a university policy could consider race as one variable among others in its admissions criteria if it was attempting to rectify past discrimination or to promote diversity.

After the *Bakke* decision precluded the use of quotas, admissions offices changed their strategies to retain higher numbers of black students. Some admissions offices gave minority students additional points in the admission process, as they did for students whose parents were alumni of the institution or students who possessed special skills in athletics or music. Sometimes admissions offices divided applicants into three categories—traditional, members of underrepresented racial or ethnic groups, and financially disadvantaged—and applicants were evaluated according to the national performance of their pool (Conrad and Sharpe 1996).

In the 1990s there was a steady movement away from racial preferences in admissions as the courts have become more critical of these preferences. In September 1992, the Department of Education announced that from 1988 to 1990, Berkeley's Boalt Hall School of Law shielded minority applicants from competition with white applicants to meet affirmative action quotas. Investigators asserted that the school divided applicants by race and ethnicity and compared each applicant only to others within the same group. The school denied any wrongdoing, but agreed not to separate applicants based on race or ethnicity in the future.

Three years later, affirmative action programs at all University of California campuses were further challenged when California Governor Pete Wilson told reporters he favored ending race- and gender-based preferences in government employment and college admissions. In January 1995, Ward Connerly, a member of the University of California Board of Regents, supported Wilson and announced that he would try to replace the university's affirmative action programs. In July 1995, after many hours of heated debate, the Board of Regents of the University of California system voted to eliminate the use of race, gender, color, ethnicity, and national origin in the admissions, contracting, and employment activities of the state's public universities. The ban went into effect in 1996 at graduate and professional schools, and in 1998 at the undergraduate level.

In 1996, affirmative action was challenged both in and outside of California. On March 19, the Fifth Circuit Court of Appeals nullified a University of Texas Law School admissions policy that sought to maintain certain percentages of black and Latino students. In *Hopwood v. Texas,* a three-judge panel ruled in favor of four white students who sued the University of Texas, claiming that its law school did not admit them because of their race. The court denounced the use of racial classifications and banned universities from using race as a factor in admission policies. Unlike the decision in *Bakke,* which supported some affirmative action measures, the *Hopwood* case strongly curtailed the justifications for racial preferences. In 1997 the U.S. Supreme Court refused to hear the case.

In November 1996, California voters passed Proposition 209 (the California Civil Rights Initiative) by a 54 to 46 percent majority. Proposition 209 provided that "the state shall not discriminate against, or grant preferential treatment to, any individual or group on the basis of race, sex, color, ethnicity, or national origin, in the operation of public employment, public education, or public contracting." There were many critics of both the California regents' decision and Proposition 209. The American Civil Liberties Union challenged Proposition 209, but the Ninth Circuit Court of Appeals upheld it in April 1997. This movement to eliminate racial preferences in higher education generated allegations of discrimination from minorities who were denied admission to the university system's schools. Critics expressed concern about the decrease in African American enrollment at the most competitive institutions (the University of California at Los Angeles and at Berkeley) in the state system. In contrast, those who supported using the same admissions standards for students of different races claim the program was successful, because by 2002 there was a larger percentage of minorities in the University of California's eight undergraduate campuses than in 1997, the last year racial preferences were allowed. The U.S. Supreme Court later declined to review the ACLU's appeal of Proposition 209.

In November 1998, the state of Washington passed a ballot initiative similar to California's Proposition 209 when its electorate approved Initiative 200 (I-200) by 58 to 42 percent. The approval of I-200 by the Washington voters was particularly surprising given that the proposal was opposed by the popular Democratic governor of Washington, the Washington Democratic Party, the largest employers in Washington (Boeing, Microsoft, U.S. Bank, Weyerhaeuser, and the Eddie Bauer Company), Reverend Jesse Jackson, U.S. Representative Maxine Waters (D-CA), the NAACP, the Urban League, and many others. Furthermore, Vice President Al Gore made four trips to Washington to raise funds and speak out against I-200. Virtually every newspaper in Washington, particularly the *Seattle Times,* whose publisher donated full-page ads worth more than $200,000 to defeat the measure, also opposed the initiative (Connerly 2001).

On 27 August 2001, a three-judge panel of the Eleventh Circuit Court of Appeals ruled unanimously that a University of Georgia admissions policy violated the Equal Protection clause of the Fourteenth Amendment. The university's admissions protocol was to accept about 90 percent of its enrolling class based solely on academics and test scores. The remaining 10 percent were evaluated under a policy called the Total Student Index, in which applicants received a statistical boost if they met any of twelve criteria. At this stage in the admissions process all black applicants were awarded extra points to increase their likelihood of being admitted to the university. The university supported its decision to admit students in this manner because the policy promoted diversity and helped rectify the institution's long-standing policy of excluding blacks, who were not admitted until 1961. African Americans comprise only about 6 percent of the university's students compared to about 35 percent of the state's population. The university argued that ensuring diversity in its student body was a compelling state interest and that the admissions policy would help correct the state's and university's history of racial discrimination.

In contrast, the white students who were originally denied admission and challenged the policy contended that the policy was arbitrary, inflexible, and did not give advantage to those from other diverse backgrounds, such as those who came from economically disadvantaged homes, had extensive travel experience, were from remote or rural areas, or who had overcome personal adversity or social hardship. For example, they argued, a white applicant from a disadvantaged rural area in Appalachia may promote greater diversity in the university than a black applicant from an affluent family in the Atlanta suburbs.

Although the U.S. Supreme Court ruled by a narrow margin on quotas in the *Bakke* case, it has not ruled directly since on the very important issue of constitutionality of racial preferences in college admissions. In May 2001, the Supreme Court declined to review the Ninth Circuit Court of Appeals' decision in *Smith v. University of Washington Law School,* which upheld the use of a race-conscious admissions policy at the University of Washington Law School. The admissions policy challenged in this case was abandoned while the case made its way through the courts, which may explain why the Supreme Court did not choose to hear the case. However, it leaves the constitutionality of racial preferences in admissions unresolved.

Two cases that may provide the U.S. Supreme Court with an opportunity to make a decisive ruling on racial preferences both involve the University of Michigan; one challenges the undergraduate admissions policy and the other challenges admissions to the law school. The plaintiffs argue that the university's affirmative action admissions policy unlawfully discriminates against them because the university places extra weight on being a member of a minority group. The Center for Individual Rights (CIR), a law firm located in Washington, D.C., that represented Cheryl Hopwood in Texas and plaintiffs in the case against the University of Washington Law School, represents the plaintiffs in both University of Michigan cases. Many believe these will be historic cases, and therefore, numerous groups have filed "friend of the Court," or amicus briefs that support one of the sides. General Motors, Microsoft, the American Bar Association, the United Auto Workers, and the National Organization for Women Legal Defense Fund (NOW LDEF) filed briefs to support the university. The National Association of Scholars, the Center for Equal Opportunity, and the Pacific Legal Foundation filed briefs in support of the plaintiffs.

The undergraduate case, *Gratz v. Bollinger et al.,* challenges the university's use of race in its admission process for its largest undergraduate college, the College of Literature, Science and the

Arts, which directed admissions officials to postpone or waitlist nonminority applicants and to admit minority applicants. This case was brought by Jennifer Gratz, an unsuccessful applicant for the 1995 fall term. Gratz had an adjusted grade point average (GPA) of 3.8 and an ACT score of 25; although 100 percent of the minority applicants with the same grades and test scores as Gratz ultimately were admitted, only 68 percent of nonminority applicants were admitted.

The Michigan Law School case, *Grutter v. Bollinger, et al.*, challenges the university's use of race in its admissions process for the law school. This case was brought by Barbara Grutter, an unsuccessful applicant for the 1997 entering class. In the grade and score range in which Grutter fell (GPA above 3.25 and LSAT score of 156–163), 80 percent of the minority applicants were accepted for admission, compared with 8 percent of nonminority applicants. CIR argued that the law school places too much weight on race in the admissions process. For example, in 1998, controlling for grade point average and LSAT score, an African American had more than a 100 percent greater chance of admission than a white student. The admissions data show that in some years, the difference in relative odds was even greater.

The University of Michigan contends that taking race and ethnicity into account in its admissions program is constitutionally protected under the Supreme Court's *Bakke* decision. The university claims that its desires to promote a racially diverse student body and compensate for past discrimination constitute a "compelling state interest" that justifies giving preferential treatment to minorities.

Lending further confusion to the situation is that different judges in the U.S. district courts ruled differently on the two cases—Judge Bernard Friedman ruled that the university's law school admissions policy was unconstitutional because it lacked a "race neutral" process, but Judge Patrick J. Duggan ruled in favor of the university in the case against the undergraduate admissions policy. In May 2002 in a narrow 5–4 decision, the Sixth Circuit Court of Appeals, reviewing the cases on an expedited basis, overturned the case against the law school. On 3 December 2002, the U.S. Supreme Court announced that it would review these two cases.

In light of these disparate court rulings, many academic institutions, especially highly ranked public universities, are designing new alternatives to maintain some degree of racial integration. Some institutions, like the University of California, are changing the emphasis on standardized tests, on which high-income whites score relatively higher than predominantly low-income minorities. Other institutions give extra weight to "strivers"—those who have overcome economic or family hardship to perform well in high school. Other universities give extra weight to students from economically disadvantaged backgrounds. Texas guarantees admission to its top universities to everyone in a defined class rank, regardless of which Texas high school they attended. The University of California, San Diego adds a new supplemental factor, "academic promise and potential in a limited educational and social environment" (APCV), which gives added weight to leadership, community service and special awards, talents, and interests.

Given the confusion produced by conflicting circuit court rulings and the different decisions even in district court cases involving the same university, many administrators will remain unsure of the exact degree to which race can be used in the admissions process until the U.S. Supreme Court makes a final decision. When that decision is made, it will significantly affect how educational institutions are run and will set a lasting precedent in the matter of racial preferences and affirmative action.

Employment and Wages

Closely related to racial differences in education are racial differences in employment and wages—education is one of the primary determinants of income, employment opportunities, and economic success. The racial differences in income have also differed by gender. In the twentieth century since World War II, there has been very little difference in the average incomes of black and white women, and those differences have been very stable. In contrast, there have been significant differences in the average incomes of black and white males, and those differences have changed significantly over time. Just as the educational opportunities of African Americans have been very circumscribed, so have their employment and vocational choices. In examining racial justice, an important issue to consider is the degree to which people of different races have opportunities to work and earn a living. The racial difference in labor market opportunities has deep historical roots in the United States. This section will examine the significant changes in employment prospects and outcomes of African Americans over time.

Employment under Slavery

One of the defining characteristics of slavery was that slave owners owned the rights to the value of what slaves produced. Slaves also did not have the freedom to choose their livelihood, how much they would work, or the circumstances under which they worked. Although the majority of slaves were agricultural workers with limited responsibilities, slaves were not restricted solely to the agricultural sector. Instead, slaves participated in many aspects of southern economic life, with a few notable exceptions like owning land. More than 25 percent of male slaves were managers, professionals, craftsmen, and semiskilled workers (Fogel 1989). Especially in urban areas, slaves frequently had a broader set of vocations than agriculture. For example, in Charleston, South Carolina, about 27 percent of adult male slaves were skilled artisans (Fogel and Engerman 1974). There were often life cycle differences in slave occupations. Young slaves typically spent most of their time in gang labor in the fields. As slaves aged, they often became team managers or supervisors of the many agricultural jobs. Skilled slaves could become carpenters, coopers, artisans, or blacksmiths. A complex hierarchy of positions helped provide incentives to reward slaves. However, whites remained at the top layer of plantation management and ownership.

Changes in Black-White Wages after Slavery

Like the other areas this book has discussed, African Americans made some progress in earnings in the late nineteenth and early twentieth centuries, but that progress was generally limited. Although blacks were free from slavery and could retain what they earned, they still faced large obstacles in being treated equally in the labor market.

Between 1940 and 1980, the earnings of black men increased substantially both in absolute terms and relative to whites. During this time the average real income (income adjusted for inflation) of white men increased 2.5 times while the real income of black men increased more than four times (Smith and Welch 1989). Following the passage of the Civil Rights Act of 1964 and other measures aimed at reducing labor market discrimination during the 1960s, the differential in average weekly wages between black and white men in the United States narrowed substantially from 50 percent in 1967 to 30 percent in 1974, or by about 1 percent per year (Couch and Daly 2002). However, in 2002, black men still made only 69 cents to every white man's dollar, and black women made only 63 cents per dollar.

What factors caused this decrease in the gap between the wages of African Americans and white men? One reason is the large increase in the quality and quantity of education of African Americans. In 1920, the length of the school year for southern blacks was only 75 percent of that of southern whites. However, this gap closed to 89 percent in 1940 and 96 percent in 1953 (O'Neill 1990). Also, the student-teacher ratio, which was 46 percent larger for blacks than whites in 1920, was almost equal with that of whites in 1955 (O'Neill 1990). Furthermore, in 1920 teachers who taught black students received only 55 percent of the salaries of teachers who taught white students, a difference that was nearly entirely eliminated by the mid-1960s. The resulting increase in human capital made African Americans much more productive in the labor market.

Another reason for the convergence between black and white incomes involves migration. At the end of the Civil War about 90 percent of blacks lived in the South, and most of them lived in rural areas (O'Neill 1990). Because the South in general and agricultural areas in particular had experienced significant economic trauma from the Civil War, there were relatively few vocational opportunities for freedmen. Consequently, wages were lower in southern and rural areas than in northern and urban regions. During the twentieth century, as African Americans migrated from the relatively poorly paid southern and rural areas to the relatively better paid urban and northern regions, income differences between the races closed.

A third factor in the decrease in the disparity of incomes across races is a decrease in discrimination in the labor market. There was a significant decrease in racial discrimination in the labor market even before the Civil Rights Act that was implemented in the 1960s, as the wages of blacks relative to whites increased significantly prior to 1960. However, this pre-1960 convergence proceeded least rapidly in the South. Consequently, in terms of income and employment equality, the Civil Rights Act had the most effect in the South and relatively little in the North (O'Neill 1990).

Because African Americans are more likely than whites to be

at the lower end of the income distribution, increasing the minimum wage is often touted as a strategy to reduce racial income inequality. However, the effects of the strategy are more subtle and uncertain than many think. Although those who continue to work after the minimum wage increase goes into effect are clearly made better off, the resulting increase in unemployment (which is more likely to be borne by African Americans) makes others worse off. The unintended effects work against the minimum wage increase, significantly affecting income inequality.

Although the black-white wage gap decreased during most of the twentieth century, there was a change in rate. From the late 1970s until the early 1990s the wage gap between the races remained constant or increased slightly. The difference in black and white wages remained essentially constant at 30 percent (Couch and Daly 2002). Some reasons for this rate change were shifts in industry demand, greater occupational crowding, relative deterioration of skills among blacks, and declining real wages for men. One frequently supported explanation for this trend is that the decline of the industrial sector and growth of the service sector forced many workers, especially African Americans, to accept lower-paid positions in jobs for which they had less experience. However, others believe this occupational change had relatively little impact. O'Neill (1990) shows that the black-white earnings gap increased even within industries and occupations. She instead argues that the wage premium for college education grew faster for whites than for blacks. Why would college blacks experience less wage growth than college-educated whites during this time? Smith and Welch (1984) argue that this may partially be explained by an "affirmative action bubble," which temporarily artificially increased the wages of college-educated blacks in the early 1970s, but was difficult to sustain through the late 1970s and 1980s.

Another explanation is that the earnings of less-skilled workers (defined by either education or occupation) declined in the 1980s both in an absolute sense and relative to other workers (Murphy and Welch 1989). Because African Americans on average have less schooling and are in less skilled jobs than whites, the economy-wide decline in demand for less-skilled workers would disproportionately hurt blacks.

William Julius Wilson (1996) provided another explanation and argued that the change in location of work in addition to the change in the type of work was important for understanding the growing problems of some African American individuals, families, and neighborhoods. The disappearance of work from the urban core during this period and the corresponding growth of employment in the suburbs decreased the types of jobs available to many African Americans. Many of these quickly growing jobs were located in towns that lacked public transportation and were not cheaply and easily accessible from urban areas. Consequently, although some African Americans thrived economically, others in urban settings became isolated and experienced increasing economic difficulty. The ability for blacks to migrate from rural to urban areas and from south to north earlier in the century were important determinants in narrowing the black-white wage gap. However, times are quickly changing as economic opportunities in recent years have become more plentiful in suburbia and the South. Ironically, the ability for blacks to migrate from urban to suburban and from north to south may be a significant factor in closing this gap in the future. The 2000 census shows that this type of migration is indeed occurring as more than three million blacks migrated south between 1990 and 2000 (Riley 2002). Rather than concentrating in large cities, more African Americans are now setting up residence in southern suburban areas.

Following more than a decade of stasis, the black-white wage gap once again declined during the 1990s and is now at its lowest level in U.S. history. For workers of all experience levels it is below 30 percent and for workers with less than ten years of experience it is below 20 percent (Couch and Daly 2002). Recent convergence was due to a number of factors such as equalization in the attainment of education and experience and the distribution of employment across industries and occupations. Years of tremendous growth and tight labor markets have helped raise incomes, especially at the low end of the income distribution. At the beginning of the twenty-first century, black incomes have never been higher, while unemployment and poverty rates are at all-time lows.

Current Labor Market Issues

In recent years some very prominent corporations have settled claims regarding improper conduct toward their employees based on race. In 1996, Texaco agreed to a large settlement, which required that Texaco submit its employment practices to external monitoring. In November 2000, Coca-Cola agreed to pay $192.5

million to settle a race discrimination suit. The settlement awarded $113 million in cash, $43.5 million to adjust salaries of African American employees during the next ten years, and $36 million to implement diversity initiatives. About 2,000 current and former Coke employees will receive an average of $40,000 (McKay 2000). The agreement also calls for diversity in corporate board members and for Coke to submit its employment practices to a higher level of outside scrutiny.

In addition to the improper treatment of employees on the basis of race, some firms have been criticized for improper racial treatment of customers. The insurance industry has been one of the most prominent examples. In June 2000 all fifty states agreed to examine insurance companies to determine whether their policyholders continued to be affected by discriminatory practices that were common on policies sold through the mid-1960s when life insurers, particularly those that did large amounts of business in the South, collected race-based premiums from African Americans. In 2001, about seventy-five life insurance companies were targeted for formal investigations, which led to millions of dollars in fines and reimbursements to black customers. The investigations showed that although there has been substantial improvement, a few policyholders were still receiving less in benefits because of old rules that limited blacks to substandard policies. MetLife Inc. set aside about $200 million to cover expected costs of reimbursing nonwhite customers who allegedly were victims of past racial discrimination by the company. The life insurer, based in New York, has been trying to settle both a class-action lawsuit brought by African American policyholders and an investigation by the New York State Insurance Department.

In February 2002, the U.S. Supreme Court voted unanimously to make it less difficult for workers to bring discrimination cases against their employers. In overturning a ruling of the U.S. Court of Appeals for the Second Circuit, the Supreme Court ruled that the plaintiff does not need to present direct evidence of discrimination at the time the complaint is filed to challenge initial efforts by the employer to have the case dismissed. This ruling is important because evidence of discrimination is often difficult to document at the time a complaint is filed. This ruling applies not only to racial discrimination but also to gender and age discrimination.

Living Conditions

Today we freely make numerous decisions—where to eat lunch, where to live, and how to get to work—without governmental restrictions. Unfortunately many African Americans have not always had the freedom to make such decisions. There were even racial restrictions on whom one could marry, one of the most personal decisions one can ever make. Through the late 1960s, many states had racial restrictions on marriage. In June 1958, Virginia residents Richard Perry Loving, who was white, and Mildred Jester, who was black, were married in Washington, D.C., because they could not legally marry in their home state. After returning home, they were arrested, and in January 1959 were convicted of violating the state's antimiscegenation law. Their punishment, the minimum possible sentence for this infraction, was one year each in jail, with the sentence to be suspended if they left the state for twenty-five years. The couple chose to move to Washington, D.C., and in 1963 they challenged the constitutionality of the Virginia law. In March 1966, the Virginia Supreme Court upheld the statute and the conviction. However, in June 1967, the U.S. Supreme Court unanimously ruled in the case of *Loving v. Virginia* that the Fourteenth Amendment's Equal Protection and Due Process clauses prevented states from restricting marriage on the basis of race. This Supreme Court ruling was binding on the other sixteen states with similar laws. The remaining part of this section examines issues related to housing, public areas, and transportation.

Integrating Eating Establishments

Through the 1950s and 1960s the relatively simple act of eating lunch or dinner could be disheartening for blacks, because they were separated from whites or forced to eat in another area of the restaurant. Even when a prominent athlete like Jackie Robinson was traveling with his Los Angeles Dodgers teammates, he frequently had to eat in another restaurant or have his friends bring him something to eat. The primary strategy for fighting such segregation was nonviolent sit-ins, which took place throughout the nation. The struggle for integrated eating establishments in Nashville, Tennessee, took a significant step on 12 February 1960, when about forty college students, primarily from Fisk University and the American Baptist Theological Seminary, staged a sit-in at

Woolworth's lunch counter. In spite of harassment by whites and many arrests, the number of sit-in participants increased. A biracial committee was formed to address the issue, and by May most downtown lunch counters began integrating.

Similar passive resistance protests began in Tallahassee, Florida, on 20 February 1960, when eleven Florida Agricultural and Mechanical University students and members of the Congress of Racial Equality were arrested after staging a sit-in at Woolworth's. These arrestees were charged with disturbing the peace and assembling unlawfully and were sentenced to pay $300 in fines or serve sixty days in the Leon County jail. Eight of the students chose the latter penalty, which attracted national attention and encouraged other young activists to stage nonviolent sit-ins to promote integration.

Integrating Housing

One's home is supposed to be a refuge from the difficulties and challenges one faces in everyday life. However, there have been many restrictions on where African Americans can live.

Racially restrictive covenants were extremely effective tools for separating African Americans from whites in the housing market. Covenants are legally binding clauses that govern the use of property and can include such things as limiting the height of buildings on a piece of property or preventing an industrial complex from being built in a residential area. For many years in the United States, property owners, developers, and neighborhood organizations placed restrictive covenants into deeds to segregate African Americans and people of other races, national origins, and religions from white neighborhoods. It was not until 1948, when the U.S. Supreme Court heard four cases on this issue (*Shelley v. Kraemer, McGhee v. Sipes, Hurd v. Hodge,* and *Urciolo v. Hodge*), that racially restrictive property deeds were ruled unenforceable.

The *Shelley* case, the first and most recognized of the four cases, originated in St. Louis. When the Shelleys, an African American family, purchased a home covered by a racially exclusive covenant, the Kraemers, a white family, sought an injunction to prevent the new family from occupying its recently purchased home. When the Missouri Supreme Court ruled in favor of the Kraemers, the Shelleys appealed to the U.S. Supreme Court, where the attorneys for the four cases worked together—George Vaughn (*Shelley*), Thurgood Marshall (*McGhee*), and Charles H. Houston

(*Hurd* and *Urciolo*). The Court's unanimous opinion permitted racially restrictive covenants only if they were voluntarily maintained, but prohibited a state from enforcing racial restrictions in covenants because this would violate the Fourteenth Amendment "rights to acquire, enjoy, own, and dispose of property." Because this decision stopped short of ruling completely against racially restrictive covenants, this was an incomplete victory.

The Supreme Court revisited covenants in *Barrows v. Jackson* (1953) when Mrs. Leola Jackson, a white Los Angeles property owner, was sued for damages by her white neighbors because Jackson sold property covered by a covenant to an African American. After California courts refused to award damages, Barrows appealed to the U.S. Supreme Court, which ruled in favor of Jackson and concluded that damage awards would deny the third party's right to equal protection guaranteed by the Fourteenth Amendment. Although this ruling made it more difficult to enforce restrictive covenants, it still did not disallow their use.

The Civil Rights Act of 1968, passed after a lengthy debate in Congress during the heightened racial tension following the assassination of Martin Luther King, Jr., was an extremely important turning point in the effort to establish equal public accommodations. The broad act contained several important provisions that assessed criminal sanctions against those who interfered with a person for exercising his or her rights, such as voting, using public accommodations, serving on a jury, and attending school or college. In addition, it prohibited discrimination in the rental or sale of housing. It was the first congressional act since 1866 to address open housing.

A related area that has come under intense scrutiny is the mortgage lending process. Owning one's own home has always been part of the American dream, and obtaining a mortgage increases the ability of people to own their own homes. Access to credit markets is particularly important for economically disadvantaged people who may be unable to accumulate very large savings. To ensure equal access to mortgages, the United States implemented a variety of laws, such as the Fair Housing Act of 1968 and the Equal Credit Opportunity Act of 1974, to make it illegal to discriminate against disadvantaged groups.

In spite of these laws there have been many claims that blacks are still treated unfairly in the housing market. Yinger (1986) performed an experiment that matched white and black people according to their family and economic characteristics and had them successively visit a landlord or real estate agent in search of housing. He concluded that blacks were invited to inspect 36.3 percent fewer apartments than their white counterparts. Others have shown that on average, black and Hispanic applicants have much higher rates of being denied a mortgage than do whites. Some argue this is evidence for discrimination, although others argue that other factors, such as credit history and amount of debt, account for the disparities. To try to resolve these competing explanations, Munnell, Tootell, Browne, and McEneaney (1996) used the most complete data set on lending, which was from the 1975 Home Mortgage Disclosure Act and was designed to monitor lending agencies and make them report loan information. The authors concluded that although minorities have less wealth, weaker credit histories, and higher loan-to-value ratios than white applicants, controlling for this information does not completely eliminate the gap in loan approval rates between races; African Americans were still rejected for loans at slightly higher rates than whites. Many criticized the research because of data concerns, the omission of important variables, and a lack of information about default rates, which if they were higher for African Americans would also explain the results. In evaluating all the arguments and counterarguments, Ladd (1998) asserted that there is persuasive evidence that lenders in the Boston area discriminated against minorities in 1990, even in the presence of clear laws that make racial discrimination unlawful and market pressures that should reduce discrimination, and concluded that there should be further investigation to test whether there is discrimination at the prescreening stage and in the credit scoring systems used to rank mortgages.

One more recent concern relating to home ownership is environmental racism. Proponents contend that polluting industries or waste disposal sites are more frequently placed near homes of the poor and African Americans. Also, they allege that minority communities usually take longer to obtain cleanups, and when fines are levied to punish illegal dumping, those fines are lower than fines for illegal activity in white neighborhoods. Possible explanations for this phenomenon are that neighborhoods are often segregated and that African Americans often lack the political power to contest such decisions. Bullard (1993, 1994) argues that the inequitable distribution of polluting industries in minority communities is unjustified. Those concerned about environmental racism often cite medical research showing the high rate of illness that people in host communities experience.

However, critics contend that environmental racism has been overplayed. Some question whether there is any relationship between race and waste sites, and others maintain that the causality is the reverse of what the proponents argue—that the sites are chosen in a race-neutral way and that neighborhoods deteriorate because of the location of the site. The deterioration decreases the land's value, and low-income people (who are disproportionately minorities) purchase or retain the land at greater rates than wealthier people. Baden and Coursey (1997) reexamined a 1994 study that evaluated the location of a random sample of hazardous waste sites and found no relationship between the location of hazardous waste sites and greater numbers of African Americans. Baden and Coursey (1997) analyzed more sites and studied the data for both 1960 and 1990. They concluded that waste sites tended to be located in low-population-density areas near commercial waterways and commercial highways and that there was no evidence that African Americans lived in areas with higher concentrations of hazardous waste than whites or Hispanics. This disparity in the research results is also reflected in the courts, where challenges of environmental racism brought under the Equal Protection clause of the Fourteenth Amendment or Title VI of the Civil Rights Act of 1964 have generally been unsuccessful.

Integrating Transportation

Some of the most enduring images of the civil rights movement were the many protests that involved transportation. Rosa Parks, who refused to relinquish her seat to a white man and move to the back of a bus as was mandated by the segregation ordinance in Montgomery, Alabama, is one of the most celebrated individuals of that movement. Parks's arrest sparked the 381-day Montgomery Bus Boycott, which began in December 1955 and continued until 21 December 1956, when the U.S. Supreme Court upheld an earlier three-judge federal court decision that ruled that segregation on a common carrier violated the Due Process and Equal Protection clauses of the Fourteenth Amendment (*Browder v. Gayle*). Although the boycott and Supreme Court decision resolved the contentious issue of busing in Montgomery, they also had national implications. First, the precedent-setting

Supreme Court decision laid the groundwork for the civil rights movement to effectively wield the Fourteenth Amendment against other types of segregation.

Second, the success of the peaceful protest motivated many similar protests in the South. Victory in Montgomery was achieved because of the strong grassroots organizing efforts of people like E. D. Nixon, Ralph Abernathy, and Fred L. Shuttlesworth and the support of advisors like Bayard Rustin and Stanley Levison. In Florida, the Tallahassee Bus Boycott was launched in May 1956 when Florida Agricultural and Mechanical University (FAMU) students Wilhemina Jakes and Carrie Patterson ignored the segregated seating policy of the City Transit Company and took the only remaining seats available in the white section of the bus and were arrested for "inciting a riot." In response, FAMU students overwhelmingly agreed to boycott the bus company. Although it began as a student movement, the Reverend Charles K. Steele and the Tallahassee Inter-Civic Council quickly assumed leadership of the boycott. By May 1958 the bus company had abolished its segregated seating policy.

In 1956, another important bus boycott occurred in Birmingham, Alabama. When Birmingham tried to integrate its bus system, Klansmen detonated explosives to disrupt the integration efforts. When the subsequent appeal of the twenty-one blacks convicted of violating Birmingham's segregation ordinance reached federal court, the commission repealed the law on 14 October 1958 and passed a new one that authorized the Birmingham Transit Company to enforce segregated seating. The new ordinance was challenged a few weeks later, and Police Commissioner "Bull" Connor arrested fourteen blacks, including Shuttlesworth. Connor also arrested three members of the Montgomery Improvement Association (MIA) who had traveled to Birmingham to support the jailed protesters. Connor's response united a number of organizations in a boycott of the city's buses that commenced 31 October 1958. The total dependence of Birmingham's black community on the city transit system, combined with the successful use of police intimidation and a press blackout, caused the boycott to fail. It took a federal court ruling on 14 December 1959 to finally desegregate Birmingham's buses.

The Freedom Riders also sought to ensure equal access to transportation facilities. James Farmer, the national director of the Congress of Racial Equality (CORE), planned a nonviolent ride to test whether the decision in *Boynton v. Virginia* (1960) that declared segregation in railway and bus terminal accommodations to be unconstitutional would be enforced. In May 1961, the riders left Washington, D.C., to travel through the Southeast. In Anniston, Alabama, one bus was destroyed and many riders on another were attacked. The Freedom Riders protested throughout the summer and encouraged many others to participate in similar rides. Their nonviolent protests led the Interstate Commerce Commission (ICC) to prohibit segregated accommodations in November 1961.

Another important result of the Montgomery Bus Boycott was that it helped propel Martin Luther King, Jr., into national visibility as a civil rights spokesperson. King was elected president of the newly established Montgomery Improvement Association, which organized and coordinated the protest. This visibility gave King a platform from which he could articulate his philosophy of nonviolent direct action and keep it in the forefront of civil rights tactics and ideology. As a direct and enduring legacy to the boycott, King in 1957 established the Southern Christian Leadership Conference (SCLC) to organize black clergymen to coordinate local, nonviolent protests against segregation in the South. The organization's goal was to achieve full equality for blacks through mass nonviolent resistance, to garner public sympathy and support for their cause, and use redemptive love to heal America's racial wounds. Many of the leaders, including Martin Luther King, Jr., were Baptist ministers. The SCLC mobilized blacks by organizing and leading marches and protests. Its consistent commitment to nonviolence contrasted sharply with the violence of some southern whites and other African Americans.

King led the SCLC's first action, a Prayer Pilgrimage to Washington, D.C., in 1957, which attracted 25,000 people. It was followed in 1959 by a youth march on Washington, D.C., with 40,000 participants. Dramatic televised "sit-ins" were also used to draw attention to the transgressions of segregation. The SCLC fought segregation and secured voting rights by supporting the Freedom Riders, numerous sit-ins, the Birmingham confrontation with Police Chief Bull Connor, and the 1964 St. Augustine fight against segregation and the Ku Klux Klan. The SCLC was extremely influential in the passage of the Civil Rights Act of 1964 and the Voting Rights Act of 1965. During this period, the SCLC sometimes clashed over tactics and philosophy with the more radical Student Nonviolent Coordinating Committee (SNCC). In the late 1960s, the organization focused on problems of African

Americans in northern urban areas, like segregation, poverty, and housing discrimination. After King was assassinated in Memphis, Tennessee, during the campaign to support sanitation workers, the Reverend Ralph David Abernathy became the SCLC's new leader.

Political Participation

Although their enslavement was terminated with the conclusion of the Civil War, and the constitutional amendments and civil rights acts of the late nineteenth century gave African Americans the right to participate fully in the political process, these rights were often disregarded or ignored. Black Codes and Jim Crow laws introduced new restrictions on the freedmen's participation in politics. After the Civil War, many new restrictions were placed on African Americans' rights to vote and hold public office, some of which were in effect long into the twentieth century. These long-standing restrictions on the involvement of blacks in the political process have had significant impacts on many important contemporary issues, for example the response to the 2000 U.S. presidential election.

The Right to Vote

One of the most fundamental rights in a democracy is the right to vote for an idea or individual you support. Although legislation was passed after the Civil War to ensure that blacks could participate fully in the political process, states frequently exercised immense creativity in limiting the political rights of blacks. For example, even in the early twentieth century, African Americans were prohibited from voting in the Democratic primaries in Texas. When the U.S. Supreme Court in *Nixon v. Herdon* (1927) overturned this ruling by concluding that the Fourteenth and Fifteenth Amendments were applicable to the primaries in addition to general elections, the state developed more ingenious devices. To continue excluding African Americans from voting, Texas gave the right to set voting qualifications to the Democratic State Executive Committee (DSEC) and argued that the Fourteenth and Fifteenth Amendments did not apply, because this committee was not an official part of the Texas government. When the DSEC once again excluded African American voters, it was challenged and lost in *Nixon v. Condon* (1932).

However, this setback did not stop the Texas Democrats, who rewrote the rules to let the State Democratic Convention (SDC) exclude African Americans. When this policy was challenged in *Grovey v. Townsend* (1935), the U.S. Supreme Court ruled that the exclusion was legal because the SDC decision was not an official state action and therefore did not fall under constitutional consideration. The right of African Americans to vote in the Texas Democratic primaries was not formally upheld until *Smith v. Allwright* (1944), almost eighty years after the end of the Civil War. Unfortunately, Texas was not unusual in its efforts to preclude blacks from voting despite their legal right to do so. Although African Americans had the right to vote, many informal restrictions effectively limited their rights to participate in the political process. Some examples of these strategies were poll taxes, literacy requirements, and explicit physical threats to persons and property.

The barriers preventing African Americans from voting were extremely effective. Even as late as 1960, only a fraction of voting-age southern blacks were registered to vote, and in some areas the share was less than 10 percent. The Civil Rights Act of 1957, the first civil rights law passed by Congress since Reconstruction, was a turning point in establishing racial justice in the political system. This act established the Civil Rights Office of the Justice Department, empowered federal prosecutors to obtain court injunctions against interference with the right to vote, and established a federal Commission on Civil Rights with the authority to investigate discriminatory conditions and to recommend corrections.

Additional advances on this front came quickly as voting rights became a cornerstone of the civil rights movement during the 1960s. CORE, NAACP, NUL, and the SNCC worked together to form the Voter Education Project (VEP), which started in the spring of 1962. The Project's objective was to increase voter registration and education, especially in the rural South where African Americans were effectively precluded from voting. Volunteers, many of whom were students, canvassed African Americans throughout the South, conducted literacy and citizenship clinics, and encouraged blacks to register and vote. Whites who opposed these registration projects sometimes resorted to physical violence to dissuade the volunteers from executing their mission. This discord was particularly sharp in Mississippi, where whites jailed, beat, and sometimes killed to disrupt the movement. The results of the VEP were mixed. Although the percentage of southern adult blacks registered to vote increased, the process was both time consuming and dangerous. Even after the passage of the Civil Rights Act of 1964, which tightened provisions to prevent denial of black voting rights in federal elections, there was still a significant amount of work to be done.

Promoting equal voting rights for people of all races was one of the most effective and enduring parts of the civil rights movement. In early 1965, the Reverends Martin Luther King, Jr., and Ralph Abernathy led a march from Selma, Alabama, to the state's capitol in Montgomery. The SCLC enthusiastically supported this march, which started in February. On 16 February, TV news cameras recorded Police Commissioner James G. "Bull" Connor punching a civil rights worker in the face, an image that was indelibly etched in the memories of those who viewed it. Two days later in Marion, state troopers killed Jimmy Lee Jackson. On 7 March 1965, Hosea Williams and John Lewis led about 550 marchers from Selma. After they crossed the Edmund Pettus Bridge on the edge of Selma, state troopers and officers on horseback stopped and attacked them, images that were televised throughout the nation. Selma, one of the most contentious sites of the civil rights movement, became even more polarized when white supremacists attacked three white ministers and killed the Reverend James J. Reeb. The events in Selma quickly spiraled out of control, and President Lyndon B. Johnson requested a meeting with Alabama Governor George Wallace, who was at that time an avowed segregationist. Wallace was a leading opponent of the civil rights movement who had consistently defied federal orders to integrate Alabama schools and colleges. President Johnson nationalized the Alabama National Guard and federal troops to secure the route and ensure that the marchers were protected. On 21 March, about 8,000 people started the march once again. On 25 March, about 25,000 people assembled at the Alabama State Capitol in Montgomery to see the conclusion of the march and hear speeches from some of the leaders. Later that night after the conclusion of the ceremonies, Ku Klux Klansmen killed Viola Liuzzo, who was returning with the marchers to Selma.

This voter registration campaign directly affected national voting legislation. President Johnson had been considering implementing voting rights legislation and was prompted to act quickly as a result of the Selma campaign. Congress approved the Voting Rights Act of 1965 in early August, and the president signed it on 6 August. The Voting Rights Act outlawed educational requirements for voting, empowered the U.S. attorney general to enroll voters, required a federal district court to approve all changes in voting procedures for the next ten years, and permitted the court to lift the provisions when a state proved it had not discriminated for ten years. By the end of 1965, federal examiners had registered thousands of new voters. The combined effects of protests, voter registration campaigns, and new legislation significantly increased black registration in the South.

Many of the affected southern states attempted to use a variety of devices—gerrymandering, at-large elections, more appointive offices, and higher qualifications for candidates—to reduce the influence of black voters. The poll tax—a fixed fee for exercising the right to vote—increased the cost of voting, especially for African Americans who were least able to afford it. Poll taxes were used in many southern states, including Virginia, which required prospective voters to have paid poll taxes for the previous three years before they could vote. Annie E. Harper, a retired domestic from Virginia, was one of many black southerners who brought cases in the federal courts to ban poll taxes in state elections. The U.S. Supreme Court, in a 6–3 decision in *Harper v. Virginia Board of Elections* (1966), relied on the Fourteenth Amendment's Equal Protection clause to overrule the poll tax requirement.

Although the Voting Rights Act of 1965 gave African Americans access to the polls, they continued to encounter obstacles to voting. White southerners contended that their actions were not violations of the Voting Rights Act of 1965 and that the act did not pertain to changes made in the electoral process. In *Allen v. State Board of Elections* (1968), brought by the Legal Defense and Educational Fund of the NAACP, the U.S. Supreme Court ruled against a Mississippi statute that permitted a change from district to at-large elections of county officials. Because the statute diluted the voting power of blacks and thereby curtailed their ability to elect candidates, the Mississippi law violated the Voting Rights Act.

The Right to Hold Public Office

As it took a long time for African Americans to fully gain the right to vote, it also took a long time for them to hold political offices in large number. The protests for the right to vote by Martin

Luther King, Jr., the SCLC, the SNCC, and other organizations were linked with protests for the right to hold public office. Just as whites developed extralegal methods to keep blacks from voting, they developed extralegal strategies to discourage them from holding public office. One prominent example is the case of Julian Bond, the current chair of the NAACP. After being elected to the Georgia House of Representatives, he was prohibited from taking office. Although opponents maintained that this prohibition was solely a result of Bond's comments about the Vietnam War, his supporters viewed it as a racially oriented attack. Bond took his case to the U.S. Supreme Court, which eventually upheld his right to take office in the Georgia House, where he served four terms.

The greatest strides in increasing the number of African American elected officials occurred in local positions for education and city and county government (see Chapter 5, Table 5.30). However, it was not until the late twentieth century that significant strides were made at the national level. In 1966, Edward Brooke became the first African American senator since Reconstruction when he was elected as a Republican from Massachusetts. Two years later, Shirley Chisholm, a Democratic representative from Brooklyn, became the first African American woman elected to the U.S. Congress. In 1972, Chisholm ran for the Democratic nomination for U.S. president, the first African American woman in history to do so, but as such she was not taken seriously. Although there has been significant growth in the numbers of African Americans in the U.S. House of Representatives, there has been little change in the Senate (see Chapter 5, Table 5.31). In 1992, Carol Moseley-Braun of Illinois was elected the first African American woman in the U.S. Senate, but served only one term. In 2000, Mayor of Dallas Ron Kirk ran for the Senate but was defeated. Therefore, no African Americans serve today in the U.S. Senate.

During the late twentieth century, there were also advances in the judicial branch of government. In 1967, Thurgood Marshall became the first African American Supreme Court justice in history. Before serving on the Supreme Court, Marshall had a distinguished career as a litigator, winning landmark cases like *Shelley v. Kraemer* and *Brown v. Board of Education of Topeka, Kansas.* Upon Marshall's retirement from the court in 1991, President George H. W. Bush chose Clarence Thomas to replace him. Thomas, who had been the chair of the Equal Employment Opportunity

Commission from 1982 to 1990, became the second African American on the nation's highest court.

Some progress was also made in opening the executive branch of the government. In the 1980s, Jesse Jackson campaigned for the presidency of the United States both in the Democratic primaries and as an independent in the general election. In December 2000, newly elected President George W. Bush appointed Colin Powell as secretary of state. When Powell formally assumed the position in January 2001, he became the highest-ranking African American political official in U.S. history. The secretary of state is the top cabinet position and the fourth-highest ranking position in the U.S. government. The secretary of state is the president's chief foreign affairs adviser, who executes the president's foreign policies through the U.S. State Department and the Foreign Service. Powell, who was born in the South Bronx, served thirty-five years in the military and earned the rank of four-star general. He is frequently suggested as a presidential candidate, and many polls indicate that he would have tremendous support if he ran for the nation's highest office. Although many Republicans enthusiastically endorsed him for the 1996 Republican primary, General Powell refused to run.

Redistricting on the Basis of Race

Related to the right to serve in office is the controversial issue of using race to redistrict state and national political boundaries. Redistricting occurs every ten years when the new population data from the U.S. Census Bureau are released. By law, each electoral district should include approximately the same number of residents. However, how the boundaries are drawn can significantly influence who is elected. The criteria for establishing boundaries are often vague, leading to many redistricting controversies. After the redistricting from the 1990 census, challenges were filed in forty-one states. The Voting Rights Act of 1965 provides some general guidelines about how to draw district boundaries appropriately. Boundaries cannot be drawn to reduce the chance for minorities to have their preferred candidates elected. Also, race cannot be the predominant reason for forming a district. Instead districts should be based on "communities of interest," which include an array of social, demographic, and economic characteristics. The court also emphasized that voting districts must be compact and contiguous.

Historically, redistricting was used to undermine the voting interests of African Americans—many districts were drawn to disperse African Americans in order to minimize their influence. However, recently there have been more attempts to draw boundaries so some districts have a very large share of African Americans, thus significantly increasing the likelihood that an African American will be elected. Challenges to boundaries based on racial motivations have frequently been challenged under the Equal Protection Clause. In April 2001 in a majority opinion written by Justice Sandra Day O'Connor, the U.S. Supreme Court ruled in *Easley v. Cromartie* that race could be an element in redistricting decisions as long as it was not the "dominant and controlling" factor. Clarence Thomas, the Supreme Court's only African American, wrote the dissenting opinion and maintained that packing blacks into voting districts promotes segregation. Republicans, who will essentially write off those districts because the odds of winning will be very low, will not even contest races or develop a functioning party. As a result, although black Democrats can win a few more races, they lose experience in forming multiracial coalitions, a skill necessary for succeeding beyond their districts.

Many Democrats support majority black districts because African Americans are much more likely to be elected. However, some Republicans are also very supportive of redistricting in this way because it concentrates African Americans, who are the most reliably Democratic voters, in a few districts. Concentrating African Americans into a few congressional districts allows more GOP-leaning white voters to be placed in swing districts. Substantial redistricting that increased the number of predominantly black districts helped the Republicans gain control of the House of Representatives in 1994 for the first time in decades. In 1994, the number of black congressional Democrats increased in the South from thirteen to seventeen, and Republicans gained twenty-seven seats (John Miller 2001). Prior to the 1990 census, fewer than 20 percent of blacks lived in House districts represented by blacks (John Miller 2001). However, that fraction increased dramatically to 42 percent in only a few years.

Using race to redistrict has altered the usual stances of the major political parties. Some Republicans, who generally oppose racial preferences and set-asides, have been much less forceful about attacking race-driven redistricting, which increased their influence in Congress. In contrast, some Democrats who typically support using racial preferences oppose race-driven redistricting, because although it allows a greater number of African Americans (who traditionally vote Democratic) to be elected, it reduces the likelihood that white Democrats will win other races. Some white Democrats may try to dilute majority-black districts and integrate some of those voters into their own districts, to augment their chances of defeating Republican opponents. Such uncommon political alliances can lead to unusual outcomes, as was the case in Georgia's special redistricting session in 1995, when black Democrats allied themselves with Republicans, who held a minority in the statehouse, to block white Democrats from controlling how political boundaries were redrawn (Bynum 2001).

2000 United States Presidential Election

Concerns about racial fairness were voiced after the 2000 U.S. presidential election; the closest major election in our nation's history and likely the most contentious. In a hard-fought election, Republican candidate and Texas Governor George W. Bush narrowly defeated Democratic Vice President Al Gore. On election night the TV networks and polling pundits declared victory at different times for both men. In the wee hours of the morning after the election, Gore was only minutes away from officially conceding when aides encouraged him to remain in the race. The events after the election were unparalleled. In a world that expects instant communication and instant results, it took about six weeks to officially determine the new president of the United States. Although the final vote was not tallied in a few states for many days, attention was focused most intensely on Florida, because regardless of the outcome of the elections in other states, the winner of Florida would have a sufficient number of electoral votes to become the next president.

The Florida election process was placed under intense scrutiny as many voting irregularities were examined. There were strident disagreements about undervoting, overvoting, butterfly ballots, and military votes from overseas. One of the major areas of disagreement concerned the extent to which African Americans were discouraged from voting or disproportionately had ballots that were "spoiled" (not counted because they showed either no vote or multiple votes for president. Reverend Jesse Jackson alleged that there was a clear pattern of suppressing the votes of African Americans. Jackson argued that blacks were victims of racial profiling, and went so far as to criticize Bush for using "Nazi tactics" and to compare Florida in 2000 to Selma in 1965 ("The Mouth That Roared: Jesse Jackson Will Say Anything to Inflame Passions" 2000). In turn, many people harshly criticized Jackson and argued that the ballot confusion of Florida was a far stretch from the use of Nazi storm troopers or the beatings and tear gas used in Selma. Such critics also noted that blacks could not have experienced large-scale and systematic discrimination when they outpolled (15 percent) their share of the voting-age population (13 percent) in Florida (Gigot 2000).

Concerns about disproportionate treatment of African Americans led the U.S. Commission on Civil Rights to investigate voting patterns in more detail. The chair of the commission, Mary Frances Berry, stated during the summer of 2001 that votes of African Americans were systematically excluded and made the provocative assertion that the alleged discrimination was intentional. The commission hired Allan Lichtman, a historian at American University, to do the statistical analysis. Based on this analysis, the Democrats on the commission (which constituted a majority) maintained, "The disenfranchisement of Florida's voters fell most harshly on the shoulders of black voters" (U.S. Commission on Civil Rights 2001). Its report has four primary conclusions.

1. Statewide, based upon county-level statistical estimates, black voters were nearly ten times more likely than nonblack voters to have their ballots rejected.
2. Estimates indicate that approximately 14.4 percent of Florida's black voters cast ballots that were rejected. This compares with approximately 1.6 percent of nonblack Florida voters who did not have their presidential votes counted.
3. Statistical analysis shows that the disparity in ballot spoilage rates—i.e., ballots cast but not counted—between black and nonblack voters is not the result of education or literacy differences.
4. Approximately 11 percent of Florida voters were African American; however, African Americans cast about 54 percent of the 180,000 spoiled ballots in Florida during the November 2000 election based on estimates derived from county-level data. These statewide estimates were corroborated by the results in several counties based on actual precinct data.

The commission also contended that African American voters were placed on purge lists more often and more erroneously than Hispanic or white voters and reprimanded Governor Jeb Bush and Secretary of State Katherine Harris (U.S. Commission on Civil Rights 2001).

However, both the conclusion and the process of arriving at that conclusion were immediately challenged. The report received forceful internal and external criticism. The dissenting opinion from commission members was scathing. Its opening paragraph states:

> The U.S. Commission on Civil Rights, charged with the statutory duty to investigate voting rights violations in a fair and objective manner, has produced a report that fails to serve the public interest. *Voting Irregularities Occurring in Florida During the 2000 Presidential Election* is prejudicial, divisive, and injurious to the cause of true democracy and justice in our society. It discredits the Commission itself and substantially diminishes its credibility as the nation's protector of our civil rights. The Commission's report has little basis in fact. Its conclusions are based on a deeply flawed statistical analysis coupled with anecdotal evidence of limited value, unverified by a proper factual investigation. This shaky foundation is used to justify charges of the most serious nature—questioning the legitimacy of the American electoral process and the validity of the most recent presidential election. The report's central finding—that there was "widespread disenfranchisement and denial of voting rights" in Florida's 2000 presidential election—does not withstand even a cursory legal or scholarly scrutiny. Leveling such a serious charge without clear justification is an unwarranted assault upon the public's confidence in American democracy. (Thernstrom and Redenbaugh 2001)

One of the dissenters' first concerns was that although the commission is charged with the responsibility of examining differential impacts for all minorities, the report largely ignores Florida's largest minority group (Hispanics). By treating Hispanics, Asian Americans, and Native Americans as if they were in effect white, the report excluded more Floridians of minority background than it included. After these concerns were articulated, one graph about Hispanics was added to the appendix at the last minute (Thernstrom and Redenbaugh 2001).

However, of greater concern was that the majority refused to provide the minority commissioners with any resources for a statistical analysis (Lott 2001c; Thernstrom and Redenbaugh 2001). In spite of repeated requests from the commission's minority members, the majority did not make available a copy of Lichtman's computer runs, data, and output, which under standard protocol would be available to both members of the committee and the general public. Even months after the report was first leaked to the press, the majority still had not provided the data or printouts of the statistical analysis and told the minority that such things did not exist. The majority members of the commission even refused to tell a House oversight committee how they had produced their estimates (Lott 2001c). After the Commission refused to provide the information, Lichtman was asked to supply the data. Although it is a scholarly convention that data be shared so results can be replicated and tested, Lichtman also declined to provide them (Thernstrom and Redenbaugh 2001).

Because the majority members refused to disseminate the data, the minority members requested funding for other scholars to replicate the results. In light of the majority's continued intransigence about either providing the data or funding additional studies, independent researchers agreed to work without compensation and collected the data on their own to try to verify the commission's results. Lott (2001b) compiled a much more comprehensive evaluation by analyzing Florida data from the 1992 and 1996 presidential elections in addition to the 2000 election. This analysis controls for many factors that affect spoiled-ballot rates, such as education, gender, income, age, the number of absentee votes, voting-machine type, ballot type, and whether votes were counted at the precinct or centrally. It then isolates the net effect of race on spoilage rates. The results show that the share of voters who were black was never an important factor in explaining spoiled ballots. Most estimates show that the fraction of voters who were black had no statistical impact on the spoilage rate. The estimates that most strongly support the majority's claims showed that the share of voters who were black could explain a maximum of 3 percent of the change in spoiled ballots. The dissenters argued that the majority confuses voter error and bureaucratic problems with disenfranchisement and actual discrimination.

To test the assertion that black voters were intentionally disenfranchised, Lott (2001b) examined the relationship between the spoilage rate and the party affiliation of the county supervisor. The data show that the link between the percent of voters who were black and nonvoted ballots was much stronger when the county election supervisor was a Democrat than a Republican. Furthermore, because Florida elections are the responsibility of the sixty-seven county election supervisors, the commission had inappropriately assigned the responsibility of spoiled ballots to the Florida secretary of state, Katherine Harris. Amazingly, in twenty-four of the twenty-five counties with the highest spoilage rates the election was supervised by a Democrat—the one exception was an official with no party affiliation (Thernstrom and Redenbaugh 2001). These results cast significant doubt on the belief that voting patterns were the result of intentional discrimination against African Americans, because Democratic election supervisors would not intentionally prevent African Americans, who also overwhelming vote Democratic, from voting.

Additional tests of spoiled ballots show other interesting patterns. Among white voters, Republicans were much more likely than Democrats to have spoiled ballots (Lott and Glassman 2001). In addition, the overall rate of spoiled ballots was 14 percent higher when the county election supervisor was a Democrat, and 31 percent higher when the supervisor was an African American Democrat (Lott and Glassman 2001). Therefore, if spoiled ballots are viewed as an indicator of being disenfranchised, then in Florida, Democrats were disenfranchising African American Republicans. Lott and Glassman (2001) argue, "The irony is that those who screamed discrimination the loudest may have the most to hide."

Lott (2001b) also showed that the commission's claims that blacks more often were erroneously included on the ineligible voter list are incorrect. The majority's evidence that blacks win a greater share of appeals is irrelevant for drawing such conclusions, because it does not recognize that blacks make up an even larger share of the list of ineligible voters. In reality, the rate that whites are removed from the list because they were incorrectly included to begin with is almost twice the rate of blacks (9.9 percent to 5.1 percent). Furthermore, examining only those who successfully appealed says nothing about those who did not appeal, but could have successfully done so.

In related research Lott (2001a) showed that compared to

presidential elections from 1976 to 1996, there was an unusually large decrease in Republican voting rates for Florida's western panhandle during the 2000 general elections, but little change in the rate that non-Republicans in these areas voted. These results cast doubt on the allegation that the networks discouraged all voters from going to the polls in western Florida by incorrectly announcing that the polls were closed, as was asserted by many. However, the results are more consistent with the interpretation that the networks' early calls incorrectly awarding the state to Al Gore disproportionately affected Republicans in the panhandle from voting.

The critics also asserted that the commission's partisan agenda not only destroyed the report's conclusions, but also undermined the process through which the report was compiled. For example, at the Florida hearings, Governor Jeb Bush was the only witness who was not allowed to make an opening statement. Among the other procedural problems in the drafting of the report were that Republican-appointed commissioners were never asked for any input in the composition of the witness list or in the drafting of the report, and at one point, were denied access to the witness lists altogether prior to the hearing. Also, Florida authorities who might be defamed or degraded by the report (Berry, the commission's chairman, was quoted in the Florida press as comparing Governor Bush and Secretary of State Harris to "Pontius Pilate . . . just washing their hands of the whole thing") were not given the proper time to review the parts of the report sent to them or to review the report in its entirety. Furthermore, the draft of the final report that was made available to the press included no corrections or amendments on the basis of affected agency comments (Thernstrom and Redenbaugh 2001).

After the more thorough research had been completed, there was an even more bizarre turn of events. When the commission's minority members submitted their report, the majority refused to include the work because they stated that the dissent could only include work by consultants who were paid by the commission. Despite numerous precedents to the contrary, the commission refused to allow the work of people who volunteered their time to be included in the report and decided that the dissenters could not even refer to the more exhaustive studies that discredited the majority's position. Although the majority argued that this is a statutory matter, there has been a long history of unpaid consultants to the commission. The dissenting commissioners would have been happy to have the commission pay outside scholars for their work, but that effort was also denied.

Unfortunately, the shenanigans were not finished. The commission report was leaked to the *New York Times* before minority Republican members were even given a copy. Despite promises to the U.S. Senate that the commission would disseminate the minority's statement, it originally was not available on the commission's website (Steve Miller 2001). When the commission first posted the dissenting report, it omitted references to Lott's research. In trying to resolve her concerns about the report, Thernstrom said that the commission members tried to trap her with false deadlines, claimed meetings took place when they did not, and consistently failed to respond to her queries ("Suppressing Dissent" 2001). Critics stated, "To suppress the Thernstrom-Redenbaugh dissent, Ms. Berry and her allies have been using tactics reminiscent of a junior high school food fight." They also maintained, "Ms. Berry's behavior would be like Chief Justice William Rehnquist voting with the majority in the case of *Bush v. Gore* and then maneuvering to prohibit Justice Ruth Bader Ginsburg from issuing her famously scathing dissent. We've little doubt that such a maneuver would strike most Americans as outrageous" ("Suppressing Dissent" 2001). Even after the report was finally released, Berry continued to improperly use her influence to inappropriately guide the commission. Linda Chavez, the former chief executive officer of the commission when Berry was vice chairman, criticized Berry for many things, including her refusal to allow Peter Kirsanow, appointed by President Bush to a commission seat that became vacant in November 2001, to take his rightful place as a member of the commission (Chavez 2001). Others chastised Berry for her extremely critical investigation and report of the New York City Police Department and Mayor Giuliani in the middle of the Rudolph Giuliani-Hillary Clinton Senate race. Berry's contributions to Clinton's campaign and Al Sharpton's commenting that this report "was exactly what we asked for" before the report was made public further reinforced this view ("Embarrassing Berry" 2001).

Conclusion: Policy Analysis

This chapter has outlined many important issues about racial justice in five areas—criminal justice, education, employment, living conditions, and political participation. This concluding section will discuss different types of discrimination and present the reasons for and against racial preferences and reparations for slavery.

Affirmative Action and Racial Preferences

Affirmative action gives African Americans, minorities, or underrepresented groups preferential treatment in situations like admission to college, obtaining city contracts, and hiring in firms. These controversial policies have become lightening rods in the racial justice debate. Some view affirmative action and preferential treatment for blacks as instrumental correctives for racial injustice, and others believe they exacerbate injustice. This chapter has already discussed examples of racial preferences and the manner in which they have been implemented. To conclude, I will examine the arguments for and against racial preferences.

There are many reasons for supporting the preferential treatment of minorities in admissions. Bowen and Bok (1998), in a study of more than 80,000 students at twenty-eight highly selective institutions of higher education in the United States who enrolled in college in 1951, 1976, and 1989, argue that affirmative action and racial preferences for minorities can produce many benefits for all people.

First, preferential treatment is necessary to promote diversity, which is especially important in schools. Justice William Powell's decision in *Bakke* (1978), affirmed the importance of diversity to the education of lawyers. "The law school, the proving ground for legal learning and practice, cannot be effective in isolation from the individuals and institutions with which the law interacts. Few students and no one who has practiced law would choose to study in an academic vacuum, removed from the interplay of ideas and the exchange of views with which the law is concerned." Bowen and Bok (1998) contend that a racially diverse student body will stimulate learning, improve the quality of education received by all students, and increase the cultural competence of nonminority classmates. Educators in the professional schools are adamant about the value of a diverse campus environment and often argue that a critical mass of minority students is necessary for the fruitful exchange of ideas. Some medical educators stress the importance of understanding differences in culture and social practice for the effective delivery of health care services.

Second, supporters argue that providing racial preferences to

African Americans is good for the rest of society. For example, underrepresented minority physicians practice in deprived areas more frequently than others do. African Americans who attended schools in Bok and Bowen's study were more likely to participate in and assume leadership roles in community service organizations than their white counterparts.

Third, preferential treatment generates higher returns to education, because controlling for individual characteristics, the return on a college degree is typically greater for African Americans than for whites. In Bowen and Bok's study, a higher proportion of black graduates than of white graduates went on to earn professional degrees and Ph.D.s. Bowen and Bok contend that affirmative action played an important role in the economic success of African Americans and their increasing representation in the middle class.

Fourth, affirmative action corrects for the chronic underrepresentation of minorities in institutions of higher learning, which is most acute for African Americans and Latinos. There are many reasons for this underrepresentation. As discussed earlier in the chapter, the quality of elementary and secondary education is typically much worse in urban areas. Also, African Americans graduate from high school at lower rates than whites; fewer African Americans take the college entrance examinations and apply to postsecondary institutions. Blacks who take the college entrance examinations have, on average, lower scores than their white and Asian counterparts. Differences in aspirations may also contribute to the underrepresentation.

Fifth, supporters of affirmative action contend that whites are harmed little by affirmative action because they are the majority population and have many other opportunities. For example, Bowen and Bok (1998) maintain that eliminating racial preferences would drastically reduce the number of black students at the schools (by about 50–75 percent) even though increasing the white students' chances of gaining admission from 25 to only 26.5 percent.

Last, African Americans have clearly faced explicit legal and subtle social and economic constraints that have limited their opportunities. Affirmative action and racial preferences correct these past injustices and help blacks overcome the effects of past discrimination.

Critics of affirmative action and preferential treatment disagree sharply with such arguments. First, they contend that contrary to the claims of affirmative action supporters, racial diversity among students does not generate educational benefits. Using student-level data from campuses throughout the United States, Wood and Sherman (2001) show that after controlling for other explanatory variables, there are no educationally significant positive relationships between the racial diversity of an institution and any of the eighty-two cognitive and noncognitive student outcomes included in the study. Others cast doubt on Bowen and Bok's conclusions about diversity because their sample of schools is unrepresentative and therefore suffers from sample selection bias. For example, Bowen and Bok ignore HBCUs, study primarily small institutions, and examine only twenty-eight institutions and ignore the rest. Many excluded institutions (like the University of California at Berkeley) have much measure of success for African Americans.

Second, instead of helping students, preferential treatment may harm students by reducing the quality of education. Poorly prepared students with poor motivation deteriorate the quality of education for all.

Third, it is unlikely that affirmative action played a significant role in building the black middle class. Thernstrom (1999) maintains that such a claim "isn't even plausible on its face." She argues that although 44 percent of African Americans are middle class, only a tiny number were ever admitted preferentially to highly selective institutions of higher education; the vast majority of African Americans who have achieved economic success have done so on their own merits. Also, the most significant growth in the black middle class was before 1970, when preferences had only recently begun. Furthermore, Bowen and Bok never truly examine the impact of affirmative action, which they could have done by comparing the success of blacks who gained admission solely on academic merit with the records of blacks who gained admission with the assistance of racial preferences. Consequently, Bowen and Bok cannot dismiss alternative explanations such as the one that black students graduate at higher rates on smaller campuses that provide more academic assistance and have better student bodies.

Fourth, affirmative action converts a race-neutral decision-making process into one that discriminates against whites and Asian Americans. It should be irrelevant whether whites and Asians are discriminated against a little or a lot; the key point is that they are being discriminated against. By perpetuating discrimination, affirmative action perniciously poisons race relations; some people get jobs or enter college simply because of the color of their skin.

Last, regardless of what affirmative action does to other groups, it is bad for blacks; preferential treatment has unintended consequences and hurts those it is intended to help. Many African American writers argue that affirmative action produces a paradigm of victimization that leads blacks to worry about how much they were victimized in the past rather making decisions to improve their present and future. For example, by reducing the qualifications for African Americans to get into college or be hired in a job, affirmative action reduces the incentives of blacks to go to college and develop job skills. Affirmative action may also divert minority students to institutions where they have lower levels of academic achievement. The earnings premium associated with attending a selective college can be offset by lower grade point averages and probabilities of completing their degrees or by increased perceptions among employers that members of the preferentially treated group are not as productive (Coates and Loury 1993). Preferential treatment stigmatizes blacks as people who cannot succeed on their own merits, but who depend on the assistance of government. Swain (1995) states, "Besides encouraging many to play the victim, affirmative action policy telegraphs an equally harmful subliminal message to its beneficiaries. It says in effect that you, as a woman or minority, are less capable than a white male and will need special preference to compete successfully in a world dominated by white males. . . . Affirmative action sends a message to whites that minorities and women need this help, contributing to white denigration of minorities and women."

Flag Controversy

Although not formally affecting the ability to vote or directly participate in the political process, an important symbolic political issue has been the controversy concerning the use of the Confederate battle emblem—crossed blue bars with white stars on a field of red—in the flags of some southern states. Opponents of these flags expressed frustration that these important state symbols contained direct ties to the Confederacy, which legalized the enslavement of blacks. Consequently, the current flags were constant reminders of one of the most shameful periods of U.S.

history when a significant fraction of our population was systematically excluded from fully participating in public life. This belief led many organizations to boycott states that displayed the "Stars and Bars." Many political and business leaders concerned about the effect of the boycotts contended that using the battle emblem limits outside investment, lowers economic growth, and reduces tourism and tourism dollars. In contrast, supporters argued that the flags celebrated important southern characteristics, such as honor, integrity, and states' rights, which were not directly related to slavery.

Many states that switched to the Confederate battle emblem did so in the 1950s. Although supporters of these flags argued that this change was a tribute to Confederate soldiers, critics believe the timing of the change was more consistent with its being an act of defiance against the federal government's orders to desegregate and expand the civil rights of African Americans. Although disagreements have existed since the 1950s, the intensity of the debates increased considerably in the mid- to late 1990s. Those who opposed the Confederate battle flag organized boycotts and protests to persuade states to eliminate it from their state flags. This pressure persuaded many organizations to move their conferences and competitions outside the affected states. The participation in the boycott of prominent organizations like the National Collegiate Athletic Association (NCAA) increased the movement's momentum.

Many states recently either dropped or reduced the use of the battle emblem. The Alabama legislature voted to remove the Confederate battle flag from the top of the state capitol in 1993. In 2000, the flag debate in South Carolina became more intense after the NAACP led a five-month tourism boycott of the state, which generated a loss of more than 100 conventions and conferences worth more than $20 million (cnn.com 2000). South Carolina first raised the flag over its courthouse in 1962. In May 2000, the South Carolina House approved a bill to remove the Confederate battle flag from the capitol dome and relocate it to a Civil War monument elsewhere on the capitol grounds. This topic became an important issue in the 2000 presidential election, as candidates debated whether the emblem should be removed from the state capitol.

In 1956, during the height of the civil rights movement, Georgia adopted the Confederate battle emblem as the primary component of its state flag. Although the Georgia flag issue was extremely controversial for many years, a majority of voters consistently supported retaining the flag. However, in January 2001, the Georgia House of Representatives approved a bill to change the design of the state flag. The new flag incorporates the state seal of Georgia as the centerpiece of the new design and includes the battle flag with four other flags in a smaller area titled "Georgia's History."

In 1894, Mississippi adopted its current flag design with the Confederate battle emblem in the upper left corner of the state's flag. In April 2001, Mississippi voters bucked the trend set by other southern states and voted against changing the flag by an overwhelming 65–35 percent. Businesses and employers concerned about boycotts and loss of tourist revenue strongly supported the proposed change. Many argued that if the decision in the other southern states had been left up to the voters as it was in Mississippi, the other states would not have garnered sufficient support to change their flags.

Reparations

Although the debate over whether the United States should pay reparations to African Americans has existed since the end of the Civil War, it has recently received increased attention. Supporters assert that reparations are justified as an unpaid debt for the many years blacks labored in bondage in the United States and for the actions of whites to limit the freedom of blacks in the years that followed. A less frequently mentioned type of payment is transatlantic reparations, which would be paid by Western nations to West Africa, whose countries were ravaged by colonization and the slave trade. Robinson (2000) argues that when a group of people unlawfully enriches itself by committing wrongful acts against others, the aggrieved group is entitled to be compensated. Reparations have been used to compensate many different groups for improprieties committed against them. The United States paid about $20,000 per person ($1.2 billion total) to Japanese Americans imprisoned on the West Coast of the United States after the Japanese attacked Pearl Harbor in 1941. The United States also compensated various Native Americans, such as the Ottawas in Michigan (payment of $32 million in 1986), the Chippewas of Wisconsin ($31 million in 1985), the Seminoles of Florida ($12.3 million in 1985), the Sioux of South Dakota ($105 million in 1985), and the Klamaths of Oregon ($81 million in 1980) (National Committee of Blacks for Reparations in America 2001).

International examples of reparations include compensation paid to survivors of the Holocaust.

Reparations would compensate blacks, who were enslaved in America for more than two centuries and performed extremely intensive labor under degrading conditions for no pay. Supporters also contend that the payments would help compensate African Americans who suffered after emancipation when many were still excluded from economic and political opportunities. Some have argued that damages should be paid for "post-slavery trauma syndrome," the emotional and psychological damage that results from slavery and continues after release.

These demands for reparations have led to organizations and conferences that examine how reparations would best be managed. In February 2001, the first National Reparations Convention for African American Descendants of African Slaves met in Chicago. The National Coalition of Blacks for Reparations hosts an annual reparations convention. The call for reparations has been echoed by about fifteen cities, including Baltimore, Chicago, Cleveland, Dallas, Detroit, Nashville, and Washington, D.C., all of which passed formal resolutions urging Congress to hold hearings on the continuing impact of slavery, a first step in getting the government to pay reparations. This political pressure has also affected the private sector. A California law was recently passed that requires insurance companies to make public any slave insurance policies they issued. Firms like Aetna, Inc. have apologized for selling insurance policies in the antebellum period that reimbursed slave owners for financial losses when their slaves died.

Supporters of reparations have not provided a uniformly accepted amount of compensation. A common suggestion is the present value of the "40 acres and a mule" that were to be given to freedmen after the Civil War. The precise source of this proposal is not completely clear. One possibility is the First Freedmen's Bureau Act that declared every male citizen, whether refugee or freedman, should not be assigned more than forty acres of land (Bardolph 1970). Shortly after this act was implemented, Congress rejected part of it and reclaimed lands that had been distributed to freedmen. Another possibility is a promise made to the freedmen who marched across Georgia with General Sherman. Acting under the authority of the War Department, Sherman issued an order to divide abandoned rice fields along the river near Charleston into forty-acre parcels and give the land to the freedmen (Oubre 1978). Shortly after the land was divided, it was returned to the white plantation owners. Given the long period of enslavement, the large harm done, and the length of time since the atrocities occurred, many estimates of reparations exceed $1 trillion in today's dollars. Larry Neal, a University of Illinois economist, estimated that unpaid net wages to slaves in the United States would total $1.4 trillion in current dollars (Montgomery 2001).

Similarly, proponents have not agreed upon a method for distributing the reparations. Most suggest providing cash, but others argue that reparations should be more comprehensive and used to repair the damage done to the communities, institutions, and the spirits of those who have suffered from the legacy of slavery. Among the proposals discussed are tax exemptions, grants to black economic development groups, free provision of education and health care, employment benefits, and the redistribution of public property.

In contrast, many argue that offering reparations would be a breach of justice that would do more harm than good and that such compensation would generate extensive problems. The most basic problem with reparations is defining who should receive compensation. Opponents contend that nobody has legitimate standing to receive reimbursement because no one living was directly injured by slavery. None of the potential recipients were ever slaves or even grandchildren of slaves, and therefore, cannot make a legitimate claim to direct disenfranchisement. Proponents counter that the generally disadvantaged status of blacks today testifies that descendents of slaves certainly have borne indirect costs of slavery and therefore should be compensated.

Challengers argue that even if these indirect costs exist, there is still no fair way to recompense people. Should all present-day blacks be eligible for reparations? Assigning benefits to all African Americans would be over-inclusive—it would compensate people who did not even bear indirect costs of slavery. Many potential recipients cannot make even an indirect claim to being harmed by slavery in the United States, because they immigrated or descended from immigrants who arrived after the slaves had been emancipated in the United States.

There is a similar set of problems in determining who would pay reparations (or in whose name payment would be made). Like the problems in determining recipients, none of those who would pay were slave owners or even grandchildren of slave owners, and are therefore generations removed from the wrongful actions. Also, millions of nonblack Americans immigrated or descended from immigrants who arrived after slavery had ended. Furthermore, because relatively few whites owned slaves, a very small fraction of the current population descended from slave owners. Although opponents label this intergenerational responsibility an injustice, supporters believe that it is appropriate. Typically the proponents contend that all whites benefited from slavery, so it is just to require reparations even from whites who did not descend from slaveholders. However, even if all benefited to some degree, should those who benefited most pay the most? Would southerners be required to make relatively large payments while northerners pay relatively little?

These two basic difficulties in determining whom to pay and who should pay are complicated by other issues. Should interracial citizens both pay and receive reparations? Would reparations be awarded in proportion to the degree to which one had fully black ancestry? Do blacks with white ancestry collect less than blacks who have no white ancestors? Further complicating the issue is that some blacks held other blacks as slaves. The 1830 Census counted 3,775 free blacks who owned 12,740 slaves (Jacoby 2001). Would some present-day African Americans pay reparations while others would collect? To summarize the basic arguments against reparations, it is impossible to determine exactly who benefited and how much they benefited from slavery. It is unjust to compel those who did not commit the wrong to compensate those who suffered no wrong.

Some critics of reparations go beyond this point to argue that present-day blacks in the United States have benefited from slavery—that they are much better off than had their ancestors not been enslaved and forcibly removed from Africa. Keith Richburg, an African American journalist for the *Washington Post*, documents the tremendous poverty, hopelessness, high mortality, and horrific living conditions in much of contemporary Africa. He contends that although he cannot justify the transatlantic slave trade, he acknowledged that the enslavement of his ancestors provided him with a quality of life that vastly exceeds the quality of life of Africans today (Richburg 1997). He writes, "But most of all, I think: Thank God my ancestors got out, because, now, I am not one of them." African American scholar Walter Williams argues, "Blacks have benefited from the fact of slavery, because we have far greater freedom and far higher incomes than we could ever find in Africa" (Jacoby 2001). Other African American critics contend that reparations are not an effective way to address the problems we currently face. For example, Glenn Loury, the director of the Institute on Race and Social Division at Boston University, argues, "The second-class status of African Americans is not going to get reversed by a contractual repayment. It's not going to remove ghettos. It's not going to do away with racial profiling. It's not going to get black males out of jail. The challenge is much more fundamental than demanding reparations" (John-Hall 2001).

Other critics argue that the government has already implemented a system of *de facto* reparations—affirmative action. To redress the past racial injustices, government-sanctioned preferences toward minorities have led us to reduce entrance requirements for black college students, promote African Americans in the marketplace who are not as qualified as others, and require businesses that work with the government to set aside specific shares of their businesses to minority-owned businesses. Reparation supporters respond to this contention that even affirmative action provides only a drop in the bucket of what should be restored to African Americans (Robinson 2000).

The modern reparations debate drew increased attention in early 2001 when David Horowitz, formerly a 1960s radical liberal who is now a prominent conservative cultural critic, submitted an advertisement to college newspapers. The advertisement was a full-page article that listed "Ten Reasons Why Reparations for Slavery Is a Bad Idea—and Racist Too." This article originally appeared in May 2000 in *Salon.com* (Horowitz 2000). The first advertisement was placed in February 2001 in the University of Chicago's *Maroon* newspaper. The ad was a well-reasoned argument criticizing the belief that most contemporary Americans should pay for offenses committed by a small minority more than 100 years ago. He further argued that reparations inhibit racial progress by constantly stressing grievance and victimization. This first advertisement triggered little discussion at the University of Chicago. There were no protests, and the *Maroon* received only one dissenting letter ("What's This about Reparations?" 2001).

After waiting a few weeks, Horowitz submitted the same advertisement to about fifty other college newspapers. Only about fourteen papers printed the advertisement ("What's This about Reparations?" 2001), which was rejected by dozens of school papers, including those at Harvard, Columbia, and the University of Virginia. After the *Daily Californian* at the University of California at Berkeley ran the ad, angry students stormed the newspaper office and chastised the staff before removing and destroying the remaining copies of the offending edition. Afterward, the student editor apologized for running the ad. At Brown University about 4,000 copies of the *Brown Daily Herald* were stolen. Students at the University of Wisconsin demanded the resignation of the editor of the *Badger Herald* (Lotozo 2001). In response, Julie Bosman, the editor in chief of the *Badger Herald,* stated, "The issues raised here go to the heart of a critical question: Are American university campuses free and open to a spirit of inquiry, or closed places where activist cohorts can determine what is, or isn't, acceptable?" (Bosman 2001). The rejection of the ads by some papers, the destruction of papers that carried the advertisement, and demands for resignations raise many important issues, such as whether the ability to honestly question important issues has been eliminated by a desire to push a politically correct agenda at some campuses.

Understanding the history and context of Africans in America in a few areas like education and politics, where racial justice is actively debated, and the benefits and costs of public policy decisions, such as preferential treatment, changing symbols on state flags, and reparations, may provide you with a framework you can use to think more critically about racial justice and how to tailor policies that truly reduce racial inequalities and minimize unintended consequences. I hope this chapter will help you formulate a stronger and more comprehensive view of what truly constitutes racial justice.

References

Baden, Brett, and Don Coursey. 1997. "The Locality of Waste Sites within the City of Chicago: A Demographic, Social, and Economic Analysis." Working Paper Series: 97.2.

Baldus, David C., Charles Pulaski, and George Woodworth. 1983. "Comparative Review of Death Sentences: An Empirical Study of the Georgia Experience." *Journal of Criminal Law and Criminology* 74: 661–753.

Bardolph, Richard. 1970. *The Civil Rights Record: Black Americans and the Law, 1849–1970.* New York: Crowell.

Becker, Gary S. 1957. *The Economics of Discrimination.* Chicago: University of Chicago Press.

Belknap, Michel R. 1987. *Federal Law and Southern Order: Racial Violence and Constitutional Conflict in the Post-Brown South.* Athens: University of Georgia Press.

Bellesiles, Michael A. 2000. *Arming America: The Origins of a National Gun Culture.* New York: Alfred A. Knopf.

Billet, Leonard. 1978. "The Free Market Approach to Educational Reform." Rand Paper P-6141. Santa Monica, CA: The Rand Corporation.

"Blacks v. Teachers." 2001. *The Economist,* 10 March, 27–28.

Bogus, Carl. 1993. "Race, Riots, and Guns." *Southern California Law Review* 66: 1365–1388.

Bosman, Julie. 2001. "The (No) Free Speech Movement." *Wall Street Journal,* 14 March, A22.

Bowen, William G., and Derek Bok. 1998. *The Shape of the River: Long-term Consequences of Considering Race in College and University Admissions.* Princeton, NJ: Princeton University Press.

Brown, Richard Maxwell. 1971. "Legal and Behavioral Perspectives on American Vigilantism." *Perspectives in American History* 5: 95–146.

Bullard, Robert D. 1994. *Dumping in Dixie: Race, Class, and Environmental Quality.* 2d ed. Boulder, CO: Westview Press.

Bullard, Robert D., ed. 1993. *Confronting Environmental Racism: Voices from the Grassroots.* Boston, MA: Southend Press.

Bush, Bernard, ed. 1977. *Laws of the Royal Colony of New Jersey.* Trenton: New Jersey State Library, Archives and History Bureau.

Butler, Richard, and James J. Heckman. 1977. "The Government's Impact on the Labor Market Status of Black Americans: A Critical Review." In Leonard J. Hausman, Orley Ashenfelter, Bayard Rustin, Richard F. Schubert, and Donald Slaiman, eds., *Equal Rights and Industrial Relations.* Madison, WI: Industrial Relations Research Association, pp. 235–281.

Butterfield, Fox. 2001. "Number of People in State Prisons Declines Slightly." *New York Times,* 13 August.

Bynum, Russ. 2001. "Court Rulings, Political Shifts Challenge Georgia Blacks in Redistricting." *Athens Banner Herald,* 24 June, D1 and D3.

Chavez, Linda. 2001. "Outrageous Behavior Nothing New from Head of Civil Rights Commission." *Philadelphia Inquirer,* 12 December.

Chubb, John E., and Terry M. Moe. 1990. *Politics, Markets, and America's Schools.* Washington, DC: Brookings Institution.

Cnn.com. 2000. "South Carolina House Approves Final Measure to Relocate Confederate Flag." Cited 11 May.

Coates, Stephen, and Glenn Loury. 1993. "Will Affirmative-Action Policies Eliminate Negative Stereotypes?" *American Economic Review* 83, no. 5 (September): 1220–1240.

Cohn, Elchanan. 1997. "Public and Private School Choices: Theoretical

Considerations and Empirical Evidence." In Elchanan Cohn, ed., *Market Approaches to Education.* Tarrytown, NY: Elsevier Science, pp. 3–20.

Connerly, Ward. 2001. "One Nation, Indivisible." *Hoover Digest* 1. Available at http://www.hoover.stanford.edu/publications/digest/011/connerly.html.

Conrad, Cecilia A., and Rhonda V. Sharpe. 1996. "The Impact of the California Civil Rights Initiative (CCRI) on University and Professional School Admissions and the Implications for the California Economy." *Review of Black Political Economy* 25, no. 1 (Summer): 13–15.

Cottrol, Robert, and Raymond Diamond. 1991. "The Second Amendment: Towards an Afro-Americanist Reconsideration." *Georgetown Law Journal* 80: 309–361.

Couch, Kenneth, and Mary C. Daly. 2002. "Black-White Wage Inequality in the 1990s: A Decade of Progress." *Economic Inquiry* 40, no. 1: 31–41.

Delk, James D. 1995. *Fires and Furies: The L.A. Riots—What Really Happened.* Palm Springs, CA: ETC Publications.

Donohue, John J., III, James J. Heckman, and Petra E. Todd. 2001. "The Schooling of Southern Blacks: The Roles of Legal Activism and Private Philanthropy, 1910–1960." Pennsylvania Institute for Economic Research Working Paper 01–036, University of Pennsylvania. Available at http://papers.ssrn.com/abstract=232549.

D'Souza, Dineshe. 1998. *Illiberal Education: The Politics of Race and Sex on Campus.* New York: The Free Press.

"Embarrassing Berry." 2001. Editorial. *Wall Street Journal,* 10 December, A18.

Fede, Andrew. 1992. "Legitimized Violent Slave Abuse in the American South, 1619–1865: A Case Study of Law and Social Change in Six Southern States." *American Journal of Legal History* 29: 93.

Finkelman, Paul. 1986. "Prelude to the Fourteenth Amendment: Black Legal Rights in the Antebellum North." *Rutgers Law Journal* 17: 415.

Fogel, Robert W. 1989. *Without Consent or Contract: The Rise and Fall of American Slavery.* New York: W. W. Norton.

Fogel, Robert W., and Stanley L. Engerman. 1974. *Time on the Cross: The Economics of American Negro Slavery.* New York: W.W. Norton & Company.

Friedman, Milton, and Rose Friedman. 1980. *Free to Choose.* San Diego: Harcourt, Brace.

Genovese, Eugene D. 1974. *Roll, Jordan, Roll: The World the Slaves Made.* New York: Pantheon Books.

Gigot, Paul A. 2000. "Ambivalent Warriors: Why Democrats Let Gore Fight On, and On, and . . ." *Wall Street Journal,* 1 December, A14.

Greene, Jay P. October 1999. "The Racial, Economic, and Religious

Context of Parental Choice in Cleveland." Working Paper of the Program on Education Policy and Governance, Harvard University.

———. February 2001. "An Evaluation of the Florida A-Plus Accountability and School Choice Program." Working Paper of the Program on Education Policy and Governance, Harvard University.

Hagan, John. 1974. "Extra-Legal Attributes and Criminal Sentencing: An Assessment of a Sociological Viewpoint." *Law and Society Review* 8, no. 3: 3357–3384.

Hanushek, Eric A., ed. 1994. *Making Schools Work: Improving Performance and Controlling Costs.* Washington, DC: The Brookings Institution.

Higginbotham, A. Leon, Jr. 1978. *In the Matter of Color: Race and the American Legal Process: The Colonial Period.* New York: Oxford University Press.

Hofer, Paul J., Kevin R. Blackwell, and Barry R. Ruback. 1999. "The Effect of the Federal Sentencing Guidelines on Inter-Judge Sentencing Disparity." *Journal of Criminal Law and Criminology* 90, no. 1: 239–322.

Horowitz, David. 2000. "Ten Reasons Why Reparations for Slavery Are a Bad Idea for Black People—And Racist Too." Available at http://www.salon.com. Cited 30 May.

Howell, William G., Patrick J. Wolf, Paul E. Peterson, and David E. Campbell. August 2000. "Test-Score Effects of School Vouchers in Dayton, Ohio, New York City, and Washington, D.C.: Evidence from Randomized Field Trials." Working Paper of the Program on Education Policy and Governance, Harvard University.

Hoxby, Caroline M. September 2001. "How School Choice Affects the Achievement of Public School Students." Working Paper of Harvard University. Available at http://post.economics.harvard.edu/faculty/hoxby/papers/choice_sep01.pdf

Jacoby, Jeff. 2001. "No Reparations for Slavery." *Boston Globe,* 5 February, A15.

John-Hall, Annette. 2001. "Once Unlikely, Reparations are Now a Concept Defended and Decried." *Athens Banner Herald,* 1 April, B1 and B6.

Kennedy, Randall. 1997. *Race, Crime, and the Law.* New York: Pantheon Books.

Kleck, Gary. 1981. "Racial Discrimination in Criminal Sentencing: A Critical Evaluation of the Evidence with Additional Evidence on the Death Penalty." *American Sociological Review* 46: 783–805.

———. 1997. *Targeting Guns: Firearms and Their Control.* New York: de Gruyter.

Knowles, John, Nicola Persico, and Petra Todd. 2001. "Racial Bias in Motor Vehicle Searches: Theory and Evidence." *Journal of Political Economy* 109 (February): 203–229.

Kocieniewski, David. 2000. "United States Justice Department to Open Civil Rights Inquiry in New Jersey Turnpike Shooting." *New York Times,* 4 November, 1.

Kocieniewski, David, and Robert Hanley. 2000. "Racial Profiling Routine; N.J. Documents Show Many Blacks Stopped." *Denver Post,* 28 November, A1.

Ladd, Helen F. 1998. "Evidence on Discrimination in Mortgage Lending." *Journal of Economic Perspectives* 12, no. 2 (Spring): 41–62.

Lindgren, James, and Justin Lee Heather. 2001. "Counting Guns in Early America." Working Paper of Northwestern University. Available at: http://www.law.nwu.edu/faculty/fulltime/Lindgren/Lindgren.html.

Lotozo, Eils. 2001. "David Horowitz and His Ad Bolster His Incendiary Reputation." *Athens Banner Herald,* 1 April, B1 and B5.

Lott, John R., Jr. 2000. *More Guns, Less Crime.* 2d ed. Chicago: University of Chicago Press.

———. May 2001a. "Documenting Unusual Declines in Republican Voting Rates in Florida's Western Panhandle Counties in 2000." Working Paper of Yale Law School. Available at http://papers.ssrn.com/sol3/papers.cfm?abstract_id=276278.

———. July 2001b. "Non-Voted Ballots and Discrimination in Florida" Working Paper 256 of Yale Law School Program for Studies in Law, Economics, and Public Policy. Available at: http://papers.ssrn.com/sol3/papers.cfm?abstract_id=276276.

———. 2001c. "On Thin Ice: Florida Voter Discrimination Claims Groundless." *Washington Times,* 31 July, A17.

Lott, John R., Jr., and David B. Mustard. 1997. "Crime, Deterrence, and the Right-to-Carry Concealed Handguns." *Journal of Legal Studies* 26, no. 1: 1–68.

Lott, John R., Jr., and James K. Glassman. 2001. "Whose Votes Really Didn't Count in Florida?" American Enterprise Institute, 10 November.

Lott, John R., Jr., and John E. Whitley. 2001. "Safe Storage Gun Laws: Accidental Deaths, Suicides, and Crime." *Journal of Law and Economics* 44, no. 2. Available at http://papers.ssrn.com/sol3/papers.cfm?abstract_id=228534.

McDonald, Douglas C., and Kenneth E. Carlson. 1993. *Sentencing in the Federal Courts: Does Race Matter?* Washington, DC: U.S. Department of Justice.

McKay, Betsy. 2000. "Coca-Cola Agrees to Settle Bias Suit for $192.5 Million." *Wall Street Journal,* 17 November, A3.

McWhorter, John H. 2000. *Losing the Race: Self-Sabotage of Black America.* New York: Free Press.

Mehegan, David. 2001. "New Doubts about Gun Historian." *Boston Globe,* 11 September, A30.

Miller, John J. 2001. "Segregation Forever?" *National Review,* 14, 24, 26 May.

Miller, Steve. 2001. "Civil Rights Panel's Lawyers Say Dissent Is Inadmissible." *Washington Times,* 19 July, A10.

Montgomery, Rick. 2001. "Drive for Slavery Reparations Gaining Steam across the United States." *Buffalo News,* 18 March, H1 and H4.

Morris, Thomas D. 1996. *Southern Slavery and the Law, 1619–1860.* Chapel Hill: University of North Carolina Press.

Most, Doug. 2000. "Shot through the Heart." *Sports Illustrated,* 10 July, 86–97.

"The Mouth That Roared: Jesse Jackson Will Say Anything to Inflame Passions." 2000. Editorial. *Wall Street Journal,* 14 December, A26.

Munnell, Alicia H., Geoffrey M. B. Tootell, Lynn E. Browne, and James McEneaney. 1996. "Mortgage Lending in Boston: Interpreting the HMDA Data." *American Economic Review* 86, no. 1 (March): 25–53.

Murphy, Kevin, and Finis Welch. 1989. "Wage Premiums for College Graduates: Recent Growth and Possible Explanations." *Educational Researcher* 18 (May): 17–26.

Mustard, David B. 2001. "Racial, Ethnic, and Gender Disparities in Sentencing: Evidence from the U.S. Federal Courts." *Journal of Law and Economics* 44, no. 1: 285–314.

Myrdal, Gunnar. 1944. *An American Dilemma: The Negro Problem and Modern Democracy.* New York: Harper & Brothers.

National Assessment of Educational Progress. 2001. *The Nation's Report Card, 2001.* Available at http://nces.ed.gov/nationsreportcard/

National Association for the Advancement of Colored People. 1969. *Thirty Years of Lynching in the United States, 1889–1918.* New York: Arno Press.

National Center for Education Statistics. 1996. *Historically Black Colleges and Universities, 1976–1994.* Washington, DC: Government Printing Office. Available at http://nces.ed.gov/pubs/96902.pdf.

National Commission on Excellence in Education. 1983. *A Nation at Risk: The Imperative for Educational Reform: A Report to the Nation and the Secretary of Education.* Washington, DC: U.S.Department of Education. Available at http://www.ed.gov/pubs/NatAtRisk/title.html.

National Committee of Blacks for Reparations in America. 2001. "History of Reparations Payments." Available at http://www.ncobra.com/documents/history.html.

Oubre, Claude F. 1978. *Forty Acres and a Mule: The Freedmen's Bureau and Black Land Ownership.* Baton Rouge: Louisiana State University Press.

O'Neil, June. 1990. "The Role of Human Capital in Earnings Differences between Black and White Men." *Journal of Economic Perspectives* 4, no. 4: 25–45.

Overby, Andrew. 1971. "Discrimination against Minority Groups." In Leon Radzinowicz and Marvin E. Wolfgang, eds., *Crime and Justice, Vol. II, The Criminal in the Arms of the Law.* New York: BasicBooks, pp. 569–581.

Peterson, Paul E., William G. Howell, and Jay P. Greene. June 1999. "An

Evaluation of the Cleveland Voucher Program after Two Years." Working Paper of the Program on Education Policy and Governance, Harvard University.
Pollock, Robert L. 2001. "A Day in Cincinnati." *Wall Street Journal*, 20 April, A14.
Richburg, Keith B. 1997. *Out of America: A Black Man Confronts Africa.* New York: BasicBooks.
Riley, Jason L. 2002. "Black, Successful—and Typical." *Wall Street Journal*, 13 May, A16.
Robinson, Randall. 2000. *The Debt: What America Owes to Blacks.* New York: Dutton.
Salter, John R., Jr., and Donald B. Kates, Jr. 1979. "The Necessity of Access to Firearms by Dissenters and Minorities Whom Government Is Unwilling or Unable to Protect." In Donald B. Kates, Jr., ed., *Restricting Handguns: The Liberal Skeptics Speak Out.* Croton-on-Hudson, NY: North River Press, pp. 185–193.
Satel, Sally. 2002. "I Am a Racially Profiling Doctor." *New York Times*, 5 May, 56.
Seckora, Melissa. 2001. "Disarming America: One of the Worst Cases of Academic Irresponsibility in Memory." *National Review*, 1 October, 50–54.
Sellin, Thorsten. 1928. "The Negro Criminal: A Statistical Note." *Annals of the American Academy of Political and Social Science* 140: 52–64.
Smith, James P., and Finis Welch. 1984. "Affirmative Action and Labor Markets." *Journal of Labor Economics* 2, no. 2: 269–302.
———. 1989. "Black Economic Progress after Myrdal." *Journal of Economic Perspectives* 27, no. 2: 519–564.
Stephenson, Gilbert Thomas. 1969 [1910]. *Race Distinctions in American Law.* New York: Negro Universities Press.
Stith, Kate, and Jose A. Cabranes. 1998. *Fear of Judging: Sentencing Guidelines in the Federal Courts.* Chicago: University of Chicago Press.
"Suppressing Dissent." 2001. Editorial. *Wall Street Journal*, 8 August, A12.
Sutherland, Edwin H., and Donald R. Cressey. 1970. *Principles of Criminology.* Philadelphia: Lippincott.
Swain, Carol M. 1995. "Where Do We Go from Here?" *New Democrat* 7, no. 3 (May/June): 20–21.
Thernstrom, Abigail. 1999. "An Interview with Abigail Thernstrom." *Frontline.* Available at http://www.pbs.org/wgbh/pages/frontline/shows/sats/race/
Thernstrom, Abigail, and Russell G. Redenbaugh. 2001. "The Florida Election Report: Dissenting Statement." U.S. Commission on Civil Rights. Available at http://www.usccr.gov/. Cited 19 July.
U.S. Commission on Civil Rights. June 2001. "Voting Irregularities in Florida during the 2000 Presidential Election." Available at http://www.usccr.gov/.

U.S. Office of Education. 1969. *History of Schools for the Colored Population.* New York: Arno Press.

"What's This about Reparations?" 2001. *University of Chicago Magazine* (June): 38–39.

Wilson, William Julius. 1996. *When Work Disappears: The World of the New Urban Poor.* New York: Alfred A. Knopf.

Wood, Thomas, and Malcolm Sherman. 2001. "Is Campus Racial Diversity Correlated with Educational Benefits?" National Association of Scholars. Available at http://www.nas.org/reports/umich_diversity/umich_execsum.htm

Yinger, John. 1986. "Measuring Racial Discrimination with Fair Housing Audits: Caught in the Act." *The American Economic Review* 76, no. 5 (December): 881–893.

3

Chronology

This chapter contains a chronological overview of many of the most important events concerning racial justice in U.S. history. Although many dates could be included, this chapter focuses on dates that have particular importance for the book's five major themes—criminal justice, education, employment, living conditions, and political participation. Most of the events mentioned in this chapter are discussed in greater detail in Chapters 1, 2, and 5.

1451 Africans are used as slaves in the Madeiras, Canary, and Cape Verde Islands.

1502 The first reference to blacks as slaves appears in Spanish colonial administrative documents.

1607 Jamestown, Virginia, is settled.

1620 The Pilgrims settle at Plymouth, Massachusetts.

1641 Colony of Massachusetts legalizes slavery.

1664 Slavery is introduced into law in Maryland. The law also prohibits marriage between white women and black men.

1688 The Germantown Quakers issue a condemnation of slavery, considered the first opposition to slavery and the beginning of the antislavery movement in the New World.

1758 At the annual Meeting of Quakers in Philadelphia, the Quakers not only condemn the slave trade, but decide that membership is contingent on noninvolvement in slave trade.

1775 Slavery is abolished in Madeira.

1777 Vermont becomes the first state to prohibit slavery.

1780 The Massachusetts constitution declares all men free and equal and is interpreted by the courts in 1783 to include slaves.

1784 A gradual emancipation policy is adopted in Rhode Island and Connecticut.

1787 The U.S. Constitution is ratified. To be ratified the Constitution includes compromises between the North and South about slavery. The Constitution allows the slave trade to continue until 1807, institutes a tax on imported slaves, requires that states recognize each other's laws regarding slavery, and declares that each slave counts as three-fifths of a white citizen for purposes of congressional representation.

The Northwest Ordinance is passed, prohibiting slavery in territories north of Ohio.

1790 Southwest Ordinance is passed, allowing slavery in territories south of Ohio.

1793 The Fugitive Slave Act is passed by Congress.

1794 Slaves rebel and fight for independence in Haiti.

France abolishes slavery in all its territories. This law is later repealed by Napoleon in 1802.

1799 A gradual emancipation law is adopted in the state of New York.

1800 Exporting slaves by United States citizens is outlawed.

1804 Haiti abolishes slavery. New Jersey adopts a gradual emancipation policy.

1807 International slave trade is prohibited by England and the United States.

1820 The Missouri Compromise prohibits slavery north of the 36 degree 31 minute line.

1831 *The Liberator,* a prominent newspaper, is established by William Lloyd Garrison, a white abolitionist.

Nat Turner leads a group of slaves who kill about sixty whites in Virginia. The Virginia militia captures and hangs about twenty of the slaves, including Turner. The rebellion causes the southern states to pass strict laws to control slaves.

1838 Slavery is abolished in all the British colonies.

1847 Frederick Douglass begins publishing *The North Star,* an abolitionist newspaper, in Rochester, New York.

1850 The Compromise of 1850 settles sectional concerns over slavery in the acquired territory of the Mexican War.

1854 The Kansas-Nebraska Act is passed. This action organizes western territories, nullifies the Compromise of 1850, and heightens sectionalism.

In July, disaffected former members of the Whig, Democrat, and Free-Soil Parties form the Republican Party at a convention in Jackson, Michigan. Opposition to expansion of slavery to new territories is one of the fundamental platforms of the new party.

1856 The two-year-old antislavery Republican Party becomes the leading political party in the North.

1857 In *Dred Scott v. Sandford,* the Dred Scott case, the U.S. Supreme Court rules that Congress has no power to exclude slavery from the nation's territories and that the Missouri

1857, *cont.* Compromise of 1820 is therefore unconstitutional. It also declares that the rights and privileges proclaimed in the Declaration of Independence and the Constitution do not extend to blacks.

1859 John Brown leads a group of men on a raid of the armory in Harpers Ferry, Virginia, on 16 October 1859, to obtain arms to use for a slave revolt. He is captured by a detachment of U.S. Marines under Colonel Robert E. Lee. Brown is found guilty of treason and hanged on 2 December.

1860 The antislavery Republicans win the presidential election with Abraham Lincoln.

1863 President Abraham Lincoln officially declares the Emancipation Proclamation, legally freeing slaves in the South.

1865 Originally known as the Bureau of Refugees, Freedmen, and Abandoned Lands, the Freedmen's Bureau is established on 3 March to aid and protect the freed slaves in the South.

In April, the Civil War ends when Robert E. Lee surrenders at Appomattox Courthouse.

Only a few days after the end of the Civil War, Abraham Lincoln is shot and killed by John Wilkes Booth in Ford's Theatre in Washington, D.C.

The Thirteenth Amendment to the U.S. Constitution abolishes slavery.

1866 The Civil Rights Act of 1866 is enacted on 9 April and declares that all persons born in the United States are citizens, without regard to race, color, or previous condition of slavery. Some of its language later becomes part of the Fourteenth Amendment.

1868 The Fourteenth Amendment to the U.S. Constitution is adopted, which states that people of different races should enjoy equal protection under law.

1870 The Fifteenth Amendment to the U.S. Constitution is adopted, which guarantees that the right to vote should not be denied on the basis of race (however, it is still denied on the basis of gender).

1875 The Civil Rights Act of 1875 becomes law on 1 March and promises that all persons, regardless of race, color, or previous condition of slavery, are entitled to full and equal accommodations and that no citizen can be denied the right to serve on juries.

1888 Slavery is abolished in Brazil.

1896 *Plessy v. Ferguson* upholds the doctrine that permits separate but equal facilities for blacks and whites, which essentially limits the value of the Fourteenth Amendment's Equal Protection Clause.

1909 W. E. B. Du Bois founds the National Association for the Advancement of Colored People (NAACP).

1936 Jesse Owens earns five gold medals at the Olympics in Berlin, Germany. His accomplishments undermine the assertions of Adolf Hitler, who attends the games, that white people are superior to others.

1948 *Shelley v. Kraemer* is the first of the four restrictive covenant cases decided in 1948 by the U.S. Supreme Court, which holds that racially restrictive property deeds are unenforceable.

1953 In *Avery v. Georgia,* the Supreme Court rules that the jury selection process, in which prospective white and black jurors' names are handled on different color tickets, constitutes evidence of discrimination. In *Barrows v. Jackson,* which grew out of efforts by whites to circumvent *Shelley v. Kraemer* (1948), the Court bars damage awards when racially restrictive covenants are violated.

1954 On 17 May, the U.S. Supreme Court rules unanimously to eliminate segregation in schools in *Brown v. Board of Education of Topeka, Kansas.* This ruling overturns *Plessy v.*

1954 *cont.* *Ferguson*. Thurgood Marshall, who will later become the first African American U.S. Supreme Court justice, argues the case on behalf of children Ethel Belton, Spottswood Bolling, Harry Briggs, Jr., Linda Brown, and Dorothy Davis. Four cases are consolidated under the name of this case, the first the Court decides to hear.

The White Citizens Council meets for first time on 11 July in Mississippi, with the purpose of preventing desegregation advocates from succeeding economically.

Fourteen-year-old African American Emmett Till is murdered after speaking flirtatiously to a white woman on a dare in a grocery store in Mississippi on 28 August.

1955 The Interstate Commerce Commission bans segregation in interstate travel on 25 November.

On 1 December, Rosa Parks boldly refuses to relinquish her seat on a bus in Montgomery, Alabama.

The thirteen-month Montgomery Bus Boycott to end segregation on local public transport begins on 5 December, led by Martin Luther King, Jr., among others.

1956 Martin Luther King, Jr.'s, home is bombed on 31 January.

Black student Autherine Lucy is admitted to the University of Alabama on 3 February.

On 12 March, the Southern Manifesto is presented, as more than 100 members of the U.S. Congress protest the *Brown v. Board of Education* decision.

The Tallahassee Bus Boycott begins on 27 May.

The NAACP is outlawed in Alabama on 1 June.

The U.S. Supreme Court outlaws segregation on local bus transport on 13 November; the Montgomery Bus Boycott ends the following month when the decision is enforced.

Fred Shuttlesworth, of the soon-to-be-formed Southern Christian Leadership Conference (SCLC), has his home bombed on Christmas Day.

1957 The SCLC is formally organized on 10 January to coordinate local nonviolent protests in the South. Many of the leaders are Baptist ministers, including Martin Luther King, Jr. The organization's goal is to achieve full equality for African Americans by using mass nonviolent resistance to win public sympathy and support, and to heal America's racially divided society by exhibiting redemptive love. Its consistent commitment to nonviolence contrasts sharply with the violence of some southern whites. King leads the group's first action, a Prayer Pilgrimage to Washington, which attracts 25,000 people. The SCLC fights segregation and secures voting rights by supporting the Freedom Riders, many sit-ins, the Birmingham Confrontation with Commissioner Bull Connor, and the 1964 St. Augustine fight against segregation and the Ku Klux Klan. The actions of the SCLC will be influential in the passage of the Civil Rights Act of 1964 and the Voting Rights Act of 1965.

In August, after an order is given to integrate the school, a long controversy begins at Little Rock, Arkansas's Central High School.

Congress passes the Civil Rights Act of 1957, the first civil rights law since Reconstruction.

1958 The Tallahassee Bus Boycott ends in March.

In September, the U.S. Supreme Court announces its unanimous decision in *Cooper v. Aaron*, which reaffirms that the *Brown* decision is binding on the states. It also holds that state governors or legislators cannot engage in or encourage actions (including support of segregated schools) that demonstrate a refusal to uphold the Constitution.

1960 The postcolonialism movement gathers momentum as eleven African nations gain independence, including the Ivory Coast, Nigeria, and Zaire.

1960, *cont.* On 1 February, a sit-in occurs at the segregated lunch counter in Greensboro, North Carolina. This leads to sit-ins and boycotts at establishments throughout the nation.

The Student Nonviolent Coordinating Committee (SNCC) is founded on 17 April to communicate and coordinate student protests in the South. The founders establish a Temporary Coordinating Committee that later becomes the Temporary Student Nonviolent Coordinating Committee, chaired by Marion S. Barry, the future Mayor of Washington, D.C. SNCC members and volunteers become involved with the Freedom Rides, voter registration, and protests and sit-ins throughout the South. These efforts help integrate many restaurants and other service establishments.

The Civil Rights Act is signed on 6 May. This act makes it unlawful to avoid prosecution for bombing offenses and interference with court orders for school desegregation and empowers federal judges to appoint referees to hear persons claiming that state election officials have denied them the right to register and vote.

1961 A federal district court orders the University of Georgia to be desegregated on 6 January; riots occur there on 11 January.

Biracial groups, with SNCC involvement, travel on the Freedom Rides throughout the South during the summer to generate publicity and support for racial harmony.

The Interstate Commerce Commission rules on 22 September that segregation in interstate bus and train stations is illegal.

The Albany Movement is formed on 17 November in Georgia as an umbrella organization to coordinate activists from several groups (Negro Voters League, NAACP, etc.) to protest segregation.

1962 The Los Angeles Riot occurs on 27 April.

In late September the University of Mississippi ("Ole Miss") is desegregated, which triggers riots.

1963 Governor George Wallace of Alabama stands in front of a doorway at the University of Alabama on 11 June to prevent two black students from registering and is confronted by U.S. Deputy Attorney General Katzenbach.

Sidney Poitier becomes the first African American actor to win the Academy Award for best actor. Not until 2002 does another African American win the best actor award.

In June, citizens throughout the United States are shocked as Mississippi NAACP leader Medgar Evers is brutally killed outside his home.

On 20 June, President John F. Kennedy meets with civil rights leaders planning the 28 August March on Washington, D.C., in which Reverend King makes his famous "I Have a Dream" speech. More than 200,000 people attend the march.

On 15 September, an African American church in Birmingham, Alabama, is bombed, which kills four young girls.

President Kennedy is assassinated on 22 November.

1964 On 24 January, the Twenty-fourth Amendment is passed to eliminate poll taxes on federal elections.

The Mississippi Freedom Democratic Party (MFDP) is founded on 26 April to challenge Mississippi's all-white Democratic Party.

Freedom Summer takes place in Mississippi, in which students travel throughout the state to register black voters for the fall 1964 elections.

On 21 June, Goodman, Chaney, and Schwerner, two whites and a black involved in the Mississippi voter registration effort, are murdered near Philadelphia, Mississippi.

1964 *cont.* There are massive race riots in Chicago, Philadelphia, Jersey City, and New York City.

President Lyndon B. Johnson signs the Civil Rights Act on 2 July after Republican Senator Dirksen helps to end a filibuster of Democrats opposed to the legislation. This act, one of the most recognized laws passed by Congress in the twentieth century, makes it illegal to discriminate in many public capacities.

Martin Luther King, Jr., is awarded the Nobel Peace Prize on 10 December.

1965 The Selma, Alabama, protests trigger unrest from January through March. Reverend King is arrested and jailed.

Malcolm X, the New York–based radical civil rights leader, is killed on 21 February.

The Unitarian minister James Reeb, injured in the Selma, Alabama, riots, dies on 11 March.

The Voting Rights Act is signed into law on 6 August.

In August, the Watts Riot takes place in the south-central region of Los Angeles.

1966 In *Harper v. Virginia Board of Elections,* the Supreme Court strikes down a requirement in the Virginia Constitution that prospective voters must pay poll taxes for the previous three years or forfeit the privilege of voting.

Edward Brooke, a Republican from Massachusetts, becomes the first black U.S. senator since Reconstruction.

SNCC members elect Stokely Carmichael as chair, who becomes a leader of the Black Power movement and alters the strategy of the SNCC.

1967 In *Loving v. Virginia,* the U.S. Supreme Court unanimously rules that the Fourteenth Amendment's Equal

Protection and Due Process clauses deny states the authority to use racial classifiers to determine which citizens can intermarry.

Thurgood Marshall becomes the first African American Justice of the U.S. Supreme Court.

1968 The Civil Rights Act of 1968 prohibits discrimination in the rental or sale of housing, thus becoming the first congressional act since 1866 to address open housing.

In *Allen v. State Board of Elections,* the Supreme Court prohibits restrictions limiting the right of blacks to register and vote. The Court sweeps aside a Mississippi statute that dilutes black voting power and thereby curtails their ability to elect candidates, ruling that the Mississippi law violates the Voting Rights Act.

Martin Luther King, Jr., is assassinated on 3 April in Memphis, Tennessee, where he is supporting striking sanitation workers.

Shirley Chisholm, from Brooklyn, New York, becomes the first African American woman elected to the U.S. House of Representatives.

1969 The Supreme Court decides *Alexander v. Holmes County Board of Education* on 29 October 1969, and sets a defining precedent that ensures school integration across the South within the succeeding twelve months. *Alexander* changes federal policy from "desegregation," eliminating barriers to blacks and whites attending school together, to "integration," requiring blacks and whites to attend the same schools.

1972 Shirley Chisholm is the first African American woman to run for a major party nomination for the U.S. presidency, but fails.

1978 The Supreme Court decides the *University of California Regents v. Bakke* case, on a 5–4 vote. The Court rules

1978, *cont.* that state universities cannot establish a quota system setting aside a number of spots for minorities because that process would deny nonminorities equal protection under the Fourteenth Amendment.

1987 The U.S. Supreme Court rules that a quota for black state troopers in Alabama is necessary to remedy persistent discrimination in hiring and promotion (*United States v. Paradise*).

1989 Colin Powell becomes the first African American to serve as chair of the Joint Chiefs of Staff, a position he holds until he retires from the U.S. Army in 1993.

1991 The Civil Rights Act addresses discrimination in the hiring and promotion of minorities and women and strengthens Title VII of the Civil Rights Act of 1964.

In March, Rodney King is severely beaten by the Los Angeles police. King is hit more than fifty times and suffers many broken bones. The racially motivated attack is captured on videotape and leads the news throughout the world.

President George H. W. Bush chooses Clarence Thomas to become the second African American justice on the Supreme Court.

1992 In April, the four Los Angeles police officers (Stacey C. Koon, Laurence M. Powell, Theodore Briseno, and Timothy Wind) on trial for the beating of Rodney King are acquitted. The jury's decision triggers six days of rioting in Los Angeles, which results in an estimated $700 million in property damage, 54 people killed, more than 2,300 people injured, and more than 13,212 arrested.

In September, the U.S. Department of Education announces that Berkeley's Boalt Hall School of Law has shielded minority applicants from competition with white applicants to meet affirmative action quotas. The school denies any wrongdoing, but agrees not to separate applicants based on race or ethnicity in the future.

1993 The Alabama legislature votes to remove the Confederate battle flag from the top of its capitol.

1995 O. J. Simpson, a Hall of Fame professional football player, is acquitted of the 1994 murder of his former wife and her friend. The decision highlights the sharp racial differences in the criminal justice system, as African Americans overwhelmingly believe he should be acquitted, but whites overwhelmingly believe he should be convicted.

In July, the board of regents of the University of California vote to eliminate the use of race, gender, color, ethnicity, and national origin in the admissions, contracting, and employment activities of the state's public universities.

In *Adarand Constructors, Inc. v. Pena,* the United States Supreme Court rules that government affirmative action programs must promote a "compelling state interest" and be necessarily tailored to reach their objectives. This ruling is part of a general trend by the courts to require programs that grant preferential treatment by race to meet higher standards to be ruled constitutional.

1996 In March, in its decision in the case *Hopwood v. Texas,* the Fifth Court of Appeals nullifies a University of Texas Law School admissions policy that uses racial classifications to create a more diverse student body, and rules that race cannot be used as a factor in admissions.

In November, California voters pass Proposition 209 (the California Civil Rights Initiative), which states that "the state shall not discriminate against, or grant preferential treatment to any individual or group on the basis of race, sex, color, ethnicity, or national origin in the operation of public employment, public education, or public contracting."

1997 In August, Abner Louima, a Haitian immigrant was brutally attacked and sexually assault by New York City police officers. One officer was convicted, and other officers were charged with obstruction of justice.

1998 In April, New Jersey police officers pull over a van of four unarmed African American males and shoot and seriously wound three of the passengers.

In Texas on 7 June, James Byrd, Jr., a forty-nine-year-old black man, is severely beaten and stabbed, then tied to the back of a pickup truck and dragged almost three miles until he dies. This brutal death helps generate support for national hate crime legislation.

In November, the electorate of the State of Washington overwhelmingly approves Initiative 200, a proposition similar to California's Proposition 209.

1999 On 4 February, questions about how New York City police officers treat African Americans are rekindled when officers shoot and kill Amadou Diallo. Police fire forty-one shots at this unarmed immigrant from Liberia, nineteen of which hit him. The jury later acquits four police officers in their role in the shooting.

2000 South Carolina votes to remove the Confederate Battle emblem from the top of its capitol in Columbia.

In November, the New Jersey attorney general's office releases a 91,000-page report that documents the extensive racial profiling practices of state law enforcement officers.

Newly elected President George W. Bush appoints General Colin Powell U.S. secretary of state. With his appointment, Powell becomes the highest-ranking African American public official in U.S. history.

2001 The Georgia House of Representatives votes to change the state flag and significantly reduce the size of the Confederate battle flag, which previously was the centerpiece of the state flag.

Mississippi citizens vote overwhelmingly to keep their state flag, which includes the prominent display of the Confederate battle emblem.

In April, a four-day race riot erupts in Cincinnati, Ohio, after police officer Stephen Roach shoots and kills Timothy Thomas, an unarmed African American man who had fourteen misdemeanors. The officer believed that Thomas was reaching for a gun; he is later charged with a misdemeanor.

Ex-Ku Klux Klan member Thomas Blanton, Jr., is sentenced to life in prison for the 1963 bombing of a Birmingham, Alabama, church that killed four black girls.

In *Easley v. Cromartie,* the U.S. Supreme Court rules that race can be an element in redistricting decisions provided it is not the "dominant and controlling" factor. Clarence Thomas, the Supreme Court's only African American, criticizes the opinion, arguing that packing blacks into voting districts promotes segregation.

The Supreme Court declines to review the Ninth Circuit Court of Appeals decision in *Smith v. University of Washington Law School,* which upheld the use of racial preferences for admissions at the University of Washington Law School. The law school abandons its admissions policy before the Supreme Court makes its decision to decline the case.

The U.S. Commission on Civil Rights examines whether African Americans were denied the right to vote or had their votes spoiled at a disproportionately high rate in Florida during the 2000 presidential election. Although the commission's report concludes that there is evidence of impropriety, the commission is severely criticized by its Republican members, who disagree with the Democratic majority's decision, and by many people outside the commission because the majority refuses to publish much of the evidence that casts doubt on its conclusion.

Mayor Charles Robertson of York, Pennsylvania, surrenders to face murder charges in the shooting death of a black woman during a 1969 race riot when he was a police officer.

2001, *cont.* In August, the Eleventh Circuit Court of Appeals rules that the University of Georgia's admissions policy, which gives some African American applicants extra points at a critical point in the admissions process, violates the Equal Protection clause of the Fourteenth Amendment.

2002 In December at a birthday party for 100-year-old South Carolinian Sen. Strom Thurmond, Republican Trent Lott suggests the country would have been better off if Thurmond had been elected president during his 1948 campaign. People from across political backgrounds sharply criticized Lott for supporting Thurmond, who took a pro-segregationist stance during his presidential campaign. Although Lott apologized and said that he was referring to Thurmond's promotion of a strong national defense, support for law enforcement, and commitment to fight budget deficits, he was forced to resign his position as majority leader of the United States Senate.

2003 In April, the U.S. Supreme Court hears oral arguments in two affirmative action cases involving the University of Michigan. *Grutter v. Bollinger* and *Gratz v. Bollinger* examine whether public educational institutions may grant extra points to blacks in the admissions decision. The decisions in these cases uphold the *Bakke* decision that has set forth the Court's views on affirmative action for nearly thirty years.

4

Biographical Sketches

This chapter contains brief biographical summaries of many people who contributed or are contributing to defining racial justice in areas of criminal justice, education, employment, living conditions, and political participation.

Ralph David Abernathy, Sr. (1926–1990)

Ralph Abernathy, a prominent civil rights and religious leader, was a top aide to the Reverend Martin Luther King, Jr. He grew up in Alabama and earned degrees from Alabama State University (B.S. 1950) and Atlanta University (M.A. 1951). Abernathy was a founder of the Southern Christian Leadership Conference (SCLC) in 1957 and worked closely with King until King's assassination in 1968, when Abernathy assumed leadership of the SCLC. In 1977, Abernathy resigned leadership of SCLC and ran, unsuccessfully, for the Georgia congressional seat vacated by Andrew Young. He later founded the Foundation for Economic Enterprises Development, a nonprofit organization to improve black economic opportunities. He became more active on the lecture circuit and served as pastor of West Hunter Street Baptist Church in Atlanta until the first of several strokes in 1983. Abernathy died in Atlanta in April 1990.

Maya Angelou (1928–)

Born Marguerite Johnson in St. Louis, Missouri, Angelou attended public schools in Arkansas and California as a child. In spite of an extremely difficult childhood, including rape by a family member that left her unable to talk until she was in her teens, Angelou distinguished herself at an early age. She earned a scholarship in dance and drama to the California Labor School, and became San Francisco's first African American and first female streetcar conductor.

Maya Angelou has a remarkable array of talents. She is fluent in six languages (English, French, Spanish, Italian, Arabic, and West African Fanti) and is a highly recognized author, historian, playwright, poet, civil-rights activist, producer, and director. She has received many awards and has been nominated for a Tony Award, Emmy Award, and Pulitzer Prize. Angelou has authored twelve best-selling books, including *I Know Why the Caged Bird Sings,* the story of her childhood. Maya Angelou was the first African American to be the longest-running author on the *New York Times* paperback best-sellers list (two years). In January 1993, she became only the second poet in U.S. history to write and recite original work at a presidential inauguration when she read her poem "On the Pulse of Morning."

Susan B. Anthony (1820–1906)

Susan B. Anthony was born 15 February, 1820, in Adams, Massachusetts. She was raised in a Quaker family of eight children that had a long history of being active in social causes. Both parents were passionate supporters of abolition, temperance, and women's rights.

In 1845, after her father's death, she and her mother and sister moved to Rochester, New York, where they became friends of Frederick Douglass and William Lloyd Garrison. Antislavery Quakers met regularly at her family's home, and Susan's brothers became antislavery activists in Kansas. She became friends with Elizabeth Cady Stanton and with her was instrumental in starting the campaign for women's suffrage. In 1856, Anthony became a member of the American Anti-Slavery Society. Although facing hostility and threats, she arranged antislavery meetings, made speeches, and distributed abolitionist information. In 1863, Anthony and Stanton organized a Women's National Loyal League to support and petition for the Thirteenth Amendment outlawing slavery. They also campaigned for full citizenship for both blacks and women, and were bitterly disappointed when women were excluded in the post–Civil War constitutional amendments. Anthony continued to campaign for equal rights for all U.S. citizens, including ex-slaves (but excluding immigrants), in her newspaper *The Revolution,* which she began publishing in Rochester, New York, in 1868. In this paper she also attempted to sway public opinion to eradicate lynching.

In the 1890s Anthony raised $50,000 in pledges to ensure the admittance of women to the University of Rochester. In a last-minute effort to meet the deadline, she put up the cash value of her life insurance policy. In 1900, the university fulfilled its promise to admit women. Anthony also advocated for various labor issues, such as an eight-hour workday and equal pay for equal work. She also campaigned for women's property rights and changes in divorce laws to make them fairer to women.

Anthony, a noted abolitionist, teacher, education reformer, labor activist, temperance worker, suffragist, and supporter of women's rights, actively campaigned for social justice until her death on 13 March 1906. In her last speech at eighty-six years old, she made the famous statement "With such women consecrating their lives, failure is impossible." In 1979, she became the first woman depicted on U.S. currency.

Arthur Ashe (1943–1993)

A native of Virginia, Ashe became a prominent professional tennis player and humanitarian. After graduating from high school as valedictorian, he earned a scholarship to the University of California at Los Angeles. After graduating with a B.A. degree in business administration in 1966, Ashe served in the military. In September 1968, Ashe won the U.S. Open tennis championship, becoming the first African American man to do so. He eventually was ranked the world's top player and won titles at the Australian Open and Wimbledon to claim three Grand Slam tournaments.

During his career, Ashe crusaded against racial prejudice throughout the world and against apartheid in South Africa. After his retirement in 1980, he devoted himself to promoting racial reconciliation. After Ashe learned in 1988 that he contracted HIV during a blood transfusion, he became a prominent advocate of AIDS research. Ashe succumbed to AIDS-related pneumonia on 6 February 1993. In February 1997, the National Tennis Center in Flushing, New York, which annually hosts the U.S. Open, named its 23,000-seat stadium in memory of Ashe.

Ella Josephine Baker (1903–1986)

Baker is most widely known as a civil rights activist. She was born in Norfolk, Virginia, in 1903. After graduating from Shaw University in 1927, Baker moved to New York City, where she worked to improve Harlem and joined the Young Negroes Cooperative League. In 1931, she became its national director. She took an active role in forming the Southern Christian Leadership Conference (1948), the Student Non-Violent Coordinating Committee (1960), and the Mississippi Freedom Democratic Party (1964).

Marion S. Barry (1936–)

Barry is most recognized as the longtime mayor of the District of Columbia who was sentenced to prison for his conviction on a drug charge. He was born in Itta Bena, Mississippi, and received his bachelor of science degree from Le Moyne College and a masters degree from Fisk University. In 1960 he became actively involved in the civil rights movement when he participated in the Nashville sit-ins, which included demonstrations at lunch counters. The Student Nonviolent Coordinating Committee (SNCC) chose Barry as its first national chair. He worked consistently to promote nonviolence workshops, raise funds, register voters, and plan demonstrations and boycotts.

Daisy Lee Bates (1914–)

Daisy Lee Bates, born in Huttig, Arkansas, in 1914, is best known for her efforts to integrate Central High School in Little Rock, Arkansas, in 1957. Shortly after she and her husband, L. C. Bates, arrived in Little Rock in 1952, the two became active members in the NAACP, and she became involved in advising the nine students who were the first African Americans to attend a previously all-white school. She wrote *The Long Shadow of Little Rock,* her account of "The Little Rock Nine." In 1986, the University of Arkansas Press republished the book, which became the first reprinted edition to earn an American Book Award. Little Rock eventually honored Bates by naming an elementary school after her.

Bates is recognized for her courage as she stood firm in her purpose in the midst of mobs who threatened to injure or kill the students and their supporters. Bates and other NAACP officials were arrested and charged with failing to provide information about members for the public record, in violation of a city ordinance. Bates refused to do so because publicizing such information would have endangered the students. Although Bates was fined, the NAACP appealed and eventually won a reversal in the U.S. Supreme Court. She also cochaired the state's Committee on Fair Employment Practices. Bates is the recipient of numerous awards and honorary doctorates for her work on educational integration.

Mary McLeod Bethune (1875–1955)

Born in Mayesville, South Carolina, Bethune was a noted educator and supporter of civil rights, including women's rights. A child of former slaves, she earned a scholarship to Scotia Seminary in North Carolina in 1888. Her strong conviction that education was necessary for blacks to improve led her to start the Daytona Normal and Industrial Institute in 1904, which became Bethune-Cookman College in 1929. Bethune was the founder of the National Association of Colored Women and the National Council of Negro Women. She served in the Franklin D. Roosevelt administration as director of the Division of Negro Affairs within the National Youth Administration. Throughout her career she made a strong effort to promote full citizenship rights for both blacks and women.

Julian Bond (1940–)

As a student at Morehouse College, Bond participated in Atlanta sit-ins and helped start the SNCC, for which he was the communications director for four years. Although he was elected to the Georgia House of Representatives, he was prevented from taking office because of his statements against the Vietnam War. Bond was forced to take his case to the U.S. Supreme Court, which upheld his right to take office. Bond served in the Georgia House from 1967 to 1975 and in the Georgia Senate from 1975 to 1987. In 1972, he authored *A Time to Speak, a Time to Act.* In 1998 he became chairman of the National Association for the Advancement of Colored People (NAACP).

Edward Brooke (1919–)

Elected in 1966 as a Republican, Brooke became the first African American senator since Reconstruction. In 1941, Brooke graduated from Howard University before serving in the infantry during World War II. After being discharged, he went to Boston University Law School, where he was the editor of the law review. After graduation, he remained in Massachusetts to practice law. Following unsuccessful attempts to win election to the state legislature and secretary of state, he was elected attorney general of Massachusetts in 1962.

John Brown (1800–1859)

Born in Torrington, Connecticut, as the son of a tradesman, he spent many of his early years in Hudson, Ohio. His mother, who was insane, died when John was only eight, and he received little formal schooling thereafter. During the 1830s and 1840s, Brown moved frequently and struggled financially. Although he had been an abolitionist since his youth, in the 1850s he started to become more serious about ending slavery and started to plan to emancipate slaves by force. By 1855 he and many of his family members moved to Kansas to fight to keep it a slavery-free state. On the night of 24 May 1856, in response to the burning of Lawrence, Kansas, by proslavery forces, Brown led a small group of men who killed five proslavery men. After returning to the east, Brown raided the armory in Harpers Ferry, Virginia, on 16 October 1859, to obtain arms to use for a slave revolt. However, he was captured by a detachment of U.S. Marines under Colonel Robert E. Lee. Brown was found guilty of treason and hanged on 2 December.

Stokely Carmichael (1941–1998)

Born in Port-of-Spain, Trinidad, Carmichael was best known for his leadership role in the Black Panthers Party. Carmichael immigrated to the United States in 1952, earned his undergraduate degree from Howard University, and became active in the civil rights movement. In the early 1960s he joined the SNCC and participated in demonstrations and voter registration projects in the South. As part of the more radical contingent of the SNCC, his disagreements with the SNCC's commitment to nonviolence and inclusion of whites led to his dismissal from the organization. In 1966, Carmichael made his famous Black Power speech in Greenwood, Mississippi, which helped change the emphasis of the civil rights movement from nonviolence and integration to self-defense and black nationalism. In 1969 he adopted Guinea as his home and changed his name to Kwame Ture. He died at age fifty-seven after a two-year bout with prostate cancer.

George Washington Carver (c. 1864–1943)

Carver was born into slavery in Missouri. Slave raiders kidnapped Carver and his mother when he was a six-week-old infant, but his owner allegedly ransomed back the boy with a $300 prize racehorse. Carver was the first African American student to enroll at Simpson College in Indianola, Iowa. After completing his master of science degree at the Iowa Agricultural College, Carver joined Booker T. Washington at the Tuskegee Institute, directing Tuskegee's agricultural research department until his death in 1943. At Tuskegee, Carter became an internationally recognized agricultural scientist who revolutionized southern agriculture. He taught southern farmers how to grow and preserve foods, emphasized the importance of crop rotation and diversification, and developed hundreds of products from the peanut. Upon his death, Carver willed his estate to the Tuskegee Institute to support scientific research. He was buried beside his friend and mentor, Booker T. Washington, on the Tuskegee campus.

Shirley Anita St. Hill Chisholm (1924–)

In 1968, Shirley Chisholm became the first African American woman elected to the U.S. Congress, where she served from 1969 to 1983. The child of immigrants, she grew up in Barbados and Brooklyn, where she graduated from Brooklyn College in 1946. She also earned a master's degree in childhood education from Columbia University in 1952. Chisholm was a vocal opponent of the Vietnam War and weapons development and a strong supporter of the interests of the urban poor. She ran unsuccessfully for the Democratic nomination for U.S. president in 1972.

Septima Poinsette Clark (1898–1987)

Septima Poinsette Clark was an educator and an early leader of the U.S. civil rights movement. Septima was born in 1898 in Charleston, South Carolina, and was the second of eight children. Her father was a former slave who did not become literate until adulthood. After graduating from Avery Normal Institute, a school established by missionaries to educate African American children, Septima became a teacher.

In 1918, while welcoming home troops from World War I, she met Nerie Clark, whom she married in 1919. Their first child, Victoria, died at the age of one month. Their second child, Nerie, was born in 1925, and in December of that year, Septima's husband died of kidney disease. Soon afterward Septima became an active member of the NAACP, which called for equalization of teacher salaries between blacks and whites. During this case, which the NAACP eventually won, Septima worked with NAACP lawyer Thurgood Marshall.

In 1942, at the age of forty-four, she received a bachelor's degree from Benedict College in Columbia, and in 1946 received a master's degree from Hampton Institute in Virginia. During the day Septima taught children and at night she taught adult literacy. In spite of doing an excellent job teaching, Clark was fired and her pension revoked when the state legislature passed a law prohibiting public employees from being members of civil rights organizations. Clark protested this inappropriate decision, but did not prevail until 1976. She became director of workshops at the Highlander Folk School in Tennessee, where she developed citizenship schools and literacy programs for adults. Because many states tried to limit the right to vote to those who were literate, her work had a profound effect on expanding the rights of blacks to be involved in the political process. In 1957, she became involved with the Southern Christian Leadership Conference (SCLC), formed in 1957 under the leadership of Martin Luther King, Jr., and the Voter Education Project. From 1962 to 1966 she prepared 10,000 teachers to teach in citizenship schools and helped register nearly 700,000 African Americans to vote. In 1965, King invited Clark to accompany him to Sweden when he received the Nobel Peace Prize.

Angela Yvonne Davis (1944–)

Davis, who was born in Birmingham, Alabama, is a recognized supporter of radical black causes who believes that for blacks to be liberated in the United States, there must be a complete overthrow of the capitalist class. She received a B.A. from Brandeis University in 1965 before pursuing a doctorate at the University of California at San Diego. While in California she joined the Communist Party.

Davis worked to free African American prisoners held in California during the late 1960s and befriended George Jackson, one of the prisoners. In 1970, during a failed escape attempt at Marin County's Hall of Justice, the trial judge and three people were killed, including Jackson's brother Jonathan. Although not at the crime scene, Davis was implicated when a gun used in the crime was found legally registered to her. She was later tried and acquitted on charges of conspiracy, murder, and kidnapping.

After that episode she founded the National Alliance against Racist and Political Repression and has taught at San Francisco State University and the University of California at Santa Cruz. Davis was the American Communist Party's vice presidential candidate in 1980 and 1984.

Frederick Douglass (c. 1817–1895)

Frederick Douglass was one of the most recognized and respected reform leaders of the nineteenth century, and is sometimes referred to as "the father of the civil rights movement." He was born a slave in Maryland, but escaped to Massachusetts in 1838. Once free, Douglass used his remarkable abilities as an orator and writer to challenge slavery. During the 1840s, he wrote the *Narrative of the Life of Frederick Douglass,* the first of three autobiographies. In 1847, he moved to Rochester, New York, and published his own newspaper called *The North Star,* which became *The Frederick Douglass Paper* in 1851. Douglass, who was committed to nonviolent approaches to freeing the slaves, turned down a request from John Brown to join him in a revolution against slavery. Brown was later hanged for his part in the raid on Harpers Ferry.

In addition to working against slavery, Douglass was also an outspoken supporter of women's rights (especially suffrage), temperance, and better working conditions. In 1848 at Seneca

Falls, New York, Douglass attended a women's rights meeting. Although thirty-two men attended, he was the only male to vote for the women's right to vote. Douglass strongly supported the Republican Party. President Rutherford Hayes appointed this steadfast Republican to be marshal of the District of Columbia from 1877–1880. President James Garfield appointed Douglass to the Office of the District's Recorder of Deeds from 1881 to 1886. In 1889, President Benjamin Harrison appointed him minister to Haiti, where he served until 1891. Douglass died on 20 February 1895, after attending a women's rights meeting. He is buried in Mount Hope Cemetery, next to the University of Rochester, which established the Frederick Douglass Institute for African and African American Studies to honor him.

William Edward Burghardt (W.E.B.) DuBois (1868–1963)

DuBois is most noted for founding the National Association for the Advancement of Colored People (NAACP) in 1909 and helping it to become the country's single most influential organization for African Americans. Born in Great Barrington, Massachusetts, DuBois earned a bachelor's degree at Fisk University and a master's degree at Harvard, and became the first African American to earn a doctoral degree from Harvard in 1896. He taught at Wilberforce University, the University of Pennsylvania, and Atlanta University, and was a highly respected academic and one of the most effective supporters of full rights for African Americans prior to World War II. DuBois often disagreed with people like Booker T. Washington, who pursued more accommodating strategies to obtain rights for African Americans. DuBois became frustrated by the slow pace of advancement of civil rights in the United States and increasingly turned his attention internationally. In 1959 he was awarded the Soviet Union's Lenin Peace Prize before joining the Communist Party. He later emigrated to Ghana, where he died.

Marion Wright Edelman (1939–)

Marian Wright Edelman was born in Bennettsville, South Carolina. She was one of five children, and her father was a Baptist preacher who died when Marian was a teenager. While at Spelman College, she became involved in the civil rights movement. After graduation she studied law at Yale and worked on a project to register African American voters in Mississippi. Edelman worked for the NAACP Legal Defense and Educational Fund in both New York and Mississippi. In 1973, she established the Children's Defense Fund (CDF), which lobbys for children's rights to quality education and health care. Edelman was the first African American admitted to the Mississippi state bar.

Minnie Joycelyn Elders (1933–)

Born into an impoverished family in Schaal, Arkansas, Elders was the oldest of eight children. In spite of her humble upbringing, Elders became the first African American U.S. surgeon general when President Clinton appointed her in 1991. She attended Philander Smith College, served in the army, and graduated from the University of Arkansas Medical School before entering residency at the University of Minnesota. She returned to the University of Arkansas Medical School as a professor and later became director of the Arkansas Department of Health.

Medgar W. Evers (1925–1963)

Medgar Evers was one of the central figures in the civil rights movement. After serving in the military during World War II, he graduated from Alcorn A&M College. He helped revitalize the Mississippi NAACP and in 1954 became its state field secretary. Evers frequently opposed the less radical NAACP national leadership and generally pursued a more aggressive strategy to promote the rights of African Americans. He often led large sit-ins and demonstrations and economic boycotts to mobilize blacks. On 11 June 1963, he was killed in the driveway of his home.

Myrlie Evers-Williams (1933–)

Myrlie was born 17 March 1933, in Vicksburg, Mississippi. In 1950, she enrolled at Alcorn A&M College, where she met Medgar, an Army veteran. She left school before earning her degree, and they married on Christmas Eve, 1951. After Medgar was named the Mississippi state field secretary for the NAACP in 1954, Myrlie became his secretary and worked with him to organize voter registration drives and civil rights demonstrations. In 1963, Evers was murdered in the driveway of his home in

Jackson. After Medgar's murder, Myrlie and her three children moved to California, where in 1967 she authored a book about her husband, *For Us, the Living,* and graduated from Pomona College in 1968. In 1975 she married Walter Williams.

After Evers's murder, his wife continued to promote his work and undertook a long and arduous journey to bring his killer to justice. Byron De La Beckwith, a white supremacist who denied the shooting but publicly expressed his support for the murder, was tried twice for the crime. However, both juries were deadlocked and Beckwith was released. Evers-Williams pressured the state to retry the case and aided the prosecutors by providing new witnesses and an original transcript of the case. On 4 February 1994, thirty-one years after the murder, Beckwith was found guilty and sentenced to life in prison, where he died in 2001. In 1995, the same year her second husband died of prostate cancer, Myrlie Evers-Williams became the first woman to chair the NAACP, a position she held until 1998.

William Lloyd Garrison (1805–1879)

In 1805, Garrison was born in Newburyport, Massachusetts. He had a difficult childhood as his father deserted the family in 1808, and William was forced to work at an early age to help support his family. In 1818, Garrison began working for the *Newburyport Herald* as a writer and editor. This job provided him with the skills he would eventually need to start his own newspaper years later.

When he was twenty-five, Garrison joined the abolition movement. He helped organize the New England Anti-Slavery Society and the American Anti-Slavery Society, which promoted immediate emancipation. He continued his career in journalism by working as coeditor of an antislavery paper in Maryland. On 1 January 1831, he published the first issue of his own antislavery newspaper, *The Liberator,* which became a very influential and noted supporter of abolition. During the thirty-five years of his paper's existence, Garrison spoke eloquently and effectively against slavery and in support of the rights of blacks.

Lani Guinier (1950–)

Lani Guinier is as a prominent civil rights attorney who in 1998 became the first black woman to be appointed to a tenured professorship at Harvard Law School. Guinier is a graduate of

Radcliffe College of Harvard University and Yale Law School. During the 1980s she was head of the voting rights project at the NAACP Legal Defense and Educational Fund and served in the U.S. Office of Civil Rights during the Carter administration as special assistant to then Assistant Attorney General Drew S. Days. She was a professor for ten years at the University of Pennsylvania Law School. In 1993 President Clinton nominated her to head the Civil Rights Division of the Department of Justice, and later nominated her for the Supreme Court, but concerns about her personal life derailed the latter opportunity. Guinier has received numerous awards, including the Champion of Democracy Award from the National Women's Political Caucus, the Rosa Parks Award from the American Association for Affirmative Action, and eight honorary degrees.

Fannie Lou Hamer (1917–1977)

Fannie Lou, the youngest of twenty children, grew up in the midst of poverty as the child of sharecroppers. Although she had only an elementary school education, she had a tremendous impact on desegregating the Mississippi Democratic Party. Her civil rights activism began in 1962, when she volunteered for the SNCC to help challenge voter registration procedures that excluded African Americans. She became a field secretary for SNCC before assuming the role of vice chair of the Mississippi Freedom Democratic Party (MFDP) in 1964. During her tenure with the MFDP, she frequently brought attention to incidents of violence and injustice suffered by civil rights activists, including her own beating in a jailhouse, which crippled her. In her autobiography, *To Praise Our Bridges,* Hamer recounted her commitment to bring economic and political justice to people of all races in Mississippi.

Dorothy Height (1912–)

Dorothy Height was born in 1912 in Richmond, Virginia. She was educated in the public schools in Rankin, Pennsylvania. Height worked as a civil rights advocate to prevent lynching, desegregate the armed forces, and reform the criminal justice system. She also worked with Mary McLeod Bethune to promote equal opportunities for women in education and the marketplace. Height was the president of the National Council of Negro

Women for more than forty years and worked for many years for the national Young Women's Christian Association (YWCA). In her capacity with the YWCA she promoted interracial education and helped provide equal opportunity and facilities for women of all cultures and nationalities.

Alexis M. Herman (1947–)

On 1 May 1997, Alexis M. Herman became the nation's twenty-third secretary of labor and the first African American to hold this position. During her tenure at the Department of Labor, she oversaw an organization with a $39 billion annual budget and 17,000 employees.

Born in Mobile, Alabama, Herman began her career working for Catholic Charities helping young out-of-school men and women find work in Mississippi. At the age of twenty-nine, she joined the Carter administration as the youngest director of the Women's Bureau in the history of the labor department. Herman now serves as chair and chief executive officer of New Ventures, Inc. She has received more than a dozen honorary degrees from major colleges and universities, and serves as a trustee her alma matter, Xavier University. She is also chair of the Coca-Cola Company's Human Resources Task Force, chair of the Toyota Diversity Advisory Board, and a member of the board of directors of Cummins Inc. and MGM/Mirage Inc.

bell hooks (1952–)

Gloria Jean Watkins, now known as bell hooks, was born in Hopkinsville, Kentucky. She received her B.A. from Stanford University in 1973, her M.A. from the University of Wisconsin in 1976, and her Ph.D. from the University of California at Santa Cruz in 1983. When she started writing, she chose her pseudonym, which was her great-grandmother's name. Her writings have examined issues of race and gender.

In 1985 hooks taught African and Afro-American studies and English at Yale University, in New Haven, Connecticut. In 1988 she was an associate professor of women's studies and American literature at Oberlin College in Oberlin, Ohio, and in 1994 she accepted the post of distinguished professor of English at the City College of New York.

Charles Hamilton Houston (1895–1950)

Concerning Charles Houston, Thurgood Marshall stated, "A large number of people never heard of Charles Houston . . . [but] when Brown against the Board of Education was being argued in the Supreme Court . . . there were some two dozen lawyers on the side of the Negroes fighting for their schools. . . . Of those lawyers, only two hadn't been touched by Charlie Houston. . . . That man was the engineer of it all." Houston attended Amherst College at age sixteen, where he was the only black student in his class. He was elected to Phi Beta Kappa and graduated with honors before serving in the U.S. Army as a judge advocate. In 1919, Houston enrolled at Harvard Law School and became the first black elected to the editorial board of the *Harvard Law Review.* He received his law degree in 1922 and his doctoral degree in 1923. One of Houston's mentors was Felix Frankfurter, a founder of the American Civil Liberties Union and later a justice on the U.S. Supreme Court. Houston, the first African American to win a case before the U.S. Supreme Court, was particularly concerned about the dramatic disparity between black and white southern schools.

Charlayne Hunter-Gault (1942–)

In January 1961, after almost two years of legal challenges, Charlayne Hunter-Gault and Hamilton Holmes became the first two African American students to attend the University of Georgia, where she earned her B.A. in journalism. After graduation, she worked for the *New Yorker,* and in 1967 received a Russell Sage Fellowship to study social science at Washington University. Later she accepted a position with the *New York Times,* and in 1978, she joined the staff of Public Broadcasting Station's *MacNeil/Lehrer Newshour,* where she remained for nineteen years. She now works with her husband, Ron Gault, in South Africa as a reporter for National Public Radio. Hunter-Gault has received numerous awards, including the *New York Times* Publishers Award, Emmy awards for national news and documentary, and two George Foster Peabody Awards awarded to her by the University of Georgia.

Jesse L. Jackson (1941–)

Jackson, originally from Greenville, South Carolina, is one of the most publicly recognized and controversial people of the late twentieth century. Jackson ran unsuccessfully for mayor of Chicago in 1971 and the Democratic Party nomination for president in 1984 and 1988. Jackson began his activism as a student leader in the sit-in movement and continued as a young organizer for the SCLC as an assistant to Martin Luther King, Jr. In 1971, Jackson formed People United to Save Humanity (PUSH) to economically empower and expand educational and employment opportunities for the disadvantaged. In 1984, he started the National Rainbow Coalition, a national social justice organization. The two merged into the Rainbow/PUSH Coalition in 1996. Jackson has often been criticized for being divisive and by interjecting race as an issue where it is not relevant. Also, his tax problems with the Internal Revenue Service and fathering children out of wedlock have undercut his messages to encourage economic independence and discourage teenage pregnancy. Reverend Jackson has been awarded many honors, among them the prestigious NAACP Spingarn Award and more than forty honorary doctorate degrees.

Barbara Charline Jordan (1936–1996)

Barbara Jordan was born 21 February 1936, in Houston, Texas. Her father was a Baptist preacher who made a strong impression on his daughter. Jordan attended Texas Southern University (TSU), where she graduated magna cum laude in 1956. After graduation she went to Boston University Law School. In 1959 she finished law school and passed both the Massachusetts and Texas bar examinations. Upon returning to Texas she became more involved in the civil rights movement and sought to become a lawmaker in order to end segregation. Although she lost two elections for the Texas House of Representatives, she won a seat in the Texas Senate in 1966. She was the first African American woman elected to the Texas Senate and the first African American to serve there since Reconstruction.

In 1972 when she was elected to the U.S. House, she became the first African American female from the South to serve there. Jordan played a prominent role as a member of the House Judiciary Committee when it held President Richard M. Nixon's impeachment hearings. A skilled orator, she gave the keynote address at the Democratic Party National Conventions in 1976 and 1992. She became the first African American ever selected to deliver this address. In 1994, she received the Medal of Freedom from President Clinton. Jordan died on 17 January 1996, in Austin, Texas.

June Jordan (1936–2002)

A noted poet and author who often addressed racial issues in her writings, Jordan won numerous awards such as a Rockefeller Foundation grant, the National Association of Black Journalists Award, and fellowships from the Massachusetts Council on the Arts, the National Endowment for the Arts, and the New York Foundation for the Arts. Jordan was born in New York City and studied at Barnard College (1953–1955; 1956–1957) and the University of Chicago (1955–1956). While at the University of California, Berkeley, she founded Poetry for the People. June Jordan died of breast cancer on 14 June 2002.

Coretta Scott King (1929–)

The wife of one of America's greatest leaders, Reverend Martin Luther King, Jr., she consistently worked with her husband to promote civil rights. Born in Alabama, Coretta Scott received a scholarship to Boston's New England Conservatory of Music. In Boston, she met Martin, whom she married in June 1953. Since Martin's assassination in 1968, Coretta has continued to be actively involved in the civil rights movement. She founded the Martin Luther King, Jr., Center for Nonviolent Social Change in Atlanta and served as the center's president and chief executive officer until transferring the position to her son Dexter in 1995. She established the annual Coretta Scott King Award to honor an African American author of children's literature.

Martin Luther King, Jr. (1929–1968)

The most influential leader in modern civil rights was born in Atlanta. His father was a Baptist minister at nearby Ebenezer Baptist Church and provided strong religious training for Martin. King graduated from Morehouse College in 1948 and then graduated from Crozer Theological Seminary as valedictorian and president of the student body. He obtained his Ph.D. from Boston University, where he met and married Coretta Scott.

King quickly became a prominent participant in the civil rights movement. He led the boycott of Montgomery's segregated buses, which led to a U.S. Supreme Court decision in 1956 against Alabama's segregation laws. Shortly thereafter, King was made president of the newly formed SCLC. In 1959, King moved to Atlanta to head the new organization and became copastor with his father at Ebenezer. Throughout his career, King led many civil rights demonstrations and protests. He often endured physical threats and was often incarcerated for his leadership role in the protests. His experience with being arrested gave him the opportunity to write *Letter from a Birmingham Jail.* King was also an articulate and persuasive orator, whose famous "I Have a Dream" address before the Lincoln Memorial in Washington, D.C., is one of the most quoted speeches in U.S. history. In 1964, he was awarded the Nobel Peace Prize. Martin Luther King, Jr., was assassinated on 3 April 1968, in Memphis, Tennessee, where he was supporting striking sanitation workers.

John Mercer Langston (1829–1897)

John Mercer Langston was born on 14 December 1829. After earning bachelor's, master's, and theology degrees, he was admitted to the Ohio bar in 1854. Langston helped create the Republican Party and participated in various antislavery activities, including the Underground Railroad. He became the first black elected official in the United States in 1855 when he was elected clerk of a rural Ohio township. During the Civil War he recruited black soldiers for the Union army and, after the war ended, was appointed inspector general for the Freedmen's Bureau, a federal agency created to assist freed slaves. In 1868 Langston moved to Washington, D.C., to become dean of Howard University Law School, the first black law school in the nation. He also became the first black to practice before the U.S. Supreme Court. In 1872 Langston was named acting president of Howard, and in 1877 was named U.S. minister to Haiti. Langston returned to Virginia in 1885 to serve as the first president of what is now Virginia State University. After winning in Virginia's Fourth Congressional District, Langston was elected Virginia's first black member of Congress. Langston retired to Washington, D.C., where he died in 1897. The town of Langston, Oklahoma, home of Langston University, is named after him.

Malcolm X (1925–1965)

As a leader of the Nation of Islam, Malcolm X was one of the most controversial figures in the civil rights movement. To many whites, he was a teacher of hate; to many blacks he was the only one who truly articulated their deep frustration. Born Malcolm Little in Omaha, Nebraska, he spent much of his childhood in institutions and foster homes. As a youth, Malcolm moved to the East Coast, spending time in Boston and New York, where he became involved in drugs, gambling, and prostitution. After receiving a ten-year sentence for burglary in 1946, he radically changed his life by becoming a follower of Elijah Muhammad's Nation of Islam. After his parole in 1952, he replaced his "slave name" of Little with an X, and became more actively involved in the Nation of Islam.

In 1954 he became minister of Harlem's Temple Number 7, organized mosques throughout the nation, and quickly became nationally prominent. In 1958 he married Betty Shabazz, with whom he had six children. He did not follow Martin Luther King, Jr.'s nonviolent strategies for reform. After extensive disagreements with Elijah Muhammad, Malcolm resigned and traveled to the Middle East. On 21 February 1965 he was shot during a speech in New York. Although three black Muslims were found guilty of the crime, there is still extensive disagreement about the perpetrators of the assassination.

Burke Marshall (1922–2003)

Burke Marshall was born in Plainfield, New Jersey, and graduated from Yale in 1943. While serving in the Army he worked in the intelligence corps as a Japanese linguist and met Violet Person, a civilian linguist, whom he later married. After World War II, Marshall earned a law degree from Yale and worked in private practice. By 1970 he was a deputy dean and professor at Yale Law School.

Marshall was very influential during the civil rights era. He was assistant attorney general in charge of the U.S. Department of Justice Office of Civil Rights under Presidents John F. Kennedy and Lyndon B. Johnson. He was the government's legal strategist on the freedom rides, the Birmingham church bombing, and the March on Washington. He was also a key contributor to civil rights advances that included the government's 1961 ban on segregation in interstate travel, the desegregation of the University of Mississippi, and the adoption of the Civil Rights Act of 1964, which barred discrimination in public accommodations.

Marshall was a skilled negotiator who regularly met with people from across the political spectrum such as Martin Luther King, Jr., and Governor George C. Wallace. John Lewis, a congressmember from Georgia, recalled in a speech at Yale in 1995 that leaders of the civil rights movement had been on a first-name basis with Marshall, whose skills helped avert more severe racial discord in the American South. Marshall died of a bone marrow disorder at age eighty.

Thurgood Marshall (1908–1993)

As a lawyer, federal judge, solicitor general, and U.S. Supreme Court justice, Thurgood Marshall is one of the most recognized people in U.S. civil rights history. In 1933 he graduated at the top of his class from Howard University Law School. Shortly after graduation he started to work for the NAACP and try civil rights cases. Marshall served as legal director of the NAACP from 1940 to 1961. With his mentor Charles Hamilton Houston, Marshall developed a long-term strategy for eradicating segregation in schools. They first concentrated on graduate and professional schools and then focused on primary and secondary schools. In 1948 Marshall won *Shelley v. Kraemer,* where the Supreme Court struck down the legality of racially restrictive covenants.

His most celebrated case was the landmark 1954 decision *Brown v. Board of Education of Topeka, Kansas,* which overthrew *Plessy v. Ferguson* (1896) and declared segregation of public schools unconstitutional. Marshall won twenty-nine of the thirty-two civil rights cases he and his aides argued before the Supreme Court, a record that earned him the reputation of the nation's best civil rights lawyer. In 1961, President John F. Kennedy appointed Marshall to the U.S. Court of Appeals for the Second Circuit. From 1965 to 1967, Marshall served under President Lyndon Johnson as the first African American U.S. solicitor general. In 1967 he became the first African American U.S. Supreme Court justice, where he served until his retirement in 1991. He died 24 January 1993.

Lucretia Coffin Mott (1793–1880)

Mott was born on 3 January 1793, to Quaker parents in Nantucket, Massachusetts. When she was thirteen, Lucretia went to a coeducational Quaker school in Dutchess County, New York, where she met James Mott, her future husband. James and Lucretia married in 1811 and became parents to six children.

A social reformer who was involved with many issues, Mott was recognized for her commitments to abolishing slavery, expanding women's rights, promoting educational and prison reforms, and supporting the temperance movement. She was a friend of both Elizabeth Cady Stanton and Susan B. Anthony. In 1818, Mott began to speak at Quaker meetings and three years later was recognized as a minister in the Quaker Society of Friends in Philadelphia, where she lived most of her life.

Mott was a founder of the American Anti-Slavery Society and an early president of the Philadelphia Anti-Slavery Society. Chosen as one of only six women delegates from U.S. antislavery societies, she traveled to the World Anti-Slavery Convention in London in 1840. During the conference the women delegates were refused seats despite protests from prominent people like William Lloyd Garrison. Mott met Elizabeth Cady Stanton at this conference. Upon her return to the United States, she worked with other prominent antislavery leaders such as Frederick Douglass, William Lloyd Garrison, and Lucy Stone. The Quakers were strongly committed to both nonviolence and the abolitionist movement. Consequently, like many Quakers, Mott opposed the Civil War, but hoped that it would end slavery.

After the war, Mott continued her struggle for equal rights for both women and blacks. In May 1866, she was chosen the first president of the Equal Rights Association. Widowed in 1868, Mott continued her work until the time of her death.

Elijah Muhammad (1897–1975)

Also known as Elijah Poole, Elijah Muhammad was a son of sharecroppers and former slaves who became the spiritual leader of the Nation of Islam. Poole, born and raised in Georgia, met W. D. Fard, who claimed to be "Allah," the self-anointed leader of the Nation of Islam. After Fard's unexplained disappearance in 1934, Poole assumed control of the organization, a position he held officially or unofficially until his death. Under Muhammad's leadership, the Chicago-based group grew into a religious/nationalistic organization. Muhammad supported doctrines of racial separation, self-help, and self-defense, which foreshadowed the Black Power movement. Muhammad generated significant controversy for his militant racial views and derogatory view of whites. Before his death in 1975, he was the source of additional controversy for his well-publicized feud with his former lieutenant, Malcolm X, whose assassination in 1965 has been attributed to three of Poole's followers.

Eleanor Holmes Norton (1937–)

A civil rights activist born in Washington, D.C., Norton became a prominent attorney for the American Civil Liberties Union (ACLU) and represented the free speech rights of both Julian Bond and George Wallace. She has also served on the New York Human Rights Commission and the Equal Employment Opportunities Commission. In 1982 she became a law professor at Georgetown University. In 1991 Norton became the District of Columbia's elected, nonvoting delegate to the U.S. Congress.

Rosa Parks (1913–)

Rosa grew up in racially segregated Montgomery, Alabama, where she married Raymond Parks, a barber, at age twenty. Parks became an active member of the Montgomery Voters League and NAACP, where she was secretary of the Montgomery chapter. She is most recognized for her decision on 1 December 1955, when she refused to relinquish her seat on a bus to a white man. Parks was arrested and jailed for her transgression. News of her arrest spread quickly, and the Women's Political Council protested her treatment by organizing a bus boycott for the day of Parks's trial. Many civil rights leaders from around the nation joined the Montgomery Bus Boycott, which lasted 381 days, until the U.S. Supreme Court ruled the Montgomery segregation law illegal. Since the bus boycott, Parks has continued her work to improve the black community. She has given numerous talks and is particularly devoted to youth. In 1987, she established the Rosa and Raymond Parks Institute for Self-Development, a training school for Detroit teenagers. In 1996, she was awarded the Presidential Medal of Freedom by President William Clinton, and in 1999 she received the Congressional Medal of Honor.

Colin Powell (1937–)

Powell, appointed by President George W. Bush as secretary of state, is the highest-ranking African American public official in U.S. history. Born and raised in New York City, Powell became one of the country's best-known figures during Operation Desert Storm, as he led the United Nations offensive against Saddam Hussein's Iraq in 1990–1991. Upon graduation from the City University of New York in 1958, Powell received a second lieutenant's commission and became a career army officer, serving with distinction in Vietnam. He rose quickly through the military ranks and served as a presidential assistant for national security in the Reagan administration from 1987 to 1989. In 1988 he was nominated to become one of only ten four-star army generals. During the Reagan years he advised the president at summit conferences in both Moscow and Washington, D.C. In 1989 he became the first African American chair the Joint Chiefs of Staff, a position he held until he retired from the army in 1993. Upon retirement from the military he was awarded the Presidential Medal of Freedom. President George H. W. Bush appointed Powell U.S. secretary of state in the year 2000.

A. Philip Randolph (1889–1979)

Asa Philip Randolph was a union and civil rights leader dedicated to obtaining pay increases and shorter hours for African American employees. He sought to organize black workers in New York City to strengthen their standing against employers. During World War I, Randolph consistently called for more positions for African Americans in the armed forces and increased employment in war-related industries. After the war, he founded the Brotherhood of Sleeping Car Porters, the first successful black trade union. He fought passionately with the American Federation of Labor (AFL), which often barred blacks from membership. He eventually left the AFL and joined the newly formed Congress of Industrial Organizations (CIO). He was instrumental in persuading President Franklin D. Roosevelt to issue Executive Order 8802, which banned discrimination in defense industries and federal bureaus and created the Fair Employment Practices Committee. He also played a key role in the passage of President Harry S. Truman's Executive Order 9981, which banned segregation in the armed forces. When the AFL merged with the CIO in

1955, Randolph was made a vice president and member of the executive council of the combined organization. He formed the A. Philip Randolph Institute to promote cooperation between organized labor and the African American community.

Jackie Robinson (1919–1972)

A football, baseball, basketball, and track star at the University of California at Los Angeles, Robinson gained national prominence in 1947 when he broke the color barrier in major league baseball, which had been segregated since the 1880s. In 1945, the Brooklyn Dodgers purchased Robinson's contract from the Negro League Kansas City Monarchs. After his brilliant season with their Montreal farm team, the Dodgers promoted him to the majors in 1947, where he won rookie of the year. Robinson, who endured taunts from players and fans, become the league's most valuable player in 1949. In 1962, he became the first African American in the Baseball Hall of Fame. Robinson's opening of baseball to African Americans paved the way for increased employment opportunities in many other sectors of the economy.

Bayard Rustin (1910–1987)

Rustin was recognized for his passionate opposition to racial segregation and his strong commitment to pacifist protests. In New York City he organized a branch of the Congress on Racial Equality (CORE) in 1941 and worked for the Fellowship of Reconciliation, a nondenominational religious organization, from 1941 to 1953. He later became a trusted adviser to Martin Luther King, Jr., and a leader in the SCLC. In 1963, Rustin was the chief organizer of the March on Washington, a massive demonstration to rally support for civil rights legislation pending in Congress. One year later he directed a one-day student boycott of New York City's public schools to protest racial imbalances in the schools. Between 1966 and 1979, Rustin served as president of the A. Philip Randolph Institute, a civil rights organization in New York City.

Dred Scott (1795–1858)

Dred Scott was the focal point of one of the most important cases in U.S. history, involving the bitterly contested issue of the status of slavery in the new territories. In 1834, Scott, a slave of John Emerson, was taken from Missouri, a slave state, to Illinois, a free state, and then to the Wisconsin Territory, where the Missouri Compromise prohibited slavery. While there, Scott married before returning with Emerson to Missouri in 1838. After Emerson's death, Scott sued Emerson's widow for freedom on the ground that residence in a free state and a free territory had ended his bondage. He won his suit before a lower court in St. Louis, but the Missouri Supreme Court reversed the decision and was upheld by a federal district court. In February 1857, the U.S. Supreme Court reportedly decided to avoid the question of the constitutionality of the Missouri Compromise and to rule against Scott on the ground that under Missouri law as now interpreted by the supreme court of that state, he remained a slave despite his previous residence in free territory. However, when it became known that two justices, John McLean and Benjamin R. Curtis, planned to write dissenting opinions vigorously upholding the constitutionality of the Missouri Compromise (which had been voided by the Kansas-Nebraska Act of 1854), the court's southern members, constituting the majority, decided to consider the whole question of federal power over slavery in the territories. They decided in the case of *Scott v. Sandford* that Congress had no power to prohibit slavery in the territories. Three of the justices also held that a black "whose ancestors were . . . sold as slaves was not entitled to the rights of a federal citizen and therefore had no standing in court." This verdict further inflamed the North/South schism that was growing rapidly, and was denounced by the growing antislavery movement.

Elizabeth Cady Stanton (1815–1902)

With Susan B. Anthony, Elizabeth Cady Stanton was an abolitionist and one of the most influential leaders in the nineteenth-century women's rights movement. Stanton was born in Johnstown, New York, and married Henry Stanton, whom she met at her cousin's home. Soon after their wedding they traveled to London, where Henry Stanton was a delegate to the World Anti-Slavery Convention in 1840. While she was in London, Stanton met Lucretia Mott, who served with her in many organizations devoted to temperance, abolition, and women's rights.

In 1847, the Stantons moved to Seneca Falls, New York, where one year later Stanton and Mott organized the 1848

"Woman's Rights Convention." At this conference they drafted a "Declaration of Sentiments and Resolutions" modeled after the Declaration of Independence. In May 1869, Stanton formed the National Women's Suffrage Association, which called for women's voting rights. After her husband's death in 1887, Stanton moved to New York City, where she was involved in the National American Woman Suffrage Association and contributed to newspapers and magazines. Elizabeth Cady Standon died in 1902 at the age of eighty-six.

Lucy Stone (1818–1893)

Lucy Stone was a prominent abolitionist and influential women's rights activist. Born in West Brookfield, Massachusetts, she was the eighth of nine children. At age twenty-five, she entered Oberlin College. When she graduated in 1847 she was the first Massachusetts woman to earn a college degree. Shortly thereafter she began lecturing for the American Anti-Slavery Society. Stone started the American Woman Suffrage Association, which she later merged with a group led by Elizabeth Cady Stanton and Susan B. Anthony to form the National American Woman Suffrage Association.

Carol M. Swain

Carol M. Swain was born in Bedford, Virginia, one of twelve children. Although she never attended high school, she later earned a GED and many other degrees. She received a B.A. degree from Roanoke College in 1983, an M.A. from Virginia Tech in 1984, and a Ph.D. from the University of North Carolina at Chapel Hill in 1989. After graduating from Duke she spent ten years teaching at Princeton University's Woodrow Wilson School of Public and International Affairs. After leaving Princeton, she earned an MSL from Yale Law School in 2000, and she is currently a professor of political science and a law at Vanderbilt University.

Swain has written extensively about race, affirmative action, and voting. She has authored or edited many books and more than twenty articles in scholarly journals, including *Black Faces, Black Interests: The Representation of African Americans in Congress* and *Race Versus Class: The New Affirmative Action Debate*. She regularly writes op-eds and appears on television in prominent media outlets. She has won a number of awards for her writing, including one of the seven outstanding academic books by Library Journal, the Woodrow Wilson prize, the V.O. Key Award, and the D. B. Hardeman Prize.

Mary Church Terrell (1863–1954)

Terrell was born in Memphis, Tennessee, during the Civil War and died the year of the *Brown* decision. After graduating from Oberlin College in 1884, she moved to Europe to seek greater freedom both as a black and as a woman. Upon her return to the United States she helped start the National Association of Colored Women (NACW) in 1896, which assists mothers and children. In the 1950s she fought to desegregate restaurants in Washington, D.C. On 8 June 1953, the district court declared Washington's segregated restaurants illegal.

Abigail Thernstrom (1936–)

Abigail Thernstrom, who received her Ph.D. from the Department of Government at Harvard University, is a senior fellow at the Manhattan Institute in New York, a commissioner on the U.S. Civil Rights Commission, and a member of the Massachusetts State Board of Education. Thernstrom and her husband, Harvard historian Stephen Thernstrom, are prominent commentators on contemporary race problems and solutions. She has authored or edited numerous books and articles, including *America in Black and White* and *Whose Votes Count? Affirmative Action and Minority Voting Rights.*

She has earned many awards for excellence in writing, including top awards in law, public policy, and race and ethnicity. Thernstrom frequently appears in the media on shows such as *Fox News Sunday, Good Morning America, The Jim Lehrer News Hour, Both Sides with Jesse Jackson,* and *Black Entertainment Television.* She has written for the *Economist,* the *Wall Street Journal,* the *New York Times,* the *Washington Post,* and the *Public Interest.* She serves on several boards: the Center for Equal Opportunity and the Institute for Justice among others. President Clinton chose her as one of three authors to participate in his first "town meeting" on race in Akron, Ohio, on 3 December 1997.

Sojourner Truth (1797–1883)

Born into slavery as Isabella Baumfree in Ulster County, New York, Sojourner Truth obtained her freedom and moved to New York City in 1829. In New York she worked for decades with women's abolitionist, suffrage, and temperance organizations. After the death of her son, she took the name Sojourner Truth to signify her new role as traveler telling the truth about slavery. She quickly developed a reputation as a powerful preacher, known for her commitment to human rights for slaves and women, and for her quick wit and refusal to be intimidated. In 1850, she published an account of her early years in *The Narrative of Sojourner Truth,* which became popular abolitionist reading after Harriet Beecher Stowe publicized it in an article for *Atlantic Monthly.* Because she was unable to read or write, Truth dictated her memories of slavery to her neighbor Olive Gilbert, who wrote the book. Truth also fought for the desegregation of public transportation in Washington, D.C., during the Civil War, and spoke before Congress and two presidents. Later she served as a counselor for the National Freedman's Relief Association, retiring in 1875 to Battle Creek, Michigan.

Clarence Thomas (1948–)

In 1991, when President George H. W. Bush nominated Clarence Thomas to the Supreme Court to replace Thurgood Marshall, he became the second African American associate justice of the U.S. Supreme Court. A prominent black conservative, Thomas graduated from Yale Law School in 1974. He chaired the Equal Employment Opportunity Commission (1982–1990) during the Reagan and Bush administrations. In 1990 he was appointed a judge on the Court of Appeals for the District of Columbia Circuit. In October 1991, when approval was all but assured, the Senate Judiciary Committee reopened confirmation hearings to examine charges by Anita Hill, a law professor at the University of Oklahoma, who claimed that Thomas sexually harassed her while she was an EEOC employee in the 1980s. After extensive testimony and debate about the charges televised nationally, the Senate approved Thomas by a vote of 52–48. This led to an election season known as "The Year of the Woman," when more women were elected to the U.S. Congress than ever before.

Harriet Tubman (c. 1820–1913)

Harriet was born on the eastern shore of Maryland and had ten brothers and sisters. Harriet, who received no formal education, labored in physically demanding jobs. In 1844, at age twenty-four, she married John Tubman, and in the summer of 1849 she decided to escape from slavery. Because her husband refused to leave with her, she made her way to freedom on her own. She later returned to Baltimore to rescue her sister and began guiding others to freedom. Neither the Fugitive Slave Act nor large rewards for her capture deterred Tubman from her objective. Referred to as the "Moses" of her people, Underground Railroad conductor Tubman became a legend by leading thousands of slaves to freedom and never losing a person on her trips.

Tubman is also noted for her role in the Civil War, when she spied on the South as a scout for the Union Army. Her directions and knowledge of geography remained an asset as she explored the countryside in search of Confederate fortifications. Although she received official commendation from Union officers, she was never paid for her work. After the war she returned to Auburn, New York, where she established a home for indigent aged blacks and became involved in the women's suffrage movement. She was buried with military rites, with Booker T. Washington serving as the funeral speaker.

Nat Turner (1800–1831)

Turner was born on a plantation in Southampton County, Virginia. His parents and grandmother encouraged him to become educated and to fight slavery. The son of one of his masters taught him to read and write. Turner became a forceful preacher who believed that God wanted him to free the slaves, a conviction that led him to plan the most famous slave revolt in U.S. history. In 1831, Turner and about sixty-five other slaves killed about sixty whites in Virginia. The victims included the family of Joseph Travis, Turner's owner. The Virginia militia captured and hanged about twenty of the slaves, including Turner. The rebellion caused the southern states to pass strict laws to the control slaves, especially those who were preachers.

Madame C. J. Walker (Sarah Breedlove) (1867–1919)

Madame C. J. Walker manufactured and distributed hair care and skin products for African Americans and became the first American woman millionaire. With her significant economic resources she supported antilynching legislation and gave generously to the National Association for the Advancement of Colored People, to whom she willed her estate.

Walker was born Sarah Breedlove on 23 December 1867, in Delta, Louisiana, to emancipated slaves who worked as sharecroppers. She overcame many obstacles to achieve her success. At the age of six Sarah was orphaned. When she was only fourteen years old Sarah married Moses McWilliams, who died when Sarah was just twenty. They had one daughter who as an adult worked in her mother's business. Her second husband, Charles Joseph Walker, whom she married in 1906, helped to finance and develop her business. She adopted her husband's initials and surname as her professional name, calling herself Madam C. J. Walker for the rest of her life, even after they were divorced. On 25 May 1919, she died of hypertension at age fifty-one. Mary McLeod Bethune delivered the eulogy at Walker's funeral service.

Booker Taliaferro Washington (1856–1915)

Up from Slavery, Booker T. Washington's best-selling autobiography, recounts his life from childhood as a slave in Virginia, through the founding of the Tuskegee Institute and the National Negro Business League. After graduating from the Hampton Institute in 1875, he taught in West Virginia and studied at Wayland Seminary before returning to Virginia to teach. At Tuskegee, one of his most distinguished professors was George Washington Carver. Booker T. Washington was the most prominent spokesperson for African Americans after the death of Frederick Douglass. He sought social improvement for African Americans through economic progress. His conciliatory stances on issues such as the "separate but equal" doctrine sometimes led other African American leaders to criticize him. He died on the campus at Tuskegee in 1915 and was buried there.

Harold Washington (1922–1987)

Washington did his undergraduate work at Roosevelt University in Chicago and graduated with a law degree from Northwestern University before entering private practice. Washington held many political positions, including precinct captain, state labor arbitrator, representative in the Illinois House and Senate, and representative in the U.S. House of Representatives. At the end of his second term in Congress, Washington ran for mayor of his home city. In the 1983 Democratic primary, he upset Richard M. Daley, the son of four-term mayor Richard J. Daley. In the general election Washington narrowly defeated Bernard Epton to become the first African American mayor of Chicago, a position he held until his death in 1987.

Ida B. Wells-Barnett (1862–1931)

Ida B. Wells, a passionate journalist and speaker, was most recognized as a activist against lynching and a strong supporter of the nascent women's rights movement. She was born in Holly Springs, Mississippi, during the Civil War. The oldest of eight children, Wells supported her siblings after her parents died of yellow fever by becoming a teacher. She attended Rust College and later moved to Memphis, Tennessee, to live with her aunt. While in Memphis, she became editor and co-owner of a black newspaper called *The Free Speech and Headlight*. When some friends of hers were lynched, she started a lifelong odyssey to eliminate lynching.

In June of 1895 she married Ferdinand Barnett, a prominent Chicago attorney. She was a devoted mother to her two sons and two daughters. In 1906, she joined W.E.B. DuBois in the Niagara Movement. She was one of two African American women founding members of the National Association for the Advancement of Colored People (NAACP) and became one of the first black women to run for public office, when in 1930 she campaigned for the Illinois State legislature. She died in Chicago in 1931 at the age of sixty-nine.

William Wilberforce (1759–1833)

Wilberforce studied at Cambridge University, where he befriended William Pitt the Younger, the former prime minister of Britain, a relationship that would be extremely important for his future success. In 1780, Wilberforce was elected to the British Parliament, and four years later converted to Christianity, a decision that profoundly affected his entire outlook on life. He became a leading humanitarian and started the campaign for the abolition of the slave trade in 1788. Every year for eighteen years, Wilberforce introduced antislavery motions in Parliament. Wilberforce's unpopular beliefs made him the subject of constant allegations by fellow members of Parliament to discredit him and his objectives. His perseverance paid off when in 1807 Parliament ended the slave trade. However, eliminating the slave trade failed to eliminate the institution of slavery, and Wilberforce redirected his efforts to suppress the institution throughout the British Empire. To that end he was a founding member of the Anti-Slavery Society. Unfortunately Wilberforce did not live to see this goal accomplished; Parliament passed the bill to eliminate slavery in the British Empire one month after he died. Afterward London, which hosted the World Anti-Slavery Convention in 1840, became the center for antislavery campaigns, and many people whom Wilberforce influenced were important abolitionists throughout the world. Wilberforce is buried next to his friend Pitt in Westminster Abbey.

Lawrence Douglas Wilder (1931–)

The grandson of slaves and the youngest of ten children, Douglas Wilder was born in Richmond, Virginia. After graduating in 1951 from Virginia Union University with a bachelor of science degree in chemistry, Wilder was drafted by the U.S. Army and stationed in Korea, where he won a Bronze Star. After returning from the war, Wilder decided to earn a law degree. However, because all the Virginia law schools still barred African Americans, he chose to attend Howard University in Washington, D.C. In 1969, Wilder became the first African American in Virginia's Senate since Reconstruction. His aggressive style and strong support helped him to quickly become one of the most influential members of the Senate. Sixteen years later, Wilder won the election for lieutenant governor (1986–1990) and became the first African American to win a statewide election in Virginia. In 1989, Wilder won Virginia's closest election for governor (1990–1994) and became the first African American governor of any state in the nation. In 1998 Wilder was chosen to head Virginia Union University.

Oprah Winfrey (1954–)

From humble beginnings in rural Mississippi, Oprah Winfrey has become one of the most prominent, influential, and highly compensated entertainers in the world. She started her career in broadcasting in Nashville at age nineteen, when she became the youngest person and first African American woman to anchor the news in Nashville. In 1984 she moved to Chicago where her career took off. Winfrey is the producer and host of *The Oprah Winfrey Show,* the highest-rated talk show in television history, seen by more than 20 million people per week in the United States and broadcast in more than 115 nations. This show's excellence has been recognized as it has received thirty-four Emmy Awards. In addition, Winfrey has received many of the most prestigious awards in broadcasting, including the George Foster Peabody Award (1996), the IRTS Gold Medal Award (1996), and the National Academy of Television Arts and Sciences' Lifetime Achievement Award (1998).

Winfrey's impact has transcended her show. She has also made many important contributions in philanthropy, education, health and fitness, and social justice. In 1996, she began "Oprah's Book Club" to generate interest in reading. Every book she has featured on this segment has instantly hit the best-seller's list. She also started Oprah's Angel Network, which generates college funds for needy students, funded more than 200 Habitat for Humanity homes, and was active in passing legislation to establish a national database of convicted child abusers. *Time* magazine recognized Winfrey as one of the 100 most influential people of the twentieth century.

Carter Godwin Woodson (1875–1950)

In his distinguished academic career, Carter G. Woodson earned bachelor's and master's degrees from the University of Chicago and a doctoral degree in 1912 from Harvard University, becoming only the second African American to receive such a degree. Convinced that scholars were generally ignoring or misrepresenting the role of blacks in history, Woodson devoted his career to changing this situation. He was instrumental in developing the field of African American studies. During his career he published many scholarly books and journal articles, began the scholarly *Journal of Negro History,* wrote the *Encyclopedia Africana,* and helped organize the Associated Publishers, the oldest black publishing company in the country. One of his most noted accomplishments was the founding of the Association for the Study of Negro Life and History, which sponsored the first Negro History Week during February 1926. He chose the second week of February because the two people he believed had most significantly impacted the lives of African Americans were born during that month: Abraham Lincoln and Frederick Douglass. This event has grown consistently, and in 1976 was changed to Black History Month to help Americans reflect on both the history and teachings of African Americans whose contributions are too little known.

Andrew Young (1932–)

A dynamic clergyman and civil rights leader, with an outstanding record as a public official, Andrew Young attended Dillard University, in New Orleans, Louisiana, before he earned a bachelor of science degree at Howard University in 1951 and a B.D. degree from Hartford Theological Seminary in 1955. Active in interracial and civil rights projects since his seminary days, Young joined the staff of the SCLC in 1961. A skilled strategist and negotiator, Young soon gained prominence as one of Martin Luther King, Jr.'s, lieutenants. From 1964 to 1970 Young served as the executive director of SCLC and between 1967 and 1970 as the organization's executive vice president as well. He now sits on its board of directors and on the board of the Martin Luther King, Jr., Center for Social Change. In 1972 Andrew Young became the first African American to be elected to the U.S. House of Representatives since Reconstruction. In 1977, President Jimmy Carter appointed him the first black U.S. ambassador to the United Nations. Between 1982 and 1990 he served as mayor of Atlanta, but, in 1990, Young lost his bid to become Georgia's first African American governor.

5

Laws, Cases, Statistics, and Quotations

This chapter contains four sections. The first segment contains many of the laws that were important for defining and securing equal treatment across races. Because many important strides toward racial justice involved the legal system, it is extremely important to have some knowledge of these influential cases, which the second section contains. The third portion includes, in table form, statistical comparisons and contrasts by race of the primary themes of this book. The last part consists of quotations from prominent people about racial issues.

Laws

U.S. Declaration of Independence, 1776

We hold these truths to be self-evident, that all men are created equal, that they are endowed by their Creator with certain unalienable Rights, that among these are Life, Liberty, and the pursuit of Happiness.

U.S. Constitution, Article 1, Section 2 (1787)

Clause 3. Representatives and direct Taxes shall be apportioned among the several States which may be included within this

Union, according to their respective Numbers, which shall be determined by adding to the whole Number of free Persons, including those bound to Service for a Term of Years, and excluding Indians not taxed, *three fifths of all other Persons.* The actual Enumeration shall be made within three Years after the first Meeting of the Congress of the United States, and within every subsequent Term of ten Years, in such Manner as they shall by Law direct. The Number of Representatives shall not exceed one for every thirty Thousand, but each State shall have at Least one Representative; and until such enumeration shall be made, the State of New Hampshire shall be entitled to choose three, Massachusetts eight, Rhode-Island and Providence Plantations one, Connecticut five, New-York six, New Jersey four, Pennsylvania eight, Delaware one, Maryland six, Virginia ten, North Carolina five, South Carolina five, and Georgia three.

U.S. Constitution, Article 1, Section 9 (1787)

Clause 1. The Migration or Importation of such Persons as any of the States now existing shall think proper to admit, shall not be prohibited by the Congress prior to the Year one thousand eight hundred and eight, but a Tax or duty may be imposed on such Importation, not exceeding ten dollars for each Person.

U.S. Constitution, Article 4, Section 2 (1787)

Clause 3. No Person held to Service or Labour in one State, under the Laws thereof, escaping into another, shall, in Consequence of any Law or Regulation therein, be discharged from such Service or Labour, but shall be delivered upon Claim of the Party to whom such Service or Labour may be due.

First Morrill Act (1862)

The First Morrill Act, enacted by Congress on 2 July 1862, created public land-grant colleges and universities.

Emancipation Proclamation (1863)

Issued by the first Republican President, Abraham Lincoln, the Emancipation Proclamation freed all slaves in Confederate states. Although the document had been written for many weeks,

Lincoln delayed its publication pending a significant Union victory. The Battle of Antietam provided such an opportunity, and on 22 September 1862 Lincoln issued the Preliminary Emancipation Proclamation announcing his intention of freeing all slaves in places that had not returned to their allegiance within the following three months. He presented the final document on 1 January 1863. Clearly indicating that he was acting in his capacity as commander in chief of the army in times of actual armed rebellion, the president declared free all slaves in areas still in rebellion and invited blacks to enlist in the armed forces. Tennessee and part of Louisiana and Virginia were specifically exempted, so that on the day of issue only a few slaves in the South were legally affected by the document. However, as the Union gained control over more land, the proclamation became effective in the rest of the Confederacy.

Whereas on the 22nd day of September, A.D. 1862, a proclamation was issued by the President of the United States, containing, among other things, the following, to wit:

That on the 1st day of January, A.D. 1863, all persons held as slaves within any State or designated part of a State the people whereof shall then be in rebellion against the United States shall be then, thenceforward, and forever free; and the executive government of the United States, including the military and naval authority thereof, will recognize and maintain the freedom of such persons and will do no act or acts to repress such persons, or any of them, in any efforts they may make for their actual freedom.

That the executive will on the 1st day of January aforesaid, by proclamation, designate the States and parts of States, if any, in which the people thereof, respectively, shall then be in rebellion against the United States; and the fact that any State or the people thereof shall on that day be in good faith represented in the Congress of the United States by members chosen thereto at elections wherein a majority of the qualified voters of such States shall have participated shall, in the absence of strong countervailing testimony, be deemed conclusive evidence that such State and the people thereof are not then in rebellion against the United States.

Now, therefore, I, Abraham Lincoln, President of the United States, by virtue of the power in me vested as Commander-In-Chief of the Army and Navy of the United States in time of actual armed rebellion against the authority and government of the United States, and as a fit and necessary war measure for suppressing said rebellion, do, on this 1st day of January, A.D. 1863, and in accordance with my purpose so to do, publicly proclaimed for the full period of one hundred days from the first day above mentioned, order and designate as the States and parts of States wherein the people thereof, respectively, are this day in rebellion against the United States the following, to wit:

Arkansas, Texas, Louisiana (except the parishes of St. Bernard, Palquemines, Jefferson, St. John, St. Charles, St. James, Ascension, Assumption, Terrebone, Lafourche, St. Mary, St. Martin, and Orleans, including the city of New Orleans), Mississippi, Alabama, Florida, Georgia, South Carolina, North Carolina, and Virginia (except the forty-eight counties designated as West Virginia, and also the counties of Berkeley, Accomac, Northhampton, Elizabeth City, York, Princess Anne, and Norfolk, including the cities of Norfolk and Portsmouth), and which excepted parts are for the present left precisely as if this proclamation were not issued.

And by virtue of the power and for the purpose aforesaid, I do order and declare that all persons held as slaves within said designated States and parts of States are, and henceforward shall be, free; and that the Executive Government of the United States, including the military and naval authorities thereof, will recognize and maintain the freedom of said persons.

And I hereby enjoin upon the people so declared to be free to abstain from all violence, unless in necessary self-defence; and I recommend to them that, in all case when allowed, they labor faithfully for reasonable wages.

And I further declare and make known that such persons of suitable condition will be received into the armed service of the United States to garrison forts, positions, stations, and other places, and to man vessels of all sorts in said service.

And upon this act, sincerely believed to be an act of justice, warranted by the Constitution upon military necessity, I invoke the considerate judgment of mankind and the gracious favor of Almighty God.

Black Codes

After the Civil War, most of the southern states passed Black Codes to limit the ability of the freedmen to participate fully in society. These laws ensured an immobile, dependent black labor force for each state's agricultural interest by disempowering black laborers. Failure to adhere to strict stipulations resulted in arrest and being hired out for a period not to exceed one year. One provision made it a misdemeanor to lure an employee under contract away from his employer. Although most Black Codes made no distinction based on race, they were worded to exempt white workers. Furthermore, some counties and towns passed ordinances that were blatantly discriminatory. When Reconstruction ended, the Black Codes were made illegal. The maintenance of such southern practices as the convict lease system, black peonage, and contract labor laws well into the twentieth century, however, ensured continuing forms of forced labor in the South.

Thirteenth Amendment (Ratified in December 1865)

Section 1. Neither slavery nor involuntary servitude, except as a punishment for crime whereof the party shall have been duly convicted, shall exist within the United States, or any place subject to their jurisdiction.

Section 2. Congress shall have power to enforce this article by appropriate legislation.

Civil Rights Act of 1866

Enacted on 9 April 1866 by an increasingly radical Congress over President Andrew Johnson's veto, the act declared that all persons born in the United States were citizens, without regard to race, color, or previous condition. As citizens, they could make and enforce contracts, sue and be sued, give evidence in court, and inherit, purchase, lease, sell, hold, and convey real and personal property. Persons who denied these rights to former slaves were guilty of a misdemeanor and upon conviction faced a fine not exceeding $1,000, or imprisonment not exceeding one year, or both. Authority for prosecuting the cases was given to U.S. district attorneys, marshals, and deputy marshals. Although the law did not mention the rights of blacks with regard to public education or public accommodations, some of its language became part of the Fourteenth Amendment. However, in the midst of political turmoil, the law failed to protect the civil rights of freedmen.

Fourteenth Amendment (Ratified in July 1868)

Section 1. All persons born or naturalized in the United States, and subject to the jurisdiction thereof, are citizens of the United States and of the State wherein they reside. No State shall make or enforce any law which shall abridge the privileges or immunities of citizens of the United States; nor shall any State deprive any person of life, liberty, or property, without due process of law; nor deny to any person within its jurisdiction the equal protection of the laws.

Section 2. Representatives shall be apportioned among the several States according to their respective numbers, counting the whole number of persons in each State, excluding Indians not taxed. But when the right to vote at any election for the choice of electors for President and Vice President of the United States, Representatives in Congress, the Executive and Judicial officers of a State, or the members of the Legislature thereof, is denied to any of the male inhabitants of such State, being twenty-one years of age, and citizens of the United States, or in any way abridged, except for participation in rebellion, or other crime, the basis of representation therein shall be reduced in the proportion which the number of such male citizens shall bear to the whole number of male citizens twenty-one years of age in such State.

Section 3. No person shall be a Senator or Representative in Congress, or elector of President and Vice President, or hold any office, civil or military, under the United States, or under any State, who, having previously taken an oath, as a member of Congress, or as an officer of the United States, or as a member of any State legislature, or as an executive or judicial officer of any State, to support the Constitution of the United States, shall have engaged in insurrection or rebellion against the same, or given aid or comfort to the enemies thereof. But Congress may by a vote of two-thirds of each House, remove such disability.

Section 4. The validity of the public debt of the United States, authorized by law, including debts incurred for payment of pensions and bounties for services in suppressing insurrection or rebellion, shall not be questioned. But neither the United States nor any State shall assume or pay any debt or obligation incurred in aid of insurrection or rebellion against the United States, or any claim for the loss or emancipation of any slave; but all such debts, obligations, and claims shall be held illegal and void.

Section 5. The Congress shall have power to enforce, by appropriate legislation, the provisions of this article.

Fifteenth Amendment (Ratified in February 1870)

Section 1. The right of citizens of the United States to vote shall not be denied or abridged by the United States or by any state on account of race, color, or previous condition of servitude.

Section 2. The Congress shall have power to enforce this article by appropriate legislation.

Civil Rights Act of 1875

The bill, which became law on 1 March 1875, promised that all persons, regardless of race, color, or previous condition, were entitled to full and equal employment of accommodations in "inns, public conveyances on land or water, theaters, and other places of public amusement." Nor could any citizen be denied the right to serve on grand or petit juries. The federal and district courts were given responsibility to enforce the law; those convicted faced a fine of between $500 and $1,000 for each offense, and a forfeiture of $500 to the aggrieved individual. Excluded from the law was a section concerning equal enjoyment of public education. Although blacks asserted their rights under the law, federal officials were often indifferent to their claims of discrimination. In 1883, the U.S. Supreme Court struck down the law by declaring that Congress did not have the power to regulate the conduct and transactions of individuals.

Second Morrill Act (1890)

The Second Morrill Act required states with dual systems of higher education to provide land-grant institutions for both systems.

Civil Rights Act of 1957

This act established the Civil Rights Office of the U.S. Department of Justice, empowered federal prosecutors to obtain court injunctions against interference with the right to vote, and established a federal Commission on Civil Rights with the authority to investigate discriminatory conditions and to recommend corrective measures. The first civil rights law passed by Congress since Reconstruction, it significantly encouraged African Americans.

Civil Rights Act of 1960

This act made unlawful avoiding prosecution for bombing offenses and interference with court orders for school desegregation. It also empowered federal judges to appoint referees to hear persons claiming that state election officials had denied them the right to register and vote. The law was difficult to enforce, because before a finding could be made and penalties implemented, the Justice Department had to bring forth specific cases to prove that qualified citizens had been denied the vote because of race or color.

Civil Rights Act of 1964

This is one of the most recognized laws passed by Congress in the twentieth century. The act prohibited discrimination by businesses serving the public, forbade discrimination by employers or labor unions in employment decisions, authorized government agencies to withhold federal money from any program permitting discrimination, and authorized the U.S. attorney general to file suit to force desegregation of public areas. The act also tightened provisions to prevent denial of black voting rights in federal elections, established a federal agency to assist local communities in settling racial disputes; and granted additional powers to the Commission on Civil Rights. The most controversial section of the act addressed public accommodations. Under threat of prosecution, most businesses generally accepted that separate public accommodations for the races was settled permanently. Desegregated public facilities became the norm throughout the nation.

Voting Rights Act of 1965

In 1964 President Lyndon B. Johnson began to plan voting rights legislation, and the president called for legislation in his 1965 State of the Union address. The voting rights campaign in Selma, Alabama, led by Martin Luther King, Jr., prompted the administration to act more quickly. In a 15 March address to Congress at the height of the Selma demonstrations that climaxed with the

Selma to Montgomery march, the president employed the phrase "we shall overcome" to call for voting rights legislation. Congress approved a voting rights bill in early August, which was signed by the president on 6 August.

The Voting Rights Act outlawed educational requirements for voting in states or counties where less than half of the voting age population had been registered on 1 November 1964 or voted in the 1964 presidential election, and empowered the U.S. attorney general to have the Civil Service Commission assign federal registrars to enroll voters. Other parts of the bill required a federal district court in Washington, D.C., to approve all changes in voting procedures in the affected jurisdictions for the next ten years and permitted the court to lift the provisions when a state proved it had not discriminated for ten years. Implementation began on 10 August when, at the direction of Attorney General Nicholas Katzenbach, federal registrars began registering voters in nine southern counties. By the end of 1965, federal examiners had registered nearly 80,000 new voters. Many of the affected southern states attempted to use a variety of devices—gerrymandering, at-large elections, more appointive offices, higher qualifications for candidates—to dilute or negate the effect of black voters. Largely as a result of enforcement of the Voting Rights Act, black registration soared in the South. In Mississippi, for example, black registrants went from 28,500 in 1964 to 251,000 in 1968. The percentage of voting-age blacks registered to vote in the South grew from 43 percent in 1964 to 62 percent in 1968. The larger number of black voters produced more black officeholders and white officials more receptive to black constituents. In 1966 the U.S. Supreme Court upheld the Voting Rights Act in *South Carolina v. Katzenbach* and *Katzenbach v. Morgan.* Congress renewed the Voting Rights Act in 1970, 1975, and 1982.

Civil Rights Act of 1968

This law was finally passed after a lengthy debate in Congress during the heightened racial tension following the assassination of Martin Luther King, Jr. Its most important section prohibited discrimination in the rental or sale of housing, thus becoming the first congressional act since 1866 to address open housing. The act also contained several important provisions protecting civil rights and upholding civil obedience. It provided criminal penalties for anyone who interfered with or injured a person for exercising specified rights, such as voting, using public accommodations, serving on a jury, and attending school or college. Civil rights workers who encouraged citizens to exercise the above and other fundamental rights were similarly protected. An antiriot provision provided criminal penalties for persons utilizing interstate commerce facilities to incite, organize, or take part in a riot.

Civil Rights Act of 1991

This bill addressed discrimination in the hiring and promotion of minorities and women, and strengthened Title VII of the Civil Rights Act of 1964 by providing stronger guarantees against discrimination in employment. Anyone suffering from job discrimination because of race, religion, national origin, or gender was permitted to bring suit against the employer, not just for job reinstatement and back pay, as provided for in the 1964 legislation, but also for punitive damages.

Court Cases

Roberts v. City of Boston, 59 Mass. 198 (1850)

The Supreme Court of Massachusetts denied that school segregation violated the state constitution's guarantees of equality of persons. The Boston school system prohibited black children from attending schools with whites. Five-year-old Sarah Roberts brought a suit through her father. She argued that Massachusetts law neither created nor recognized racial distinctions and that separate schools for blacks were inconvenient because of their distance from the children's homes. Shortly after the case, in 1855, the city abolished the system.

Dred Scott v. Sandford, 19 How. 393 (March 6, 1857)

In a 7–2 vote, the U.S. Supreme Court ruled that Congress had no power to exclude slavery from the nation's territories and that the Missouri Compromise of 1820 was therefore unconstitutional. It also declared that the rights and privileges proclaimed in the

Declaration of Independence and the Constitution did not extend to blacks.

The case concerned a slave, Dred Scott, who had traveled into a "free soil" state with his master. At that time a "free soil" state was one where slavery was prohibited. The court declared the "free soil" federal laws, which held that any slave on free soil was no longer the property of his master, were unconstitutional because they deprived a slave owner of the right to receive just compensation from the government for deprivation of property. Justice Taney summed up the court's argument when he wrote "Though Congress could acquire territories and prepare them for statehood it does not have a broader police power within the areas." No word in the Constitution can be found that gives Congress a greater power over slave property, or that entitles property of that kind to less protection, than property of any other description. The Court also held that blacks could not become citizens and therefore were not entitled to the privileges and immunities held by white Americans. This decision on citizenship was later overturned by the Fourteenth Amendment.

Plessy v. Ferguson, 163 U.S. 537 (1896)

This 1896 Supreme Court decision firmly established the separate but equal formula that endured until being overturned in 1954 by *Brown v. Board of Education of Topeka, Kansas.* The decision was one of a long series of Court opinions beginning in the 1870s—the *Slaughterhouse Cases, United States v. Reese,* and *United States v. Cruikshank*—that eroded the rights and privileges gained by blacks during Reconstruction and guaranteed by the Fourteenth and Fifteenth Amendments. This doctrine significantly weakened the Fourteenth Amendment's Equal Protection clause and provided the constitutional basis for many Jim Crow laws.

This case involved an 1890 Louisiana statute that required all railroad companies operating in the state to provide equal but separate accommodations for black and white passengers. Homer A. Plessy, an African American who often passed as white, was arrested for refusing to vacate a seat in a white compartment of a Louisiana train. He challenged the law, contending that it violated the Equal Protection clause of the Fourteenth Amendment. After losing in the state courts, he appealed to the U.S. Supreme Court, which also upheld the constitutionality of the law. The Court ruled that laws permitting or even requiring separation of the races did not necessarily imply the inferiority of either race to the other. Such laws were clearly authorized by the Constitution under the police power of the states and there was nothing unreasonable in the Louisiana statute requiring the separation of the two races in public conveyances. Justice John Marshall Harlan's prophetic dissent stated, "Our Constitution is color-blind, and neither knows nor tolerates classes among citizens," and predicted that "the judgment this day rendered will, in time, prove to be quite as pernicious as the decision made by this tribunal in the Dred Scott case."

Shelley v. Kraemer, 334 U.S. 1 (1948)

This case was the first of the four restrictive covenant cases (the other three being *McGhee v. Sipes, Hurd v. Hodge,* and *Urciolo v. Hodge*) decided in 1948. In it the U.S. Supreme Court held racially restrictive property deeds unenforceable. Developers and neighborhood organizations placed restrictive covenants into deeds to segregate African Americans (and others by race, national origin, and religion) from white neighborhoods. In St. Louis, where the *Shelley* case originated, covenants restricted more than five square miles. When the Shelleys, an African American family, purchased a home covered by a covenant, the Kraemers, a white family, sought an injunction to block occupancy. The circuit court refused, but the Missouri Supreme Court reversed this decision. The NAACP coordinated the work of lawyers George Vaughn (*Shelley*), Thurgood Marshall (*McGhee*), and Charles H. Houston (*Hurd* and *Urciolo*). Chief Justice Frederick Vinson's unanimous opinion found racially restrictive covenants, voluntarily maintained, permissible, but state action to enforce them violated Fourteenth Amendment "rights to acquire, enjoy, own, and dispose of property." Although a major victory, *Shelley* failed to stop private housing discrimination—neither the Federal Housing Administration nor the Public Housing Administration fully complied.

Avery v. Georgia, 345, U.S. 559 (1953)

This U.S. Supreme Court case clarified what constituted racial discrimination as prescribed by the Equal Protection clause of the Fourteenth Amendment in a state's jury selection process. James Avery, an African American, was tried and convicted of rape in the Superior Court of Fulton County, Georgia, in 1952. He appealed on the grounds that racial discrimination in the selection of the trial jury had deprived him of the equal protection of the law. On 25 May 1953, the U.S. Supreme Court upheld his appeal. The Court ruled that although the petitioner may not be able to identify particular acts of discrimination, the jury selection process, in which prospective white jurors' names were handled on white tickets and prospective black jurors' names were handled on yellow tickets, constituted "*prima facie* evidence of discrimination." The burden of proof in such instances falls upon the state, and in the absence of countervailing evidence of blacks actually serving on juries, convictions obtained before juries so selected had to be reversed.

Barrows v. Jackson, 346 U.S. 249 (1953)

This decision barred damage awards when racially restrictive covenants were violated. This case grew out of efforts by whites to circumvent *Shelley v. Kraemer* (1948), and maintain segregated neighborhoods or gain damages from covenant violations. In *Shelley*, the U.S. Supreme Court forbade state action to enforce a deed restriction that would block African Americans and others from occupying property. In *Barrows*, Leola Jackson, a white Los Angeles property owner, faced suit for damages from neighbors for selling property covered by a covenant to an African American. Although both parties were white and no discrimination was directly involved, Loren Miller of the NAACP defended Jackson; plaintiffs gained support nationwide from white property owners' associations. When California courts refused to award damages, Barrows appealed to the U.S. Supreme Court. In his majority opinion, Justice Sherman Minton concluded that damage awards would deny the third party's right to equal protection guaranteed by the Fourteenth Amendment.

Brown v. Board of Education of Topeka, Kansas, 347 U.S. 483 (1954)

Brown, one of the most notable legal cases in U.S. jurisprudence, removed the most important constitutional obstacle to equal rights for blacks. During Reconstruction, Congress inserted the Equal Protection clause into the Fourteenth Amendment so that blacks and whites would be equal before the law. However, the federal government and states refused to enforce the Fourteenth Amendment. In 1896 the Supreme Court held in *Plessy v. Ferguson* that as long as transportation facilities were theoretically equal, separation based on race was lawful under the Equal Protection clause. Shortly thereafter, this ruling was extended to educational facilities.

The NAACP Legal Defense and Educational Fund, led by Thurgood Marshall, attacked the *Plessy* doctrine in grade schools. Seeking to demonstrate the widespread nature of racial injustice, Marshall and the NAACP initiated suits simultaneously in Delaware, Kansas, South Carolina, Virginia, and Washington, D.C. The cases reached the Supreme Court in December 1952, and the Court consolidated the four state suits under the Kansas litigation, and treated separately the federal questions raised in the Washington appeal.

In 1954 the Court concurred unanimously in Chief Earl Warren's reversal of *Plessy,* holding that "in the field of public education the doctrine of 'separate but equal' has no place." The Court ruled that black children had been deprived of the equal protection of the laws guaranteed by the Fourteenth Amendment and that separate facilities based on race were "inherently unequal."

Cooper v. Aaron, 358 U.S. 1 (1958)

After *Brown v. Board of Education,* some areas, like Little Rock, Arkansas, integrated their schools very slowly. At the beginning of the 1957–1958 school year, nine African American children were chosen to attend the previously all-white Central High School. The state legislature, governor, and the general public adamantly opposed desegregation. Many people attempted to prevent these students from entering the school. Federal troops were sent to protect the students during the school year. The next year, the Little Rock Board petitioned the District Court to suspend the desegregation plan for two and one-half years, because of the extremely hostile public reaction that desegregation generated. The District Court ruled in favor of the school district. However, the U.S. Court of Appeals for the Eighth Circuit reversed, and the U.S. Supreme Court upheld the Appeals Court's decision. The Court rejected the argument that threatened violence or disorder justified delay in desegregating the schools, especially when the state was instrumental in threatening that violence. This was a key ruling in expediting the integration of public schools.

Harper v. Virginia Board of Elections, 383 U.S. 663 (1966)

Annie E. Harper, a retired domestic, was one of many black southerners who brought cases in the federal courts seeking a decision to ban poll taxes in state elections. In Virginia, a poll tax had been imposed since 1902. In a 6–3 decision in March 1966, the U.S. Supreme Court relied on the Fourteenth Amendment's Equal Protection clause to overrule *Breedlove v. Suttles* (1937) and struck down a requirement in the Virginia Constitution that required prospective voters to have paid poll taxes for the previous three years before they could vote. By the time the court made its ruling, lower federal courts had recently outlawed the poll tax as a requirement for voting in Texas and Alabama, and the tax had remained in effect only in Mississippi and Virginia. The decision culminated a series of significant changes in the electoral and legislative environments in Virginia and other southern states.

Loving v. Virginia, 388 U.S. 1 (1967)

Virginia prohibited the marriage of Richard Perry Loving, who was white, and Mildred Delores Jester, who was not. The couple were married in Washington, D.C., in June 1958, and returned to Caroline County, Virginia. Convicted in January 1959 of violating the state's antimiscegenation law, they were given the minimum sentence the law permitted, one year each in jail, such sentence to be suspended if they left the state for twenty-five years. They moved to Washington, D.C., but in 1963 they challenged the constitutionality of the law that had led to their banishment. In March 1966, the Virginia Supreme Court of Appeals upheld the statute and the conviction. However, in June 1967, the U.S. Supreme Court unanimously ruled that the Fourteenth Amendment's Equal Protection and Due Process clauses denied any state the authority to use racial classifiers to determine which citizens could intermarry. Such statutes fell in the sixteen states where they were still on the books.

Allen v. State Board of Elections, 393 U.S. 544 (1968)

Although the Voting Rights Act of 1965 gave African Americans access to the polls, they continued to encounter obstacles to voting. To dilute the political power of the newly enfranchised blacks, white southern politicians changed electoral laws and practices to reduce the effect of the black vote. It was not clear that the Voting Rights Act of 1965 prohibited such electoral manipulations. Southern conservatives argued that the act simply prohibited restrictions limiting the right to register and vote but did not pertain to changes made in the electoral process. In *Allen v. State Board of Elections,* a suit brought by the Legal Defense and Educational Fund of the NAACP, the U.S. Supreme Court swept aside a Mississippi statute that permitted a change from district to at-large elections of certain county officials. Because the statute diluted black voting power and thereby curtailed their ability to elect candidates, the Mississippi law violated the Voting Rights Act.

Alexander v. Holmes County Board of Education, 396 U.S. 1218 (1969)

On 29 October 1969, the U.S. Supreme Court unanimously declared that public school desegregation at "all deliberate speed," as allowed in the second *Brown v. Board of Education* case in 1955, was no longer acceptable. In *Alexander* the court ordered that the dual school systems in Mississippi's thirty-three school districts be eliminated and replaced immediately with integrated school systems. State officials argued futilely that such a large integration during the middle of the academic year would significantly disrupt the educational process. *Alexander* was particularly important because it changed federal policy from emphasizing desegregation to promoting integration. This ruling substantially increased the rate of integration in public schools in the South.

University of California Regents v. Bakke, 438 U.S. 265 (1978)

This case led to a 5–4 U.S. Supreme Court decision in favor of Alan Bakke, a white man who had been twice rejected by the University of California at Davis medical school. The Court ruled that the admissions policy of reserving seats for minority applicants denied fair access to education for nonminorities.

Hopwood v. Texas, 518 U.S. 1033, 116 S. Ct. 2581 (1996)

The 1996 case of *Hopwood v. Texas* significantly undermined the constitutionality of affirmative action programs. Cheryl J. Hopwood, Douglas W. Carvell, Kenneth R. Elliott, and David A. Rogers, a white female and three white males, brought suit against the University of Texas, alleging violations of the equal protection clause of the Fourteenth Amendment. The University of Texas Law School used separate evaluative processes for minority and nonminority applicants. On 19 March, the Fifth Circuit Court of Appeals nullified a University of Texas Law School admissions policy that sought certain percentages of black and Latino students. The Court concluded that the admission procedure used was impermissible and unnecessarily harmed the rights of the plaintiffs. Two of the three appellate judges denounced the practice of using racial classifications and argued that the goal of creating a diverse student body was insufficient to legally justify the policy. On 1 July 1996, the U.S. Supreme Court denied the petition for a writ of certiorari; it refused to hear the case. This ruling went beyond *Bakke*, which supported some affirmative action measures. *Hopwood* essentially prohibited any use of racial preferences in admissions.

Statistics

This section provides information about racial differences as they pertain to the five substantive divisions—criminal justice, education, employment, living conditions, and political participation—discussed in Chapter 2.

Criminal Justice

Table 5.1 Estimated Rate (per 1,000 Persons Age 12 and Older) of Personal Victimization, 1998

	White	Black
All Crimes	37.5	43.7
All Violent Crimes	36.3	41.7
Rape/Sexual Assault	1.5	2.0
Robbery	3.7	5.9
Assault	31.1	33.7
Personal Theft	1.2	2.1

Source: Sourcebook of Criminal Justice Statistics, 1999, Table 3.7, p. 182.

Table 5.2 Death Rates for Homicide and Legal Intervention, by Sex and Age, 1998

	Male		Female	
Ages	White	Black	White	Black
All	6.4	43.1	2.2	8.6
Under 1 year	6.7	21.8	5.9	22.1
1–14 years old	1.1	4.9	1.1	3.4
15–24 years old	12.2	96.5	2.8	12.6
25–44 years old	8.7	59.0	3.2	13.0
45–64 years old	4.7	25.8	1.7	5.0
65 years old and over	2.8	11.9	1.7	4.0

Note: Death rate is the number of deaths per 100,000 people.
Source: Black Americans: A Statistical Sourcebook, 2001, Palo Alto, CA: Information Publications, Table 2.17.

Table 5.3 Percent of People Arrested by Offense Charged and Race, 1998

Type of Crime	White	Black
Total	68.0	29.7
Violent Crimes	57.7	40.2
Murder and Nonnegligent Manslaughter	44.5	53.4
Forcible Rape	60.2	37.5
Robbery	43.0	55.3
Aggravated Assault	61.6	36.3
Property Crimes	65.3	31.9
Burglary	68.3	29.5
Larceny/Theft	65.3	31.8
Motor Vehicle Theft	58.0	39.2
Other Crimes:		
Weapons Carrying	59.3	39.1
Drug Abuse	61.5	37.3
Prostitution and Commercialized Vice	60.4	37.6
Fraud	67.3	31.5
Forgery and Counterfeiting	66.4	31.8
Offenses against Family and Children	68.2	29.2
Embezzlement	63.1	35.0
Vandalism	73.6	24.2
Driving under the Influence	86.9	10.5

Source: Sourcebook of Criminal Justice Statistics, 1999, Table 4.10, p. 408.

Table 5.4 Percent of Federal Defendants Convicted in U.S. District Courts by Race, Fiscal Year 1998

Type of Crime	White %	Black %
All Crimes	67.0	27.7
All Violent Crimes	52.0	30.2
Drug Offenses	63.3	34.3
Fraudulent Property Offenses	64.5	28.9
Misdemeanors	64.6	25.2

Source: *Sourcebook of Criminal Justice Statistics,* 1999, Table 5.23, p. 421.

Table 5.5 Number and Rate (Per 100,000 Adult Residents in Each Group) of Adults Held in State or Federal Prisons or Local Jails, 1997

1997	Male		Female	
	White	Black	White	Black
Number of Persons, 1997	806,300	753,600	65,200	63,000
Rate, 1997	990	6,838	76	491

Source: Sourcebook of Criminal Justice Statistics, 1999, Table 6.20, p. 497.

Table 5.6 Prisoners under Sentence of Death and Executed (1997)

	Percent		Number	
	White	Black	White	Black
On death row (as of Dec. 31, 1997)	56.3	42.2	1876	1406
Executed during 1997	60.8	36.5	45	27

Source: Sourcebook of Criminal Justice Statistics, 1999, Table 6.20, p. 497.

Education

Table 5.7 Educational Attainment of People 25 Years Old and Older by Race, 1960–1999

Year	% Completing 4 Years of High School or More		% Completing 4 Years of College or More	
	White	Black	White	Black
1960	43.2	20.1	8.1	3.1
1970	54.5	31.4	11.3	4.4
1980	68.8	51.2	17.1	8.4
1990	79.1	66.2	22.0	11.3
1999	84.3	77.0	25.9	15.4

Source: Statistical Abstract of the United States: The National Data Book, 2000, Table 249, p. 157.

Table 5.8 Student Achievement on Standardized Tests by Race and Subject, 1996

	Reading		Writing		Math		Science	
Age of Student	White	Black	White	Black	White	Black	White	Black
Age 9	219.9	190.0	216	182	237	212	239	201
Age 13	267.0	235.6	271	242	281	252	266	226
Age 17	294.4	265.4	289	267	313	286	307	260

Source: Black Americans: A Statistical Sourcebook, 2001, Palo Alto, CA: Information Publications, Tables 3.08, 3.09.

Table 5.9 Scholastic Aptitude Test (SAT) Scores, 1975–1998

	Math		Verbal	
Average Mathematics Proficiency	White	Black	White	Black
1975–1976	493	354	451	332
1980–1981	483	362	442	332
1990–1991	489	385	441	351
1994–1995	498	388	448	356
1997–1998	528	426	526	434

Note: The minimum score is 200 and the maximum score is 800. Between 1995 and 1997 the SAT scores were recalibrated, which explains the large increase in test scores between the last two rows.
Source: Black Americans: A Statistical Sourcebook, 2001, Palo Alto, CA: Information Publications, Table 3.12.

Table 5.10 Percent of All People 25 Years Old and Older Who Completed a Bachelor's Degree or More, by Race and Gender

	Males		Females	
Year	White	Black	White	Black
1970	15.0	4.6	8.6	4.4
1975	18.4	6.7	11.0	6.2
1980	22.1	7.7	14.0	8.1
1985	20.8	11.2	24.0	11.0
1990	25.3	11.9	19.0	10.8
1995	27.2	13.6	21.0	12.9
1999	30.6	14.3	25.0	16.5

Source: Black Americans: A Statistical Sourcebook, 2001, Palo Alto, CA: Information Publications, Table 3.32.

Table 5.11 Percentage of 18–24 Year Olds Enrolled in Institutions of Higher Education by Race

Year	White	Black
1975	27.4	20.4
1980	27.3	19.4
1985	29.7	19.6
1990	35.2	25.3
1995	37.9	27.5
1998	40.6	29.8

Source: Black Americans: A Statistical Sourcebook, 2001, Palo Alto, CA: Information Publications, Table 3.18.

Table 5.12 Percentage of All Students Enrolled in Professional Schools by Race, 1997–1998

	White	Black
Registered nursing	81.0	9.9
Osteopathic medicine	78.5	4.1
Podiatry	73.7	6.0
Optometry	73.0	2.4
Pharmacy	68.1	8.1
Dentistry	66.4	5.2
Allopathic medicine	66.2	7.9

Source: Black Americans: A Statistical Sourcebook, 2001, Palo Alto, CA: Information Publications, Table 3.23.

Employment and Earnings

Table 5.13 Unemployment Rates of the Civilian Labor Force 25–64 Years of Age, by Educational Attainment, 1999

Education Level	White	Black
Total	3.1	6.3
Less than a high school diploma	7.0	12.0
High school graduate, no college	3.4	6.7
Less than a bachelor's degree	2.8	5.2
College graduate	1.7	3.3

Note: Unemployment rates as a percent of the total civilian labor force (percent of the civilian labor force that is unemployed).
Source: Black Americans: A Statistical Sourcebook, 2001, Palo Alto, CA: Information Publications, Table 6.17.

Table 5.14 Mean and Median Income of Households, 1980–1999

	Median Income		Mean Income	
Year	White	Black	White	Black
1980	$30,921	$17,814	$36,264	$23,119
1985	31,529	18,758	38,302	24,474
1990	32,545	19,462	40,549	25,858
1999	42,504	27,910	56,904	38,448

Note: Median and mean money income in current dollars, as shown.
Source: Black Americans: A Statistical Sourcebook, 2001, Palo Alto, CA: Information Publications, Table 7.01.

Table 5.15 Mean and Median Money Income of Families, 1980–1999

	Median Income		Mean Income	
Year	White	Black	White	Black
1980	$37,341	$21,606	$42,514	$26,945
1985	38,011	21,887	44,822	27,850
1990	39,626	22,997	47,803	29,578
1999	51,224	31,778	65,215	42,793

Note: Median and mean money income in current dollars, as shown.
Source: Black Americans: A Statistical Sourcebook, 2001, Palo Alto, CA: Information Publications, Table 7.03.

Table 5.16 Percent Living below the Poverty Level, by Year

	Families		Children		Persons over 65	
Year	Black	White	Black	White	Black	White
1980	28.9	8.0	42.1	13.4	36.3	13.3
1985	28.7	9.1	43.1	15.6	31.5	11.0
1990	29.3	8.1	44.2	15.1	33.8	10.1
1995	26.4	8.5	41.9	16.2	25.4	9.0

Sources: Black Americans: A Statistical Sourcebook, 6th ed., 1996, Palo Alto, CA: Information Publications, Table 7.14.

Table 5.17 Fraction of Households in Which One or More Members Received Income from the Specified Sources, 1992

Category	White	Black
All households	82,083	11,190
One or more members received:		
Social Security (%)	28.5	25.1
AFDC or other non-SSI cash assistance	3.7	15.5
SSI	3.2	10.2
Food stamps	6.6	25.0
Housing assistance	3.3	14.5
Free or reduced-price school lunches	5.5	20.5
Employer subsidized health insurance	54.3	43.4
Medicare	26.6	23.1
Medicaid	10.1	30.9

Note: Number of households in thousands.
Source: Black Americans: A Statistical Sourcebook, 2001, Palo Alto, CA: Information Publications, Table 7.19.

Table 5.18 Percent of Households Owning Assets, by Type of Asset, 1998

Type of Asset	White	Black
Interest-earning assets at financial institutions:		
Total	76.6	44.5
Passbook savings accounts	64.2	40.7
Money market deposits	16.7	3.4
Certificates of deposit	19.6	4.3
Interest-earning checking accounts	37.0	13.0
Other interest-earning accounts:		
Total	10.5	1.9
Money market funds	4.0	0.5
U.S. government securities	2.5	0.1
Municipal and corporate bonds	3.1	0.3
Other interest-earning assets	3.6	1.2
Regular checking account	50.9	30.1
Stocks and mutual fund shares	23.9	7.0
Own business or profession	13.6	3.7
Motor vehicle	89.2	64.7
Own home	66.7	43.5
Rental property	9.6	4.6
Other real estate	11.4	4.4
Mortgages	2.5	0.4
U.S. savings bonds	18.5	11.0
IRA or KEOGH account	26.4	6.9
Other assets	3.6	0.8

Source: Black Americans: A Statistical Sourcebook, 6th ed., 1996, Palo Alto, CA: Information Publications, Table 7.20.

Table 5.19 Households Owning Assets: Median Value of Type of Asset, 1988

Median value by type of asset	White	Black
Interest-earning assets at financial institutions	$4,024	$939
Other interest-earning assets	11,199	3,218
Regular checking account	490	428
Stocks and mutual fund shares	4,931	2,259
Equity in own home	44,546	28,683
Rental property	38,052	28,658
Other real estate equity	18,510	10,647
Equity in own business or profession	10,751	1,033
Motor vehicle	4,593	2,868
U.S. savings bonds	583	325
IRA or KEOGH account	9,287	4,129
Other assets	16,271	17,738
Median net worth	43,279	4,169

Note: Median value of assets, by type of asset, in dollars.
Source: Black Americans: A Statistical Sourcebook, 6th ed., 1996, Palo Alto, CA: Information Publications, Table 7.21.

Table 5.20 Labor Force Participation of the Civilian Noninstitutional Population 16 Years Old and Over, By Sex and Age, 1999

	Male		Female	
By Age	White	Black	White	Black
All persons 16 years old and over	75.6%	68.7%	59.6%	63.5%
Persons 16–19 years old	56.4	38.6	54.5	38.8
Persons 65 years old and over	17.2	12.7	8.9	8.9

Note: Participation rate as percent (the civilian noninstitutional population divided by the civilian labor force).
Source: Black Americans: A Statistical Sourcebook, 2001, Palo Alto, CA: Information Publications, Table 6.02.

Table 5.21 Unemployment Rates for the Civilian Labor Force, by Age, 1999

Unemployment rate by Age	White	Black
All ages	3.7	8.0
16–19 years old	12.0	27.9
20–24 years old	6.3	14.6
25–54 years old	2.8	5.9
55–64 years old	2.5	3.9
65 years old and over	2.9	5.0

Source: Black Americans: A Statistical Sourcebook, 2001, Palo Alto, CA: Information Publications, Table 6.11.

Living Conditions

Table 5.22 Marital Status, Persons 15 Years Old and Older, 1998

	White		Black	
	Number	Percent	Number	Percent
Single, never married	44,389	25.4	10,880	43.5
Married, spouse present	97,415	55.8	8,051	32.2
Married, spouse absent	5,294	3.0	1,607	6.4
Widowed	11,457	6.6	1,752	7.0
Divorced	16,153	9.2	2,708	10.8

Note: Number in thousands of persons.
Source: Black Americans: A Statistical Sourcebook, 2001, Palo Alto, CA: Information Publications, Table 1.09.

Table 5.23 Births and Birth Rates, by Age of the Mother, 1998

	White	Black
Live births	3,122,391	610,203
Birth rate per 1,000 population	64.7	71.0
Birth rate per 1,000 women, by age group:		
10–14 years old	0.7	2.9
15–19 years old	45.4	85.3
20–24 years old	107.3	141.9
25–29 years old	119.3	101.9
30–34 years old	90.7	64.8
35–39 years old	37.8	30.5
40–44 years old	7.2	6.7
45–49 years old	0.4	0.3

Note: Live births in number of births; rates as shown.
Source: Black Americans: A Statistical Sourcebook, 2001, Palo Alto, CA: Information Publications, Table 2.01.

Table 5.24 Selected Characteristics of Live Births, 1996

	White births (%)	Black births (%)
Birth weight under 2,500 grams	6.52	13.05
Birth weight under 1,500 grams	1.15	3.08
Mother under 18 years old	3.9	8.9
Mother 18–19 years old	7.2	12.6
Births to unmarried mothers	26.3	69.1
Mother with less than 12 years of school	21.2	26.9
Mother with 16 or more years of school	25.1	11.0
Prenatal care began in first trimester	84.8	73.3
Prenatal care began in third trimester or not at all	3.3	7.0

Source: Black Americans: A Statistical Sourcebook, 2001, Palo Alto, CA: Information Publications, Table 2.08.

Table 5.25 Life Expectancy at Birth, by Sex, 1970–1998

	Male		Female	
	White	Black	White	Black
1970	68.0	60.0	75.6	68.3
1975	69.5	62.4	77.3	71.3
1980	70.7	63.8	78.1	72.5
1985	71.8	65.0	78.7	73.4
1990	72.7	64.5	79.4	73.6
1995	73.4	65.2	79.6	73.9
1998	74.6	67.8	79.9	75.0

Sources: Black Americans: A Statistical Sourcebook, 2001, Palo Alto, CA: Information Publications, Table 2.09.

Table 5.26 Infant Mortality, Fetal Deaths, and Perinatal Mortality Rates, 1996

	Black	White
Infant mortality rate	14.7	6.1
Neonatal mortality rates:		
Under 28 days	9.6	4.0
Under 7 days	7.8	3.2
Neonatal mortality rate	5.1	2.1
Fetal death rate	12.5	5.9
Late fetal death rate	5.5	3.3
Perinatal mortality rate	13.3	6.4

Source: Black Americans: A Statistical Sourcebook, 6th ed., 1996, Palo Alto, CA: Information Publications, Table 2.11.

Table 5.27 Selected Characteristics of Households, 1997

	Black	White
Marital status and type of householder		
All households, both sexes	12,474	86,106
Family households	8,408	59,511
Married couple families	3,921	48,066
Male householder, no wife present	562	3,137
Female householder, no husband present	3,926	8,308
Nonfamily households	4,066	26,596
Male householder	1,876	11,725
-living alone	1,594	9,018
Female householder	2,190	14,871
-living alone	1,982	12,980
Housing Tenure		
All tenures	12,474	86,106
Own housing unit	935	4,242
Rent housing unit	6,529	24,635
Residence		
All residences	12,474	86,106
Northeast	2,286	16,926
Midwest	2,288	21,465
South	6,814	28,948
West	1,086	18,307
Inside Metro Areas	10,761	67,800
Outside Metro Areas	1,713	18,307

Source: Black Americans: A Statistical Sourcebook, 6th ed., 1996, Palo Alto, CA: Information Publications, Table 1.18.

Table 5.28 Families with Children under 18 Years Old, 1997

	White		Black	
	Number	Percent	Number	Percent
Total	58,934		8,455	
All families with children under 18 years old	28,236	47.9	4,886	57.8
Married couple families	21,914	37.2	1,974	23.3
Male householder families	1,325	2.2	319	3.8
Female householder families	4,997	8.5	2,594	30.7

Note: Number in thousands of family households

Source: Black Americans: A Statistical Sourcebook, 6th ed., 1996, Palo Alto, CA: Information Publications, Table 4.08.

Political Participation

Table 5.29 U.S. Population, 1790–2000

Year	Total	White Number	White % of Total	Black Number	Black % of Total
1790	3,929	3,172	80.7	757	19.3
1800	5,308	4,306	81.1	1,002	18.9
1850	21,305	19,533	91.7	1,772	8.3
1900	75,994	66,809	87.9	8,834	11.6
1950	150,697	134,942	89.5	15,042	10.2
1960	179,324	158,832	88.6	18,872	10.5
1970	203,236	178,098	87.6	22,581	11.1
1980	226,546	194,713	85.9	26,683	11.8
1990	238,727	208,741	87.4	29,986	12.6
2000	275,306	226,266	82.2	35,332	12.8

Source: Statistical Abstract of the United States: The National Data Book, 2000, Table 10, p. 12.

Table 5.30 Black Elected Officials by Type of Office Held, 1970–1998

Year	Education	Law enforcement	City and county offices	U.S. and state legislatures	Total
1970	362	213	715	179	1,469
1980	1,206	526	2,832	326	4,890
1990	1,645	769	4,485	436	7,335
1998	2,008	998	5,210	614	8,830

Source: Statistical Abstract of the United States: The National Data Book, 2000, Table 473, p. 288.

Table 5.31 Members of the U.S. House of Representatives and Senate

Congress, Year	White House of Reps.	White Senate	Black House of Reps.	Black Senate
98th Congress, 1981	415	97	17	0
99th Congress, 1983	411	98	21	0
100th Congress, 1985	412	98	20	0
101st Congress, 1987	408	98	23	0
102nd Congress, 1989	406	98	24	0
103rd Congress, 1991	407	98	25	0
104th Congress, 1993	393	97	38	1
105th Congress, 1995	391	97	40	1

Source: Black Americans: A Statistical Sourcebook, 6th Ed., 1996, Palo Alto, CA: Information Publications, Table 4.02.

Quotations

"Four score and seven years ago, our fathers brought forth on this continent a new nation conceived in liberty and dedicated to the proposition that all men are created equal."

—President Abraham Lincoln,
Gettysburg Address, 1863

"I never run my train off the track, and I never lost a passenger."

—Harriet Tubman, 1865

"I freed thousands of slaves; I could have freed a thousand more, if only they had known they were slaves."

—Harriet Tubman, 1865

"Nobody needs to explain to a Negro the difference between the law in books and the law in action. . . . A lawyer's either a social engineer, or he's a parasite on society."

—Charles Hamilton Houston,
Report on Negro Lawyers, 1927

"The basic conflict is not really over the buses. It is evil we are seeking to defeat, not the persons victimized by evil. . . . As I like to say to the people in Montgomery, Alabama, 'The tension in this city is not between white people and Negro people. The tension is . . . between justice and injustice, between the forces of light and the forces of darkness.'"

—Martin Luther King, Jr.,
during the bus boycotts, 1955

"In 1963, on a sweltering August afternoon, we stood in Washington, D.C., and talked to the nation about many things. Toward the end of that afternoon, I tried to talk to the nation about a dream that I had had, and I must confess to you today that not long after talking about that dream I started seeing it turn into a nightmare."

—Martin Luther King, Jr.,
"A Christmas Sermon on Peace," *Testament of Hope,*
edited by James M. Washington,
New York: Harper Collins Publishers, 1991, p. 257

"The Equal Protection Clause commands the elimination of

racial barriers—not their creation in order to satisfy our theory as to how society ought to be organized."

—Justice William O. Douglas,
dissent from *DeFunis v. Odegaard*, 1974

"In order to get beyond racism, we must first take race into account."

—Supreme Court Justice Harry Blackmun,
Bakke, 1978

"It would be impossible to arrange an affirmative action program in a racially neutral way and have it be successful."

—Supreme Court Justice Harry Blackmun,
Bakke, 1978

"To say that race is declining in significance, therefore, is not only to argue that the life chances of blacks have less to do with race than with economic class affiliation but also to maintain that racial conflict and competition in the economic sector—the most important historical factors in the subjugation of blacks—have been substantially reduced. . . . In the final analysis, therefore, the challenge of economic dislocation in modern industrial society is for public policy programs to attack inequality on a broad class front; policy programs, in other words, that go beyond the limits of ethnic and racial discrimination by directly confronting their pervasive and destructive features of class subordination."

—William Julius Wilson,
The Declining Significance of Race, 1978, pp. 152 and 154

"Affirmative action is something we do for ourselves as an inclusive society that views diversity as a strength, not a hindrance. It has made the university a better place and it makes all our students better prepared to lead California into the 21st century."

—William Coblentz,
former chair of the University of California Board of Regents,
San Francisco Chronicle, 12 May 1995

"There are those who say we have a level playing field, but we don't yet. There are those who say that all you need is to climb up on your bootstraps, but there are too many Americans who don't have boots, much less bootstraps. And so [I] believe in affirmative action. I believe it has been good for America."

—General Colin Powell,
lecture at Bowie State University, Maryland, 1995

"Invidious discrimination is an engine of oppression, subjugating a disfavored group to enhance or maintain the power of the majority. Remedial race-based preferences reflect the opposite impulse: a desire to foster equality in society."

—U.S. Supreme Court Justice John Paul Stevens,
dissent in *Adarand Constructors, Inc. v. Pena,* 1995

"Affirmative action didn't make me qualified to become chancellor. It made the University of Colorado able to recognize my qualifications."

—Mary Frances Berry,
first African American woman chancellor
at the University of Colorado, 1996

"To change course now would be to retreat from decades of steady hope and progress, to follow pathways far less bright and far less full of promise."

—Neil L. Rudenstine,
Harvard University President,
"Why a Diverse Student Body Is So Important,"
Chronicle of Higher Education, 19 April 1996

"Employers and universities have always engaged in forms of 'preferential treatment.' It was only when race and gender became a factor in the effort to end discrimination that preferences became a problem. Yet there are many examples of long-accepted preferential treatment. University preference of veterans over non-veterans, or of children of alumnae over other youth is one example; employers hiring the sons and daughters of their economic and social equals (the 'old boys club') is another.

Requiring that qualified minorities and women be actively recruited and, whenever appropriate, hired is the only way that previously excluded minorities and women can gain a toehold in companies, occupations, and schools that were previously reserved for white men. It's fairness itself."

American Civil Liberties Union Briefing Paper 17, 1997

"The United States government did something that was wrong—deeply, profoundly, morally wrong. It was an outrage to our commitment to integrity and equality for all our citizens. . . . clearly racist."

—President William Clinton,
apology to the eight remaining survivors
for the Tuskegee Syphilis Experiment
on 16 May 1997

"We've got to realize that the revolution is not over. Color regrettably still makes a difference in this country. We need the kind of programs that break down barriers. . . . And that's why affirmative action is still so very important."

—General Colin Powell,
President's Summit for America's Future, 1997

"[The public] hasn't worked through the fact that you cannot really have a racially diverse student body without taking race into consideration in the admissions process."

—Derek Bok,
"An Interview with Derek Bok,"
coauthor of *The Shape of the River,* 1998, *PBS Frontline*

"Part of my obsession with race is that I believe race and poverty are American fault lines. And yet they are things we have difficulty talking about. A quarter of a century ago, race was part of everyday discussion. Today it haunts us silently."

—Alex Kotlowitz,
University of Georgia charter lecture, 2 November 1998

"Race is not an identity! Race is no more an identity than a taxpayer identification number. It is something that is assigned to you, like a brand on a steer. Identification from the outside often overcomes identity from the inside."

—Barbara Fields,
professor of history at Columbia University,
the Charter Lecture at the University of Georgia on 6 April 1999

"Black excellence, even superiority, is so visible in those areas where we live by high expectations and enforced consequences —sports, music, entertainment, literature. The 'inclusion' we most need now is in the realm of intellectual respect—which can be gained through merit alone."

—Shelby Steele,
"We Shall Overcome—But Only through Merit,"
Wall Street Journal, 16 September 1999, A30

"Sorting people out on the basis of one drop of blood of this racial group or that racial group or this ethnic group or that ethnic group, is very, very dangerous in a society with as rotten a history of racism as we have and, of course, racism continues to be a problem in this society. So race is special. Race is particularly dangerous."

—Abigail Thernstrom,
"An Interview with Abigail Thernstrom," *PBS Frontline,* 1999

"Since African Americans have been forcibly held back from educational opportunity for generations by racist policies written into law, affirmative efforts should be made to ensure they are able to attend universities."

—Cynthia Tucker,
Atlanta Journal Constitution editorial page editor,
Holmes-Hunter Lecture, 11 November 1999

"Race-based affirmative action as a concept is, at its core, a challenge to the relationship between individuals and their government. It is a direct threat to the culture of equality that defines the character of the nation."

—Ward Connerly,
"One Nation, Indivisible," *Hoover Digest,* 2001, No. 1.

"Nobody ever gave me any race or sex preferences. And I made it anyway—high school, college, my own big business, important friends. If I could make it, anybody can, because the playing field is a lot closer to level now. The truth is that preferences at this point are not just reverse discrimination; they're degrading to people who accept them. They've got to go."

—Ward Connerly
explaining his position on racial preferences to
B. Drummond Ayres, Jr., in the *New York Times,* 2001

"I mean, rather, the daily, constant efforts of black Americans, especially in the South, to defend themselves, their families and communities, not only through strategies of outward conformance or of invisibility, but through armed self-defense, since Reconstruction. I mean the shotgun behind the door."

—Jeffrey M. Dickemann,
New York Review of Books, 5 July 2001, p. 66

"Because principled opposition to racial preferences has been wrongly demonized as racist, many whites are hesitant to express their opposition to these programs, despite their belief that such programs are ultimately harmful."

—Shelby Steele,
"The Double Bind of Race and Guilt," *Hoover Digest,* 2001, No. 1

"We have missed the fact that most racial reforms were conceived as deferential opportunities for whites rather than as developmental opportunities for blacks. That these reforms have failed is entirely predictable."

—Shelby Steele,
"The Double Bind of Race and Guilt," *Hoover Digest,* 2001, No. 1

"Racial gerrymandering offends the Constitution."

—Supreme Court Justice Clarence Thomas,
dissent in *Easley v. Cromartie,* 18 April 2001

"As Samuel Hines notes, 'We need each other. Because of the interdependence of community, we all hold the key to other people's freedom. White people can't free themselves of their guilt, fears, and prejudices. Black people can't free themselves of the oppression and injustices. . . . Racial divisions are robbing both sides."

—Michael O. Emerson and Christian Smith,
Divided by Faith: Evangelical Religion and the Problem of Race in America, Oxford University Press, (August 2001), p. 55.

"The black community would particularly benefit if more [voucher] programs like Cleveland's were to become a reality. Half of all the participants in the Cleveland voucher system are Americans of African descent. And in most polls on the subject of school choice and expanded parental options in education, three out of four black Americans favor the very case I am making today."

—J. C. Watts, Jr.
"A Choice That Means a Chance," *Washington Times,*
21 February 2002

"In our view, the court would be wise to leave Michigan's program alone. Nobody ought to be comfortable with the state's treating people differently by race. But the question for the court is not whether preference programs are a good idea or whether their social costs outweigh their benefits. It is whether they so violate the basic ground rules of American democracy that they should be removed from the policymaking table altogether. It is certainly reasonable to demand that preference programs be carefully designed. But it would be wrong for the courts to decree that equal protection—a doctrine meant to prevent the subjugation of one race by another—demands race-blindness from all schools. Diversity may be an interest whose value is difficult to quantify. But in a multicultural democratic society, where universities often serve as training grounds for citizenship, diversity has educational benefits. For the courts to dismiss the desire to expose students to others unlike themselves as an inadequate justification for a race-conscious policy would be a heavy-handed imposition by judges."

—*Washington Post* editorial, 4 December 2002

References

Hornor, Louise L., ed. 2001. *Black Americans: A Statistical Sourcebook.* Palo Alto, CA: Information Publications.

National Center for Education Statistics. http://nces.ed.gov/

U.S. Census Bureau. 2000. *Statistical Abstract of the United States: The National Data.*

———. 2001. Population Division. Available at http://www.census.gov/population/www/cen2000/phc-t2.html. Cited April 2.

U.S. Department of Education, http://www.ed.gov/.

U.S. Department of Justice. 1995. *Sourcebook of Criminal Justice Statistics.* Washington, DC: Government Printing Office. Available at http://www.albany.edu/sourcebook/.

———. 1999. *Sourcebook of Criminal Justice Statistics.* Washington, DC: Government Printing Office. Available at http://www.albany.edu/sourcebook/.

6

Directory of Organizations

This chapter provides information about organizations that are involved in issues of racial justice. The organizations are listed alphabetically and contain brief summaries of their primary goals and objectives. Contact information is provided, which may include address, e-mail, phone, and/or website. Although all claim to promote racial justice and fairness, it is very interesting to see how little consensus exists about how fairness should be promoted. For example, some of these organizations strongly promote racial preferences and affirmative action as essential to obtaining justice, and others believe such laws are inherently racist and that there will be no racial justice until these types of laws are eliminated.

Affirmative Action and Diversity Project:
A Web Page for Research
Carl Gutiérrez-Jones
University of California at Santa Barbara
Department of English
Santa Barbara, CA 93106
E-mail: carlgj@humanitas.ucsb.edu
Website: http://www.humanitas.ucsb.edu/aa.html

This site presents diverse opinions and facilitates discussion about affirmative action, but does not take pro or con positions. It is a resource that provides scholars, students, and general readers with articles, theoretical analyses, policy documents, current legislative updates, and an annotated bibliography of research and teaching materials. It contains a substantial amount of information on California politics and Proposition 209.

AffirmNet
Christina Vargas Law, List Manager
Office for Affirmative Action
State University of New York at Stony Brook
E-mail: cvargas@vpfm.sunysb.edu

AffirmNet is a bulletin board for exchanging ideas about affirmative action and equal opportunity. AffirmNet promotes communication and interaction between men and women working at educational institutions in the areas of affirmative action and equal employment opportunity to help them create greater diversity in the workplace and eliminate discrimination.

Amadou Diallo Educational,
Humanitarian & Charity Foundation
The Amadou Diallo Educational, Humanitarian
and Charity Foundation
69-06 Grand Avenue
Maspeth, NY 11378
(718) 396-1152
http://www.amadoudiallofoundation.org/

Saikou A. Diallo started this foundation in August 1999 to honor his son Amadou, who was shot repeatedly by New York City Police officers. The foundation's primary objectives are to further education and to support humanitarian causes, charity, and efforts to eradicate police brutality and racial profiling.

American Association for Affirmative Action (AAAA)
Executive Director Jay McCrensky
5530 Wisconsin Avenue, Suite 1110
Chevy Chase, MD 20815
E-mail: jmccrensky@aol.com
Website: http://www.affirmativeaction.org

This organization advances affirmative action, equal opportunity, and the elimination of all types of discrimination. It is designed to help equal employment opportunity and affirmative action professionals be more successful and productive in their careers and to enhance access and equity in employment and economic and educational opportunities.

American Civil Liberties Union (ACLU)
125 Broad Street, 18th Floor
New York, NY 10004-2400
Website: http://www.aclu.org/

The ACLU works to preserve some parts of the Bill of Rights. It focuses on First Amendment rights, equal protection of the law, due process of law, and the right to privacy and works to extend protection of rights to many groups, including racial minorities.

American Civil Rights Coalition (ACRC)
P.O. Box 188350
Sacramento, CA 95818
Telephone: (916) 444-2278
Fax: (916) 444-2279 fax
Website: http://www.acrc1.org

The American Civil Rights Coalition is an advocacy organization that promotes racial and gender equality by eliminating preferential treatment. It provides guidance to individuals and groups who are pursuing antipreference legislation or ballot initiatives, advocates the elimination of racial and gender preferences in federal programs and policies, and monitors California's Proposition 209 lawsuits and implementation efforts.

American Civil Rights Institute (ACRI)
P.O. Box 188350
Sacramento, CA 95818
Telephone: (916) 444-2278
Fax: (916) 444-2279
Website: http://www.acri.org

This organization was created to educate the public about racial and gender preferences, and is associated with the American Civil Rights Coalition.

American Federation of Labor—Congress of Industrial Organizations (AFL-CIO)
Civil and Human Rights Department
815 16th Street, NW
Washington, DC 20006
Telephone: (202) 637-5000
Fax: (202) 508-6902
Website: www.aflcio.org

The AFL-CIO, one of the nation's most influential unions, includes more than 13 million American workers in 65 member unions working throughout the economy. Although originally two separate unions, the two merged in 1955. Unions historically discriminated against blacks or barred them from becoming members, which generated tension and forced some people like A. Philip Randolph to leave the original AFL for the newly formed CIO. However, in the last few decades the AFL-CIO has made a concerted effort to support affirmative action and preferential treatment for minorities in the workforce and education.

American Federation of Teachers (AFT)
555 New Jersey Ave., NW
Washington, DC 20001
Telephone: (202) 879-4400
E-mail: online@aft.org
Website: http://www.aft.org/

The AFT represents about one million teachers, school support staff, higher education faculty and staff, health care professionals, and state and municipal employees. Since the mid-1970s, the union has strongly supported affirmative action. It promotes minority recruitment and development programs and has been especially active in supporting preferential admissions in universities in the recent court cases and providing an amicus brief in support of the University of Michigan in *Gratz v. Bollinger* and *Grutter v. Bollinger.*

Americans United for Affirmative Action (AUAA)
400 Colony Square, Suite 200
1201 Peachtree Street, NE
Atlanta, GA 30361
Website: http://www.auaa.org/index.html

Americans United for Affirmative Action educates the public on the importance of maintaining affirmative action programs and the principles of equal opportunity in employment and education. It argues that affirmative action programs remain vital safeguards and our nation's best tools for removing the roadblocks of racial and gender discrimination. The organization's website features a civil rights library.

***Brown v. Board of Education* National Historic Site**
424 South Kansas Avenue, Suite 220
Topeka, KS 66603
Website: *http://www.nps.gov/brvb/*

This National Historic Site consists of the Monroe Elementary School, one of the four segregated elementary schools for African American children in Topeka, and the adjacent grounds. It commemorates the landmark 1954 Supreme Court decision that ended segregation in public schools.

Campaign for a Color-Blind America
9337-B Katy Freeway, Suite 223
Houston, TX 77024
Telephone: (713) 626-0943
Fax: (713) 522-7714
Website: http://www.equalrights.com

This organization challenges race-based public policies and educates the public about the injustices of racial preferences. It actively challenges racially gerrymandered voting districts throughout the country and race-based admission policies in public schools. It also conducts candidate questionnaire projects that evaluate candidates running for public office, which it distributes to voters.

Center for Equal Opportunity (CEO)
815 15th Street, NW, Suite 928
Washington, DC 20005
Telephone: (202) 639-0803
Fax: (202) 639-0827

The Center for Equal Opportunity is a think tank devoted exclusively to the promotion of colorblind equal opportunity and racial harmony by challenging race-conscious public policies. The CEO focuses on three areas in particular: racial preferences, immigration and assimilation, and multicultural education.

Center for Individual Rights
1233 20th Street, NW, Suite 300
Washington, DC 20036
Telephone: (202) 833-8400
Fax: (202) 833-8410

E-mail: cir@mail.wdn.com
Website: http://www.cir-usa.org

The Center for Individual Rights defends individual liberties and provides free legal representation to clients whose rights are threatened. Its clients have won many important court cases, such as *Rosenberger v. University of Virginia* (the free exercise of speech and religious rights extends to student newspapers) and *Hopwood v. Texas.* It is currently supporting the plaintiffs in two cases challenging the University of Michigan's use of race in admissions decisions for undergraduates and law school.

Citizens' Commission on Civil Rights (CCCR)
2000 M Street, NW, Suite 400
Washington, DC 20036
Telephone: (202) 659-5565
Fax: (202) 223-5302
E-mail: citizens@cccr.org
Website: http://www.cccr.org

The CCCR is committed to revitalizing a progressive civil rights agenda to fight bias and discrimination. It promotes equality of opportunity in education, employment, housing, and political and economic justice. It argues that the federal government has a duty and obligation to enforce civil rights laws.

Citizens' Initiative on Race and Ethnicity
Telephone: (212) 599-7000
Website: http://www.cire.org

This group examines how race affects U.S. social problems and makes recommendations on how race relations can be improved, especially in areas associated with education, economic opportunity, crime, social welfare programs, and the legal arena.

The Civil Rights Project
125 Mount Auburn St., 3rd Floor
Cambridge, MA 02138
Telephone: (617) 496-6367
Fax: (617) 495-5210
http://www.civilrightsproject.harvard.edu/

The CRP's mission is to help renew the civil rights movement by sponsoring scholarly research and resources, putting on conferences, and providing resources for journalists.

Equal Citizenship Project
Telephone: (206) 937-9691
Website: http://www.wips.org/ecp/ecp%20Intro.htm

The Equal Citizenship Project (ECP) is part of the Washington Institute Foundation and is devoted to researching public policy issues that affect the fundamental civil rights of Washington State citizens. The group does research and distributes information on its findings.

Equal Employment Opportunity Commission (EEOC)
1801 L Street, NW
Washington, DC 20507
Telephone: (202) 663-4900
Fax: (202) 663-4494
Website: http://www.eeoc.gov
The U.S. Equal Employment Opportunity Commission (EEOC) was established by Title VII of the Civil Rights Act of 1964. Its mission is to promote equal opportunity in employment through administrative and judicial enforcement of the federal civil rights laws, education, and technical assistance.

Florida Civil Rights Initiative
P.O. Box 10875
Tallahassee, FL 32302
Telephone: (800) 711-5498
Website: http://www.fcri.net

The Florida Civil Rights Initiative strives to bring fairness and equality to the practices of state and local government. It promotes an amendment that would require Florida and its political subdivisions not to discriminate against or grant preferential treatment to any person on the basis of race, gender, color, ethnicity, or national origin.

Frederick Douglass Institute for African and African American Studies
University of Rochester
Rochester, NY 14627
Website: http://www.rochester.edu/College/AAS/index.html

The Frederick Douglass Institute promotes the development of African and African American studies in undergraduate and graduate education and through advanced research at the

University of Rochester. It has served as an interdisciplinary center with a focus on the social sciences.

Habitat for Humanity
121 Habitat St.
Americus, GA 31709
Telephone: (229) 924-6935, ext. 2551 or 2552
E-mail: publicinfo@hfhi.org
Website: http://www.habitat.org

Habitat for Humanity International is a nonprofit, nondenominational Christian organization that provides affordable housing for low-income families, which are disproportionately people of color. Since 1976, Habitat has built more than 100,000 houses in more than sixty countries, including more than 30,000 homes in the United States. Habitat provides trained supervision and utilizes the labor of homeowners and volunteers to build their houses, which are sold at no profit and no interest charged on the mortgage.

Historic Places of the Civil Rights Movement
National Register of Historic Places
National Park Service
1849 C Street, NW
Washington, DC 20240
Telephone: (202) 343-9536 or 343-9500
Website: http://www.cr.nps.gov/nr/travel/civilrights

This is a National Register of Historic Places website that provides detailed information about the historic places of the civil rights movement.

Historically Black Colleges and Universities Network
Website: http://www.hbcunetwork.com

This organization provides information to promote five initiatives (community, leadership, education, economic empowerment, and networking) for the 103 Historically Black Colleges and Universities.

Institute for Justice
1717 Pennsylvania Ave., NW, Suite 200
Washington, DC 20006
Telephone: (202) 955-1300

Fax: (202) 955-1329
Website: http://www.ij.org

The Institute for Justice is a libertarian public interest law firm that pursues civil rights litigation. It supports developing individual initiative and opportunity, and attacks group rights and entitlements.

Journal of Blacks in Higher Education
200 West 57th Street, 15th Floor
New York, NY 10019
Telephone: (212) 399-1084
Fax: (212) 245-1973
E-mail: info@jbhe.com
Website: http://www.jbhe.com

The *Journal of Blacks in Higher Education,* which published its inaugural issue in August 1993, is dedicated to the investigation of the status and prospects for African Americans in higher education. The journal is designed to provide African Americans with new information about the governance, policies, and practices in U.S. colleges and universities.

Leadership Conference on Civil Rights (LCCR)
1629 K Street NW
10th Floor
Washington, DC 20006
Telephone: (202) 466-3311
Website: http://www.civilrights.org/

LCCR, founded in 1950 by A. Philip Randolph, Roy Wilkins, and Arnold Aronson, is a prominent coalition of 180 civil rights organizations. Its mission is to promote the enactment and enforcement of effective civil rights legislation and policy.

Martin Luther King, Jr., National Historic Site
450 Auburn Avenue, NE
Atlanta, GA 30312-1525
Telephone: (404) 331-6922
Website: http://www.nps.gov/malu

This is Martin Luther King, Jr.'s, boyhood home. Visitors can learn what inspired King to become a civil rights leader.

Martin Luther King, Jr., Papers Project
Cypress Hall, D-Wing
Stanford University
Stanford, CA 94305-4146
Website: http://www.stanford.edu/group/King

The King Papers Project is a major research effort to assemble and disseminate historical information concerning Martin Luther King, Jr., and the social movements in which he participated.

National Action Council for Minorities in Engineering (NACME)
Empire State Building
350 Fifth Avenue, Suite 2212
New York, NY 10118-2299
Telephone: (212) 279-2626
Fax: (212) 629-5178
Website: http://www.nacme.org/index.html

The National Action Council for Minorities in Engineering is committed to excellence in education, and promotes the utilization of human resources from all segments of our population.

National Association for the Advancement of Colored People (NAACP)
1025 Vermont Avenue, NW, Suite 1120
Washington, DC 20005
Telephone: (202) 638-2269
Website: http://www.naacp.org

The NAACP is one of the most recognized civil rights organizations in the United States. It works to ensure the political, educational, economic, and social equality of minority citizens.

National Civil Rights Museum
450 Mulberry Street (in the Lorraine Motel)
Memphis, TN 38103-4214
Telephone: (901) 521-9699
Website: http://www.216.157.9.6/civilrights/main.htm

This museum opened in 1991 to provide a comprehensive overview of the civil rights movement in exhibit form.

National Coalition of Blacks for Reparations (NCOBRA)
P.O. Box 62622
Washington, DC 20029-2622
Telephone: (202) 635-6272
Fax: (202) 635-9060
Website: http://www.ncobra.com

The primary objective of the National Coalition of Blacks for Reparations is to promote the distribution of reparations payments to African Americans in the United States.

National Council of Negro Women (NCNW)
NCNWNET.org
Website: http://www.usbol.com/ncnw/index.html

The National Council of Negro Women advances opportunities and the quality of life for African American women, their families, and their communities. It is the umbrella organization for a diverse group of African American women's organizations, ranging from sororities and professional associations to civic and social clubs.

National Education Association (NEA)
1201 16th Street, NW
Washington, DC 20036-3290
Telephone: (202) 833-400
Fax: (202) 822-7974
Website: http://www.nea.org/

Founded in 1857, the NEA is the oldest and largest union of public educators. The organization currently has 2.7 million members who work in pre-K through universities in every state throughout the nation. The NEA has sponsored many programs to support and encourage blacks to succeed as students and employees in public education. It strongly endorses the use of preferential treatment of minorities in employment and education.

National Fair Housing Alliance (NFHA)
1212 New York Avenue, NW, Suite 525
Washington, DC 20005
Telephone: (202) 898-1661
Fax: (202) 371-9744
Website: http://www.incacorp.com/nfha

The National Fair Housing Alliance is a consortium of private, nonprofit fair housing organizations throughout the United States. It is dedicated to eliminating residential segregation and promoting equal housing, lending, and insurance opportunities through education, enforcement, training, and research.

National Political Congress of Black Women (NPCBW)
8401 Colesville Road, Suite 400
Silver Spring, MD 20910
Telephone: (301) 562-8000
Fax: (301) 562-8303
Website: http://www.npcbw.org

The nonpartisan National Political Congress of Black Women seeks to politically empower African American women by encouraging them to run for public office and register to vote.

National Rainbow/PUSH Coalition
930 East 50th Street
Chicago, IL 60615-2702
Telephone: (773) 373-3366
Fax: (773) 373-3571
E-mail: info@rainbowpush.org
Website: http://www.rainbowpush.org

The National Rainbow/PUSH Coalition promotes social, racial, and economic justice by uniting people of diverse ethnic, religious, economic, and political backgrounds.

National Urban League (NUL)
120 Wall Street
New York, NY 10005
Telephone: (212) 558-5300
E-mail: info@nul.org
Website: http://www.nul.org

The National Urban League is one of the most prominent social service and civil rights organizations in the United States. The league assists African Americans in achieving social and economic equality.

National Women's Law Center (NWLC)
11 Dupont Circle NW, Suite 800
Washington, DC 20036

Telephone: (202) 588-5185
Website: http://www.nwlc.org/

The mission of the NWLC is to protect and advance the progress of females in all aspects of their lives. The organization strongly supports the use of affirmative action for both females and African Americans.

Negro Leagues Baseball Museum
1616 East 18th Street
Kansas City, MO 64108-1610
Telephone: (816) 221-1920
Fax: (816) 221-8424
Website: http://www.nlbm.com

This museum opened in 1991 to honor and celebrate the history of the Negro Leagues history, and contains information about the breakthrough of African Americans into major league baseball.

People for the American Way (PFAW)
2000 M Street, NW, Suite 400
Washington, DC 20036
Telephone: (202) 467-4999 or (800) 326-7329
E-mail: pfaw@pfaw.org
Website: http://www.pfaw.org

People for the American Way and its similarly named foundation lobby for progressive legislation and help to build communities of activists to promote diversity and equality.

Project Equality
6301 Rockhill Road, Suite 315
Kansas City, MO 64131-1117
Telephone: (816) 361-9222
Fax: (816) 361-8997
Website: http://www.projectequality.org

Project Equality is sponsored by religious, nonprofit, and for-profit organizations to assist employers to promote equal employment opportunities for all people.

Southern Christian Leadership Conference (SCLC)
334 Auburn Ave, NE
Atlanta, GA 30312

Telephone: (404) 522-1420
Fax: (404) 659-7390

In 1957, the Southern Christian Leadership Conference was organized by the Reverends Martin Luther King, Jr., Ralph Abernathy, Joseph E. Lowery, and Fred Shuttlesworth as an interfaith advocacy movement to promote social, economic, and political justice.

U.S. Commission on Civil Rights
624 Ninth Street, NW
Washington, DC 20425
http://www.usccr.gov/

The Commission's primary objectives are to investigate complaints alleging that citizens are being deprived of their right to vote, to study and collect information relating to discrimination or a denial of equal protection of the laws under the Constitution, to appraise federal laws and policies with respect to discrimination or denial of equal protection, to submit reports, findings, and recommendations to the president and Congress, and to issue public service announcements to discourage discrimination or denial of equal protection of the laws.

U.S. Department of Justice
E-mail: web@usdoj.gov
Website: http://www.usdoj.gov
The U.S. Department of Justice administers and enforce the nation's laws in areas such as consumer fraud, crime, discrimination, immigration, and probation and parole.

U.S. Department of Labor, Women's Bureau
Frances Perkins Building
200 Constitution Avenue, NW—Room S-3002
Washington, DC 20210
Telephone: (800) 827-5335; (202) 693-6710
Fax: (202) 693-6725
Website: http://www.dol.gov/wb/welcome.html

This organization's mission is to promote profitable employment opportunities for women, to enhance their skills, and improve their working conditions. The Women's Bureau believes that affirmative action must be retained to recruit and advance qualified minorities, women, persons with disabilities, and covered veterans. It supports affirmative action training programs and outreach efforts.

U.S. Supreme Court
1 First Street, NE
Washington, DC 20543
Telephone: (202) 479-3211
Website: http://www.supremecourtus.gov

The U.S. Supreme Court is the highest ranking court in our nation. It is composed of one chief justice and eight associate justices, who are nominated by the president and approved by the U.S. Senate.

7

Print Resources

Books

Bardolph, Richard. 1970. *The Civil Rights Record: Black Americans and the Law, 1849–1970.* New York: Crowell.

Provides an insightful examination of the long-term trends in civil rights for African Americans.

Becker, Gary S. 1957. *The Economics of Discrimination.* Chicago: University of Chicago Press.

This Nobel-prize winning author sets up a theory and analysis of discrimination.

Belknap, Michel R. 1987. *Federal Law and Southern Order: Racial Violence and Constitutional Conflict in the Post-Brown South.* Athens: University of Georgia Press.

This book documents the racially motivated violence that occurred in the five years immediately following the *Brown v. Board of Education* decision in 1954.

Bowen, William G., and Derek Bok. 1998. *The Shape of the River: Long-term Consequences of Considering Race in College and University Admissions.* Princeton, NJ: Princeton University Press.

This book gained national attention for one of the most compelling arguments about the benefits of affirmative action.

Bullard, Robert D. 1994. *Dumping in Dixie: Race, Class, and Environmental Quality.* 2d ed. Boulder, CO: Westview Press.

The topic of this book is environmental justice. The author argues that polluting industries follow the path of least resistance and locate in economically poor and politically powerless areas, which are disproportionately composed of low-income African Americans.

Bullard, Robert D., ed. 1993. *Confronting Environmental Racism: Voices from the Grassroots.* Boston, MA: Southend Press.

This book includes twelve chapters written by different people who address issues relating to environmental racism.

Bush, Bernard, ed. 1977. *Laws of the Royal Colony of New Jersey.* Trenton: New Jersey State Library, Archives and History Bureau.

Provides laws of the colony of New Jersey.

Butler, Richard, and James J. Heckman. 1977. "The Government's Impact on the Labor Market Status of Black Americans: A Critical Review." In Leonard J. Hausman, Orley Ashenfelter, Bayard Rustin, Richard F. Schubert, and Donald Slaiman, eds. *Equal Rights and Industrial Relations.* Madison, WI: Industrial Relations Research Association, pp. 235–281.

Examines the efficacy of legal interventions by the government on wage and employment outcomes for African Americans.

Chubb, John E., and Terry M. Moe. 1990. *Politics, Markets, and America's Schools.* Washington, DC: Brookings Institution.

Evaluates the effectiveness of educational reforms, examines how politics and markets affect educational outcomes, and offers proposals for more successful reforms.

Cohn, Elchanan. 1997. "Public and Private School Choices: Theoretical Considerations and Empirical Evidence." In Elchanan Cohn, ed., *Market Approaches to Education.* Tarrytown, NY: Elsevier Science, pp. 3–20.

Discusses market-based educational reforms.

Delk, James D. 1995. *Fires and Furies: The L.A. Riots—What Really Happened.* Palm Springs, CA: ETC Publications.

Provides a detailed examination of the riots that occurred in Los Angeles after the police officers from the Rodney King case were acquitted.

Fogel, Robert W. 1989. *Without Consent or Contract: The Rise and Fall of American Slavery.* New York: W. W. Norton.

Nobel-prize winning author provides a comprehensive account of the beginning, growth, and end of American slavery.

———. 1999. *The Fourth Great Awakening and the Future of Egalitarianism.* Chicago: University of Chicago Press.

Fogel examines how the periodic Great Awakenings have affected our views and commitments to many social issues such as slavery, inequality, poverty, and education.

Fogel, Robert W., and Stanley L. Engerman. 1974. *Time on the Cross: The Economics of American Negro Slavery.* New York: W. W. Norton.

These authors revitalized the study of slavery by using comprehensive databases to test and call into question many of the longstanding beliefs about slavery.

Friedman, Milton, and Rose Friedman. 1980. *Free to Choose.* San Diego, CA: Harcourt, Brace.

This classic book by the Nobel-prize winning author and his wife show how providing the freedom to choose through well-functioning competitive markets promotes the welfare of the society, especially those who are least well-off.

Galenson, David W. 1986. *Traders, Planters, and Slaves: Market Behavior in Early English America.* New York: Cambridge University Press.

Provides interesting insights into both the demand and supply of labor in colonial America.

Genovese, Eugene D. 1965. *The Political Economy of Slavery: Studies in the Economy and Society of the Slave South.* New York: Pantheon Books.

Provides a thorough account of the operations of slavery in America.

———. 1974. *Roll, Jordan, Roll: The World the Slaves Made.* New York: Pantheon Books.

This is one of the most highly cited and widely recognized books about slave culture and the interaction between master and slave on southern plantations during the antebellum period.

Hanushek, Eric A., ed. 1994. *Making Schools Work: Improving Performance and Controlling Costs.* Washington, DC: The Brookings Institution.

This book, written by a national panel for education reform, documents how expenditures on primary and secondary education rapidly increased in the twentieth century and how the quality remained unchanged. It then tries to explain why educational reforms are difficult to implement and outlines what conditions must be met for successful reform.

Higginbotham, A. Leon, Jr. 1978. *In the Matter of Color: Race and the American Legal Process: The Colonial Period.* New York: Oxford University Press.

Examines how colonial American law reflected beliefs and practices about race.

Hornor, Louise L., ed. 2001 [1996]. *Black Americans: A Statistical Sourcebook.* Palo Alto, CA: Information Publications.

Provides comprehensive data about many demographic, economic, and social variables of interest broken down by race.

Kennedy, Randall. 1997. *Race, Crime, and the Law.* New York: Pantheon Books.

Provides a comprehensive discussion of how race intersects with the various aspects of the criminal justice system, including enforcement, jury composition, drug crimes, and the death penalty. The book also examines the historical context of the nation's failure to protect blacks from criminals.

Kleck, Gary. 1997. *Targeting Guns: Firearms and Their Control.* New York: de Gruyter.

A member of the ACLU, Amnesty International, and many other liberal organizations provides a thorough and thoughtful examination of the role of firearms in the United States.

Kocieniewski, David. 2000. "United States Justice Department to Investigate New Jersey Turnpike Shootings." *New York Times,* 4 November, 1.

This newspaper article discusses a 91,000-page report from the New Jersey attorney general's office that examines the state's use of racial profiling.

Kocieniewski, David, and Robert Hanley. 2000. "Racial Profiling Routine; N.J. Documents Show Many Blacks Stopped." *Denver Post,* 28 November, A1.

Examines the U.S. Department of Justice investigation of a 1998 shooting that stemmed from an instance of racial profiling.

Lott, John R., Jr. 2000. *More Guns, Less Crime.* 2d ed. Chicago: University of Chicago Press.

A much-publicized book that argues that allowing law-abiding citizens to carry concealed weapons for self-defense lowers crime.

McDonald, Douglas C., and Kenneth E. Carlson. 1993. *Sentencing in the Federal Courts: Does Race Matter?* Washington, DC: U.S. Department of Justice.

Examines the degree to which sentencing in federal courts is affected by race.

McWhorter, John H. 2000. *Losing the Race: Self-Sabotage of Black America.* New York: Free Press.

This Berkeley linguistics professor contends that African Americans are not advancing economically and socially not because of racism or external matters, but primarily because of the African American culture's emphasis on victimhood, separatism, and anti-intellectualism.

Morris, Thomas D. 1996. *Southern Slavery and the Law, 1619–1860.* Chapel Hill: University of North Carolina Press.

Examines many legal aspects of slavery in the United States.

Myrdal, Gunnar. 1944. *An American Dilemma: The Negro Problem and Modern Democracy.* New York: Harper & Brothers.

This book is one of the earliest scholarly examinations of the role of African Americans in twentieth-century America.

National Association for the Advancement of Colored People. 1969. *Thirty Years of Lynching in the United States, 1889–1918.* New York: Arno Press.

One of the NAACP's first publications, this book carefully documents the lynchings in this nation for a thirty-year period.

Oubre, Claude F. 1978. *Forty Acres and a Mule: The Freedmen's Bureau and Black Land Ownership.* Baton Rouge: Louisiana State University Press.

Contends that one of the great tragedies of emancipation and Reconstruction was the failure to provide economic security for the former slaves, and examines the implications of this lack of provision.

Overby, Andrew. 1971. "Discrimination against Minority Groups." In Leon Radzinowicz and Marvin E. Wofgang, eds., *Crime and Justice, Vol. II, The Criminal in the Arms of the Law.* New York: BasicBooks.

Examines how minorities can be the object of discrimination in criminal justice proceedings.

Richburg, Keith B. 1997. *Out of America: A Black Man Confronts Africa.* New York: BasicBooks.

This book is a challenging account of murderous and gruesome events that occurred during this African American man's three-year assignment covering Africa for the *Washington Post.* The author, while making it explicitly clear that he is not justifying slavery, recognizes that he is much better off than he would be had his ancestors not been forcibly removed from Africa.

Robinson, Randall. 2000. *The Debt: What America Owes to Blacks.* New York: Dutton.

Robinson provides information about current and past disparities between African Americans and whites. He contends that reparations and restitution will help to rectify the significant racial differences in education, the labor market, criminal activity, housing, and many other areas of our culture.

Salter, John R., Jr., and Donald B. Kates, Jr. 1979. "The Necessity of Access to Firearms by Dissenters and Minorities Whom Government Is Unwilling or Unable to Protect." In Donald B.

Kates, Jr., ed., *Restricting Handguns: the Liberal Skeptics Speak Out.* Croton-on-Hudson, NY: North River Press.

Documents how people whom the government has either chosen not to protect or has been unable to protect have benefited from being able to use firearms to protect themselves.

Stampp, Kenneth Milton. 1956. *The Peculiar Institution: Slavery in the Ante-Bellum South.* New York: Knopf.

This classic book generated a renewed interest in the academic study of slavery and overturned many classical stereotypes about this "peculiar institution." Stampp argued that slavery was not primarily a method of regulating race relations, but an extremely effective method of exploiting labor.

Stephenson, Gilbert Thomas. 1969. *Race Distinctions in American Law.* New York: Negro Universities Press.

This book examines how differences in legal rights and protection have been provided for people of different races.

Stith, Kate, and Jose A. Cabranes. 1988. *Fear of Judging: Sentencing Guidelines in the Federal Courts.* Chicago: University of Chicago Press.

Authored by a federal judge and a Yale Law School professor, this book is a comprehensive examination of how judges carry out their duties in light of the federal sentencing guidelines adopted in 1987.

Sutherland, Edwin H., and Donald R. Cressey. 1970. *Principles of Criminology.* Philadelphia: Lippincott.

This text provides a basic introduction to the study of criminology.

U.S. Census Bureau. 2000. *Statistical Abstract of the United States: The National Data Book: 2000.* 120th ed. Washington, DC: Government Printing Office.

This annual statistical reference contains summary statistics of the social, political, and economic organization of the United States.

Wilson, William Julius. 1978. *The Declining Significance of Race.* Chicago: The University of Chicago Press.

One of the nation's most prominent sociologists makes an innovative and interesting argument about the importance of race for a number of socioeconomic issues.

———. 1996. *When Work Disappears: The World of the New Urban Poor.* New York: Alfred A. Knopf.

This book contends that the disappearance of work has had very detrimental effects on individual, family, and neighborhood life in urban areas and explains why the black underclass became isolated and experienced increased economic difficulty while many other African Americans thrived economically.

Woodward, C. Vann. 1974. *The Strange Career of Jim Crow.* 3d ed. New York: Oxford University Press.

Woodward, a prominent historian of the South and African Americans, examines the codes that continued to separate the races in the postbellum South.

Government Reports

National Assessment of Educational Progress. 2001. *The Nation's Report Card, 2001.* Available at *http://nces.ed.gov/nationsreportcard/.*

This government report regularly evaluates the academic performance in eight academic areas of primary and secondary students throughout the United States.

National Center for Education Statistics. September 1996. *Historically Black Colleges and Universities: 1976–1994.* Available at *http://nces.ed.gov/pubs/96902.pdf.*

This report discusses the historical context of Historically Black Colleges and Universities (HBCUs) and provides a statistical overview of their development.

National Commission on Excellence in Education. 1983. *A Nation at Risk: The Imperative for Educational Reform—A Report to the Nation and the Secretary of Education.* Washington, DC: U.S. Department of Education. Available at *http://www.ed.gov/pubs/NatAtRisk/title.html.* Cited 2 April.

This expert evaluation documents widespread failures in U.S. public elementary and secondary schools.

Thernstrom, Abigail, and Russell G. Redenbaugh. 2001. "The Florida Election Report: Dissenting Statement." U.S. Commission on Civil Rights. Available at *http://www.usccr.gov/*. Cited 19 July.

This is the report about the 2000 U.S. presidential election from the dissenting members of the U.S. Commission on Civil Rights.

U.S. Census Bureau Population Division. 2001. Available at *http://www.census.gov/population/www/cen2000/phc-t2.html*. Cited 2 April.

Provides population data about cities, states, and metropolitan areas in the United States.

U.S. Commission on Civil Rights. 2001. "Voting Irregularities in Florida during the 2000 Presidential Election." Available at *http://www.usccr.gov/*. Cited in June.

This is the majority report about the 2000 U.S. presidential election from the members of the U.States Commission on Civil Rights.

U.S. Department of Education, *http://www.ed.gov/*.

This website contains comprehensive information about education in the United States.

U.S. Office of Education. 1969. *History of Schools for the Colored Population*. New York: Arno Press.

Provides an extensive history of the development of schools for African Americans.

U.S. Department of Justice. 1999. *Sourcebook of Criminal Justice Statistics*. Washington, DC: Government Printing Office. Available at *http://www.albany.edu/sourcebook/*.

This annual publication is a comprehensive catalog of the crime data compiled by the U.S. Department of Justice.

Journal and Periodical Articles

Baden, Brett, and Don Coursey. 1997. "The Locality of Waste Sites within the City of Chicago: A Demographic, Social, and Economic Analysis." Working Paper Series: 97.2.

Contains empirical tests of whether waste sites are more likely to be placed in minority neighborhoods.

Baldus, David C., Charles Pulaski, and George Woodworth. 1983. "Comparative Review of Death Sentences: An Empirical Study of the Georgia Experience." *Journal of Criminal Law and Criminology* 74: 661–753.

This study examined more than 2,000 murder cases in Georgia between 1973 and 1979 and concluded that there was no discrimination on the basis of the race of the offender, but the race of the victim was significant.

Billet, Leonard. 1978. "The Free Market Approach to Educational Reform." Rand Paper P-6141. Santa Monica, CA: The Rand Corporation.

Describes how public education has generally failed, especially for the lowest income people in the nation, and argues that a market-based approach will improve school quality.

"Blacks v. Teachers." 2001. *Economist,* 10 March, 27–28.

An examination of how two of the Democrats' bedrock constituencies are fighting over allowing low-income people the ability to choose where to send their children to school.

Bogus, Carl. 1993. "Race, Riots, and Guns." *Southern California Law Review* 66: 1365–1388.

Argues that African Americans have been particularly victimized by guns and the right to bear arms and that all citizens should be subject to stricter gun control regulations.

Bosman, Julie. 2001. "The (No) Free Speech Movement." *Wall Street Journal,* 14 March, A22.

This editor in chief of the *Badger Herald* at the University of Wisconsin examines the controversy over David Horowitz's article that criticized reparations.

Brown, Richard Maxwell. 1971. "Legal and Behavioral Perspectives on American Vigilantism." *Perspectives in American History,* Vol. 5.

Examines why people take the law into their own hands and the implications of doing so.

Butterfield, Fox. 2001. "Number of People in State Prisons Declines Slightly." *New York Times,* 13 August.

This article discusses a U.S. Justice Department report that was released 12 August 2001 about prison population.

Bynum, Russ. 2001. "Court Rulings, Political Shifts Challenge Georgia Blacks in Redistricting." *Athens Banner Herald,* 24 June, D1 and D3.

This article examines how U.S. Supreme Court rulings that allow race as one factor in redistricting decisions sometimes lead to unusual political alliances between liberal African Americans and conservative whites.

Chavez, Linda. 2001. "Outrageous Behavior Nothing New from Head of Civil Rights Commission." *Philadelphia Inquirer,* 12 December.

Discusses how the head of the U.S. Commission on Civil Rights would not allow a presidential appointee to serve on the commission.

cnn.com. 2000. "South Carolina House Approves Final Measure to Relocate Confederate Flag." Cited May 11.

This article discusses the decision by South Carolina's legislature to remove the Confederate battle emblem from the top of the capitol.

Coates, Stephen, and Glenn Loury. 1993. "Will Affirmative-Action Policies Eliminate Negative Stereotypes?" *American Economic Review* 83, no. 5 (September): 1220–1240.

Examines the conditions under which affirmative action policies eliminate or exacerbate the negative stereotypes of the recipients of preferential treatment.

Connerly, Ward. 2001. "One Nation, Indivisible." *Hoover Digest.* No. 1.

Argues that affirmative action works against producing a unified nation and that it produces a mind-set of victimization that impedes the development of African Americans.

Conrad, Cecilia A., and Rhonda V. Sharpe. 1996. "The Impact of the California Civil Rights Initiative (CCRI) on University and

Professional School Admissions and the Implications for the California Economy." *Review of Black Political Economy* 25, no. 1 (Summer): 13–15.

This article uses data from the University of California to determine how ending affirmative action affects undergraduate admissions.

Cottrol, Robert, and Raymond Diamond. 1991. "The Second Amendment: Towards an Afro-Americanist Reconsideration." *Georgetown Law Journal* 80: 309–361.

These authors argue that many gun control laws were designed to or have been enforced in racially discriminatory ways.

Couch, Kenneth, and Mary C. Daly. 2002. "Black-White Wage Inequality in the 1990s: A Decade of Progress." *Economic Inquiry* 40, no. 1: 31–41.

Use data from the current population survey to show that the gap between the wages of black and white males declined during the 1990s by about 6 percent.

Donohue, John J., III, James J. Heckman, and Petra E. Todd. 2001. "The Schooling of Southern Blacks: The Roles of Legal Activism and Private Philanthropy, 1910–1960." Pennsylvania Institute for Economic Research Working Paper 01–036, University of Pennsylvania. Available at *http://papers.ssrn.com/abstract=232549.*

This paper investigates the sources of improvement in black education in the South in the first half of the twentieth century, and demonstrates the important roles of social activism, especially NAACP litigation and private philanthropy, in improving the quality and availability of public schooling.

"Embarrassing Berry." 2001. Editorial. *Wall Street Journal,* 10 December, A18.

Criticizes the head of the U.S. Commission on Civil Rights for inappropriate behavior.

Fede, Andrew. 1992. "Legitimized Violent Slave Abuse in the American South, 1619–1865: A Case Study of Law and Social Change in Six Southern States." *American Journal of Legal History* 29: 93.

A six-state study of how violence toward blacks was legitimized.

Finkelman, Paul. 1986. "Prelude to the Fourteenth Amendment: Black Legal Rights in the Antebellum North." *Rutgers Law Journal* 17: 415.

Examines the legal rights of African Americans in the antebellum period. Justice was impeded by the inability of blacks to be members of juries. Prior to the Civil War, Massachusetts was the only state that allowed blacks to serve on juries.

Gigot, Paul A. 2000. "Why Democrats Let Gore Fight On, and On, and . . ." *Wall Street Journal,* 1 December, A14.

Examines the 2000 U.S. presidential election in Florida.

Greene, Jay P. October 1999. "The Racial, Economic, and Religious Context of Parental Choice in Cleveland." Working Paper of the Program on Education Policy and Governance, Harvard University.

Shows that despite the claims of critics, school vouchers in Cleveland contribute to racial integration by providing families with access to private schools that, on average, are better racially integrated than are the public schools in the Cleveland metropolitan area.

———. February 2001. "An Evaluation of the Florida A-Plus Accountability and School Choice Program." Working Paper of the Program on Education Policy and Governance, Harvard University.

Shows that low-quality public schools that will lose funding if their students continue to do poorly significantly improve student performance. Schools respond when they know their students might be provided with vouchers to attend higher quality schools.

Hagan, John. 1974. "Extra-Legal Attributes and Criminal Sentencing: An Assessment of a Sociological Viewpoint." *Law and Society Review* 8, no. 3: 3357–3384.

Provides a helpful summary of research about racial differences in the criminal justice system.

Hofer, Paul J., Kevin R. Blackwell, and Barry R. Ruback. 1999. "The Effect of the Federal Sentencing Guidelines on Inter-Judge

Sentencing Disparity." *Journal of Criminal Law and Criminology* 90, no. 1: 239–322.

These authors examine how the U.S. federal sentencing guidelines have affected sentencing disparities across judges.

Horowitz, David. 2000. "Ten Reasons Why Reparations for Slavery Are a Bad Idea for Black People—And Racist Too." Available at *salon.com*. Cited 30 May.

Horowitz generated significant controversy in early 2001 by publishing an advertisement in college newspapers based on this article.

Howell, William G., Patrick J. Wolf, Paul E. Peterson, and David E. Campbell. August 2000. "Test-Score Effects of School Vouchers in Dayton, Ohio, New York City, and Washington, D.C.: Evidence from Randomized Field Trials." Working Paper of the Program on Education Policy and Governance, Harvard University.

This paper shows that the vast majority of beneficiaries of vouchers in Dayton, Ohio, New York City, and Washington, D.C. are African American and Hispanic. It also shows that the overall test scores of African Americans students who switched from public to private schools improved in all three cities.

Hoxby, Caroline M. September 2001. "How School Choice Affects the Achievement of Public School Students." Working Paper of Harvard University. Available at *http://post.economics.harvard.edu/faculty/hoxby/papers/choice_sep01.pdf.*

This is one of the first papers to determine how school alternatives like charter schools and vouchers affect the performance of the students who do not choose or are not eligible to move.

Jacoby, Jeff. 2001. "No Reparations for Slavery." *Boston Globe,* 5 February, A15.

This two-part article by a *Boston Globe* journalist examines the difficulties of creating a just reparations policy.

John-Hall, Annette. 2001. "Once Unlikely, Reparations are Now a Concept Defended and Decried." *Athens Banner Herald,* 1 April, B1 and B6.

Studies the general trend toward a greater willingness of

people to consider reparations for slavery and other types of reparations.

Kleck, Gary. 1981. "Racial Discrimination in Criminal Sentencing: A Critical Evaluation of the Evidence with Additional Evidence on the Death Penalty." *American Sociological Review* 46: 783–805.

Examines the degree to which race affects death penalty outcomes.

Knowles, John, Nicola Persico, and Petra Todd. 2001. "Racial Bias in Motor Vehicle Searches: Theory and Evidence." *Journal of Political Economy* 109 (February): 203–229.

The authors thoroughly analyze vehicle search data from Maryland and conclude that police do not exhibit racial prejudice in their arrest patterns.

Ladd, Helen F. 1998. "Evidence on Discrimination in Mortgage Lending." *Journal of Economic Perspectives* 12, no. 2 (Spring): 41–62.

Provides a comprehensive summary of the research on racial differences in mortgage lending.

Lindgren, James, and Justin Lee Heather. 2001. "Counting Guns in Early America." Working Paper of Northwestern University. Available at *http://www.law.nwu.edu/faculty/fulltime/Lindgren/Lindgren.html.*

This paper tries to replicate the results about gun ownership in the early colonial period published by Michael A. Bellesiles in *Arming America.* The authors show that data from probate records directly contradict Bellesiles's claims, and that he significantly understated the rate of gun ownership in colonial America.

Lotozo, Eils. 2001. "David Horowitz and His Ad Bolster His Incendiary Reputation." *Athens Banner Herald,* 1 April, B1 and B5.

Examines the controversy surrounding the decisions of college newspapers to print an advertisement that listed ten reasons why reparations for slavery is a bad idea.

Lott, John R., Jr. 2001. "On Thin Ice; Florida Voter Discrimination Claims Groundless." *Washington Times,* 31 July, A17.

Discusses how the U.S. Commission on Civil Rights provided

neither financial assistance for independent research about the U.S. presidential election results nor the statistical analysis of their own work.

———. May 2001. "Documenting Unusual Declines in Republican Voting Rates in Florida's Western Panhandle Counties in 2000." Working Paper of Yale Law School. Available at *http://papers.ssrn.com/sol3/papers.cfm?abstract_id=276278.*

Examines the allegations about how the media influenced the voting in the Florida panhandle during the evening of the 2000 presidential election.

———. July 2001. "Non-Voted Ballots and Discrimination in Florida." Yale Law School Program for Studies in Law, Economics and Public Policy, Research Paper #256. Available at: *http://papers.ssrn.com/sol3/papers.cfm?abstract_id=276276.*

This paper includes statistical analyses of the spoiled ballots during the 2000 presidential election.

Lott, John R., Jr., and David B. Mustard. 1997. "Crime, Deterrence, and the Right-to-Carry Concealed Handguns." *Journal of Legal Studies* 26, no. 1: 1–68.

This exhaustive study examines data from every county in the United States for sixteen years and shows that implementing laws that permit law-abiding citizens to carry concealed weapons lowers violent crime rates.

Lott, John R., Jr., and James K. Glassman. 2001. "Whose Votes Really Didn't Count in Florida?" American Enterprise Institute, 10 November.

Documents that the ballot spoilage rates in the 2000 presidential election in Florida were highest in counties with African American election supervisors who were Democrats.

Lott, John R., Jr., and John E. Whitley. 2001. "Safe Storage Gun Laws: Accidental Deaths, Suicides, and Crime." *Journal of Law and Economics* 44, no. 2. Available at *http://papers.ssrn.com/sol3/papers.cfm?abstract_id=228534.*

This paper examines the effect safe storage gun laws have on various outcomes.

McKay, Betsy. 2000. "Coca-Cola Agrees to Settle Bias Suit for $192.5 Million." *Wall Street Journal,* 17 November, A3.

This article summarizes Coca-Cola's settlement of charges of racial bias in employment practices.

Mehegan, David. 2001. "New Doubts about Gun Historian." *Boston Globe,* 11 September, A30.

Discusses questions raised about the book *Arming America.*

Miller, John J. 2001. "Segregation Forever?" *National Review,* 14, 24, 26 May.

This article argues that permitting the use of race as a criterion for redistricting promotes segregation and produces many negative consequences for both blacks and whites.

Miller, Steve. 2001. "Civil Rights Panel's Lawyers Say Dissent Is Inadmissible." *Washington Times,* 19 July, A10.

Examines the effort by the U.S. Commission on Civil Rights to suppress dissenting opinions.

Montgomery, Rick. 2001. "Drive for Slavery Reparations Gaining Steam across the United States." *Buffalo News,* 18 March, H1 and H4.

Studies the origins and historical arguments about reparations for slavery.

Most, Doug. 2000. "Shot through the Heart." *Sports Illustrated,* 10 July, 86–97.

A detailed report of how four young men who were going to try out for a college basketball team were pulled over and shot by New Jersey police in April 1998.

"The Mouth That Roared: Jesse Jackson Will Say Anything to Inflame Passions." 2000. Editorial. *Wall Street Journal,* 14 December, A26.

This editorial examines Jesse Jackson's role in the U.S. presidential election of 2000.

Munnell, Alicia H., Geoffrey M. B. Tootell, Lynn E. Browne, and James McEneaney. 1996. "Mortgage Lending in Boston: Interpreting the HMDA Data." *American Economic Review* 86, no. 1 (March): 25–53.

Much publicized study that utilizes the most comprehensive data set available to examine the racial differences in mortgage lending.

Murphy, Kevin, and Finis Welch. 1989. "Wage Premiums for College Graduates: Recent Growth and Possible Explanations." *Educational Researcher* 18 (May): 17–26.

This paper documents the recent increase in wages for highly skilled workers compared to lower skilled workers and examines possible explanations for this trend.

Mustard, David B. 2001. "Racial, Ethnic, and Gender Disparities in Sentencing: Evidence from the U.S. Federal Courts." *Journal of Law and Economics* 44, no. 1: 285–314.

This study, which analyzes every federal offender sentenced between 1991 and 1994, is the most comprehensive analysis of racial differences in sentencing.

National Committee of Blacks for Reparations in America. 2001. "History of Reparations Payments." Available at *http://www.ncobra.com/documents/history.html.*

This table provides information about the history of reparations payments to various groups.

O'Neil, June. 1990. "The Role of Human Capital in Earnings Differences between Black and White Men." *Journal of Economic Perspectives* 4, no. 4: 25–45.

This paper comprehensively documents the differences in earnings between blacks and whites between 1940 and 1990.

Peterson, Paul E., William G. Howell, and Jay P. Greene. June 1999. "An Evaluation of the Cleveland Voucher Program after Two Years." Working Paper of the Program on Education Policy and Governance, Harvard University.

This paper shows that compared to public schools, private schools in Cleveland use vouchers to enroll more African Americans, low income students, and students from single parent households. It also shows that parents are more satisfied with the private schools in the areas of academic program, safety, school discipline, fighting, vandalism, racial conflict, parental involvement, and teaching of moral values.

Pollock, Robert L. 2001. "A Day in Cincinnati." *Wall Street Journal*, 20 April, A14.

This article examines the shooting of Timothy Thomas by a Cincinnati police officer.

Riley, Jason L. 2002. "Black, Successful—and Typical." *Wall Street Journal*, 13 May, A16.

Discusses the rapidly growing economic opportunities for African Americans.

Satel, Sally. 2002. "I Am a Racially Profiling Doctor." *New York Times*, 5 May, 56.

Satel explains that by using racial profiling, she can improve the medical care she provides to African American patients.

Seckora, Melissa. 2001. "Disarming America: One of the Worst Cases of Academic Irresponsibility in Memory." *National Review*, 1 October, 50–54.

Documents the concerns and inconsistencies about the book *Arming America.*

Sellin, Thorsten. 1928. "The Negro Criminal: A Statistical Note." *Annals of the American Academy of Political and Social Science* 140: 52–64.

This article was one of the first scholarly works to examine racial differences in criminal justice.

Smith, James P., and Finis Welch. 1984. "Affirmative Action and Labor Markets." *Journal of Labor Economics* 2, no. 2: 269–302.

This paper examines the impacts of affirmative action on minority wages and employment. It finds that a substantial increase in wages for blacks occurred before affirmative action and that black employment increased the most in firms that were most vulnerable to monitoring and potential sanctions of affirmative action.

———. 1989. "Black Economic Progress after Myrdal." *Journal of Economic Perspectives* 27, no. 2: 519–564.

Provides a broad overview of the economic progress of blacks since Gunnar Myrdal's classic work on race relations *An American Dilemma: The Negro Problem and Modern Democracy.*

"Suppressing Dissent." Editorial. 2001. *Wall Street Journal,* 8 August, A12.

This article examines how Mary Frances Berry and the majority of the U.S. Commission on Civil Rights took very unorthodox strategies to suppress dissenting evidence that blacks were not disenfranchised in Florida during the presidential election of 2000.

Swain, Carol M. 1995. "Where Do We Go from Here?" *New Democrat* 7, no. 3 (May/June): 20–21.

Argues that the costs of affirmative action outweigh the benefits.

Thernstrom, Abigail. 1999. "An Interview with Abigail Thernstrom." *Frontline.* http://www.pbs.org/wgbh/pages/frontline/shows/sats/race/.

Thernstrom critiques *The Shape of the River* by Bowen and Bok, which argues that affirmative action and preferential admissions to colleges have provided substantial benefits to both African Americans and the U.S. population in general.

"What's This about Reparations?" 2001. *University of Chicago Magazine* (June): 38–39.

University's student newspaper was the first to publish David Horowitz's article, "Ten Reasons Why Reparations for Slavery is a Bad Idea—And Racist Too."

Wood, Thomas, and Malcolm Sherman. 2001. "Is Campus Racial Diversity Correlated with Educational Benefits?" National Association of Scholars. Available at http://www.nas.org/reports/umich_diversity/umich_execsum.htm.

These authors use student-level data to empirically test and reject the claim that racial diversity increases the educational benefits.

Yinger, John. 1986. "Measuring Racial Discrimination with Fair

Housing Audits: Caught in the Act." *American Economic Review* 76, no. 5 (December): 881–893.

This paper examines the results of experiments where individuals from white and minority groups, who have been matched according to their family and economic characteristics, successively visit a landlord or real estate broker in search of housing.

8

Nonprint Resources

Hollywood has frequently used issues related to racial justice as the foundation for documentaries, comedies, and dramas. These descriptions are based on my own viewing, Christopher Case's *The Ultimate Movie Thesaurus* (New York: Henry Holt and Company, 1996), James Pallot's *The Movie Guide,* 2d ed. (New York: The Berkley Publishing Group, 1998), *http://www.movies.com, http://www.allmovie.com,* and http://www.tvguide.com/movies.

The movie title is listed in bold, followed by the director, stars, type of film, length of the film in minutes, date of release, the source, and a short description. If two companies are listed in the source, they are in the form original studio/distribution company. If there is only one entry in the source, it means that there is no information available about the distributor.

When watching these films, it is very interesting to notice the striking difference in how racial themes are addressed over time. In the 1940s through 1960s, relatively few films had race as a primary theme. The films that were made at this time were often very subtle in the way they addressed racial justice. Many of these early films featured characters that were either biracial or very light-skinned African Americans. One common theme of these early films was how these light-colored blacks tried to pass themselves off as white and the confusion that resulted from this deception. In the later part of the century, the focus on race became much more explicit, culminating with many films by Spike Lee in the 1990s. Although known mostly for directing hard-hitting films about race, Lee has also acted in numerous movies.

Many of these films are documentaries or historical dramas and are based on extraordinary actions of both African Americans and whites to promote integration or equal treatment based on race. Wars (especially the Civil War and World War II) were frequent backdrops for how African Americans engaged in heroic activity. The military was a natural setting because it started the integration process fairly early. The civil rights movement also provided the setting for numerous films. The integration of schools, dealing with the Ku Klux Klan and recounting the lives of prominent civil rights activists were compelling themes.

Although many actors, actresses, and directors have played a significant role in placing a greater emphasis on racial themes in film, a few people stand out. Sidney Poitier broke many color barriers in the film and entertainment industry. His acting and directing careers span many decades, and he was the first African American to win an Academy Award for best actor for *Lilies of the Field* in 1963.

In the last decade of the twentieth century, many people criticized Hollywood for the lack of African Americans in feature roles. Others expressed concern that even when African Americans excelled they were insufficiently recognized. However, Spike Lee, Denzel Washington, and Halle Berry have emerged as stars of the film industry. At the turn of the century, Washington was one of the most popular actors. He has exhibited an ability to act effectively in a variety of types of films that transcend race and has been acclaimed for his roles in family movies, dramas, action pictures, documentaries, and biographies. In 2002, Washington became the first African American to win the best actor award since Sidney Poitier, for his role in *Training Day.* Also in 2002, Halle Berry became the first African American actress to win the Academy Award for best actress for her outstanding performance in *Dorothy Dandridge.*

Films

Abraham Lincoln: The Presidency
Type: Educational
Length: 24 m.
Date: 1997
Source: Edudex.com

This video profiles the struggles between abolitionist and proslavery forces that engulfed the presidential term of Abraham Lincoln, profiles the individuals and battles of the Civil War, and discusses Gettysburg and the Emancipation Proclamation.

Africans in America
Type: Educational
Length: four 90 m. videos
Date: 1988
Source: Edudex.com, Social Studies School Services/WGBH Boston

This educational series comprises four separate films—*Terrible Transformation, Revolution, Brotherly Love,* and *Judgment Day*—and documents how the struggle over slavery and freedom shaped U.S. history. The program examines the economic and intellectual foundations of slavery in colonial America and reveals how African Americans and their fight for freedom have transformed our nation. The series includes narratives by many prominent people such as John Edgar Wideman, Barry Unsworth, and Colin Powell.

The first film covers 1450 to 1750 and discusses the origins of indentured servitude in Europe, the Portuguese search for gold in Africa and the capture of African laborers, and the growth of the Caribbean and North American colonies. The "terrible transformation" of the title refers to the New World's change from using indentured servants to slaves for labor.

The second film covers 1750 to 1805 and examines slavery in the context of colonial America's fight for independence from Britain. It studies how second and third generation slaves were integrated into their new culture by receiving Christian names, going to Christian churches, learning English, and having less knowledge of Africa than the previous generation.

The third film examines how between 1791 and 1831 the new nation's Enlightenment commitment to equality and freedom directly conflicted with its position on slavery. It discusses the Haitian slave revolt, organized rebellions in America, and how the urbanization of America and Eli Whitney's invention of the cotton gin transformed the lives of American slaves.

Judgment Day is the last installment and examines the period leading to the Civil War (1831–1865). It documents the lives and writings of many prominent African Americans, such as Sojourner Truth, Frederick Douglass, Harriet Tubman, and Dred

Scott. It discusses the Underground Railroad, slave narratives, the rapid growth of the western United States and the controversy about whether these new areas should be slave or free states when granted their statehood. The series concludes by studying the battles and political implications of the Civil War.

All the Young Men
Director: Hal Bartlett
Stars: Sidney Poitier, Alan Ladd
Type: Drama
Length: 87 m.
Date: 1960
Source: Col/RCA

Set near the 38th Parallel, the dividing line between North and South Korea, this movie examines the relationships of U.S. soldiers trapped without reinforcements in an old farmhouse. These soldiers are outnumbered and casualties begin to mount. After the lieutenant dies, black Sergeant Towler (Sidney Poitier) assumes command, which causes friction among the white soldiers. Knowing that racial tension can cause extensive harm during battle conditions, Sergeant Towler defuses the situation when his nemesis, Kincaid (Alan Ladd), is wounded, and Towler gives him a life-saving transfusion.

Amistad
Director: Steven Spielberg
Stars: Morgan Freeman, Anthony Hopkins, Matthew McConaughey, Nigel Hawthorne, and Djimon Hounsou
Type: Historical/Drama
Length: 152 m.
Date: 1997
Source: DreamWorks Pictures

This film, nominated for four Golden Globe and four Academy Awards, recounts the 1839 rebellion aboard the Spanish slave ship *Amistad,* the initial trial, and the case's movement to the U.S. Supreme Court. The slaves who attempt the rebellion are captured and imprisoned in New England. The film's opening scene shows the Africans in a violent takeover of the *Amistad*. The slaves are captured and then imprisoned in New England where former slave Theodore Joadson (Morgan Freeman) attempts to help the slaves by arguing that they were kidnapped. Running for reelection, President Martin Van Buren overturns the lower court's decision in favor of the Africans. Former President John Quincy Adams reluctantly becomes involved for the defense when the case progresses to the Supreme Court.

Amos and Andrew
Director: E. Max Frye
Stars: Nicholas Cage, Samuel Jackson, and Michael Lerner
Type: Comedy/Satire
Length: 96 m.
Date: 1993
Source: Columbia

When African American professional Andrew Sterling (Samuel L. Jackson) moves to an island of mostly white residents, the populace believes he is a crook simply because of his color. The inhabitants contact law enforcement officials, who break into Sterling's limousine and trip its security alarm. When Sterling responds and pulls out his keys to open the car, a skittish policeman believes he is reaching for a gun and opens fire. The police chief, who is running for reelection, arranges a cover-up to maintain his reputation. He hires a drifter to pose as a thief so the cops will have a legitimate reason for "protecting" the vacationing Sterling.

Assault at West Point: The Court-Martial of Johnson Whittaker
Director: Harry Moses
Stars: Mary Jefferson, Peter Maloney, Samuel L. Jackson, and Jim Grimshaw
Type: Drama
Length: 95 m.
Date: 1994
Source: Republic

This film depicts how an African American cadet at West Point endures the harassment from his officers and fellow cadets.

Attack on Terror: The FBI versus the Ku Klux Klan
Director: Marvin J. Chomsky
Stars: Ned Beatty, John Beck, George Grizzard, Rip Torn, and Dabney Coleman
Type: Drama
Length: Each part is 97 m.

Date: 1975
Source:

This made-for-TV movie, based on the book by Don Whitehead, is a two-part series that examines the 1964 murders of three civil rights workers in Mississippi and the subsequent search for justice. Part One shows the FBI's investigation of the trio's disappearance. Upon the discovery of the bodies in August 1964, the authorities follow a trail of evidence that leads to the local chapter of the Ku Klux Klan. In Part Two of the movie, the FBI arrests several local members of the Ku Klux Klan, among them some police officers. However, the suspects are acquitted of all charges.

The Autobiography of Miss Jane Pittman
Director: John Korty
Stars: Cicely Tyson
Type: Drama
Length: 110 m.
Date: 1974
Source: CBS/Prism

This made-for-TV movie was based on the novel by Ernest J. Gaines and won nine Emmy Awards, including best actress, director, and screenplay. In the film, Cicely Tyson portrays Jane Pittman, a fictional African American woman whose life began in slavery and ended at the beginning of the civil rights movement. The viewers learn about Pittman's life through a northern journalist's interview of Pittman who recalls the events of her life.

Bamboozled
Director: Spike Lee
Stars: Damon Wayans, Savion Glover, Jada Pinkett, Tom Davidson, and Michael Rapaport
Type: Comedy/Drama
Length: 135 m.
Date: 2000
Source: 40 Acres and a Mule Filmworks

Spike Lee writes and directs this film about a Harvard-educated African American writer who is trying to develop new shows for African American audiences. As the writer becomes increasingly frustrated with his supervisor and associates, he devises a strategy to get fired. He writes a show he believes is so offensive that he will surely be fired. However, instead of being fired, the show is a put into syndication and becomes very popular.

Band of Angels
Director: Raoul Walsh
Stars: Clark Gable, Yvonne DeCarlo, and Sidney Poitier
Type: Drama/Tragedy
Length: 127 m.
Date: 1957
Source: Warner Brothers

This movie is based on a novel written by Robert Penn Warren and is set in the antebellum South. After her father's unexpected death, Amantha learns that she is deep in debt, and is forced to drop out of her exclusive girls' school. However, even more unsettling is that she learns that one of her ancestors was African American, which under the existing legal system, means she should be sold into slavery. Hamish Bond, a wealthy landowner played by Clark Gable, purchases Amantha, and the two become romantically involved. However, Hamish is impoverished by the Civil War and eventually he must share a secret with Amantha.

Beloved
Director: Jonathan Demme
Stars: Oprah Winfrey, Danny Glover, Thandie Newton, and Kimberly Elise, Beah Richards, Lisa Gay Hamilton
Type: Drama, Historical
Length: 172 m.
Date: 1998
Source: Buena Vista

In this movie, Jonathan Demme adapts Toni Morrison's Pulitzer Prize-winning novel. The story takes place in the late 1800s and focuses on former slave Sethe (Oprah Winfrey) and her daughter Denver (Kimberly Elise) who live near Cincinnati. A strange girl named Beloved (Thandie Newton) enters their lives and casts a spell over the family.

Betrayed
Director: Constantin Costa-Gavras
Stars: Debra Winger, Tom Berenger, John Heard, Betsy Blair, John Mahoney, and Ted Levine

Type: Action
Length: 123 m.
Date: 1988
Source: MGM-UA

A female FBI agent (Debra Winger) infiltrates a Klan-like white supremacist organization in the South. Winger falls in love with a local farmer, who turns out to be a fanatical racist.

The Bingo Long Travelling All Stars and Motor Kings
Director: John Badham
Stars: Billy Dee Williams, James Earl Jones
Type: Comedy/Drama
Length: 110 m.
Date: 1976
Source: MGM/MCA-U

Based on the novel by William Brasher, this movie is about an all-black baseball team in the 1940s. African American baseball pitcher Bingo Long (Billy Dee Williams) forms a barnstorming team. Though boycotted by powerful Negro League manager Sallison Porter, the Bingo Long Traveling All-Stars and Motor Kings flourish, gaining loyal and enthusiastic fan support, thus cutting into the league's profits. Finally, Porter offers Long a deal: if the Motor Kings can win one big game with the Negro All-Stars, Long's team will be allowed to join the league.

Birth of a Nation
Director: D. W. Griffith
Stars: Henry B. Walthall, Mae Marsh, and Miriam Cooper
Type: Drama
Length: 159 m.
Date: 1915
Source: Griffith/Republic

This film tells the story of the Civil War and its aftermath, as seen through the eyes of two families—the Stonemans from the North and the Camerons from the South. The movie highlights the Ku Klux Klan's fight against the new post–Civil War government. This controversial movie sparked protests and riots when it was released, and subsequent showings were picketed and boycotted. As recently as 1995, Turner Classic Movies cancelled a showing in the wake of the racial tensions around the O. J. Simpson trial verdict.

Black and White in Color
Director: Jean Jacques Annaud
Stars: Jean Carnet, Jacques Dufilho, and Catherina Rouvel
Type: Satire
Length: 90 m.
Date: 1976
Source: Lorimar-Warner Brothers

At the outbreak of World War I, a French trading post in West Central Africa attacks a formerly peaceful German post, because France and Germany are at war. This film won the Academy Award for Best Foreign Film of 1976.

Black Legion
Director: Archie Mayo
Stars: Humphrey Bogart, Erin O'Brien Moore
Type: Drama
Length: 83 m.
Date: 1937
Source: Warner Brothers

This socially conscious drama involves a factory worker named Frank Taylor (Humphrey Bogart), who becomes a member of a secret organization called the Black Legion, which uses violent means to drive out immigrants and minorities. The relationship between Frank and his wife is strained by his illegal activity. The tension heightens when the legion orders one of Frank's friends to be executed.

Blazing Saddles
Director: Mel Brooks
Stars: Cleavon Little, Mel Brooks, and Harvey Korman
Type: Comedy, Western
Length: 90 m.
Date: 1974
Source: Warner Brothers

A black man is made sheriff of an old-West town run primarily by Jews. This unusual movie, directed by Mel Brooks and cowritten by Richard Pryor, often utilizes racial humor and is a spoof of Westerns.

A Bronx Tale
Director: Robert De Niro
Stars: Chazz Palmintieri, Robert De Niro, and Lillo Brancato
Type: Drama/Tragedy
Length: 120 m.
Date: 1993
Source: 20th-Savoy

This film explores the life of a young man who grew up in the Bronx during the 1960s and developed a relationship with a mob leader after the young man witnessed a murder the man committed and did not turn him in to legal authorities. It was Robert De Niro's directorial debut and was based on Chazz Palminteri's one-character play.

Brother from Another Planet
Director: John Sayles
Stars: Joe Morton, Daryl Edwards, Steve James, Leonard Jackson, Bill Cobbs, and Maggie Renzi
Type: Fantasy/Science Fiction
Length: 110 m.
Date: 1984
Source: Cinecom

A black escaped slave from a faraway planet, who is the narrator of the film, appears in Harlem. Some people dismiss him because he is unable to speak, while others are impressed by his technical wizardry. He is eventually adopted as a "brother."

Brother John
Director: James Goldstone
Stars: Sidney Poitier, Will Geer
Type: Comedy Drama, Satire
Length: 94 m.
Date: 1972
Source: Columbia

An African American male (Sidney Poitier) visits the Alabama town where he was born and makes it his priority to rid the community of prejudice.

Buck and the Preacher
Director: Sidney Poitier
Stars: Sidney Poitier, Harry Belafonte, and Ruby Dee

Type: Western, Action
Length: 103 m.
Date: 1971
Source: Columbia

Sidney Poitier directs his first feature film and stars as a trail guide who helps a wagon train of former slaves in their journey westward.

Cadence
Director: Martin Sheen
Stars: Charlie Sheen, Martin Sheen
Type: 1990
Length: 97 m.
Date: 1990
Source: Ind/Republic

A young white soldier is sent to African American barracks for punishment and slowly earns the respect of his peers, who must learn how to deal with their prejudiced sergeant.

Carbon Copy
Director: Michael Schultz
Stars: George Segal, Susan Saint James, and Denzel Washington
Type: Comedy, Satire
Length: 93 m.
Date: 1981
Source: Hemdale/Col

George Segal plays a rich executive who is astonished to learn that he has a seventeen-year-old African American son. After meeting his son (Denzel Washington), the father tries to pass him off to his neighbors in his all-white suburb. When he finally acknowledges his parenthood to his wife he suffers many problems, including the loss of his job and a breakdown in his marriage. As a result, he is forced to work in manual labor, which helps him understand the challenges his son faced.

Chocolat
Director: Claire Denis
Stars: Isaach De Bankole, Giula Boschi
Type: Drama
Length: 105 m.

Date: 1988
Source: Orion

A French woman who was raised in a West African colonial plantation family recalls her childhood and remembers the cruel racism directed by the French against the indigenous blacks.

Civil Rights: The Long Road to Equality
Type: Educational
Length: Two 25 m. videos
Date: 2000
Source: Edudex.com

This educational documentary examines the history of the American Civil Rights movement, and includes a teacher's guide.

Civil War: Why, Who, What, When, and Where
Type: Educational
Length: 44 m.
Date: 1997
Source: Edudex.com

This educational film presents a detailed portrait of the Civil War's causes and major actors and explores how issues of race separated the United States.

The Color Purple
Director: Steven Spielberg
Stars: Whoopi Goldberg, Oprah Winfrey, and Danny Glover
Type: Drama
Length: 150 m.
Date: 1985
Source: WB/WB

This movie is based on Alice Walker's Pulitzer Prize-winning novel by the same name. It takes place in the South during the first half of the twentieth century and documents the life of an African American woman who struggles with her abusive husband. The film was nominated for eleven Oscars.

Conrack
Director: Martin Ritt
Stars: Jon Voight, Paul Winfield
Type: Drama

Length: 106 m.
Date: 1974
Source: 20th/Fox

This movie is based on Pat Conroy's book *The Water is Wide,* which describes Conroy's experiences as a teacher in South Carolina. In the late 1960s, a white teacher takes a new position on a small South Carolinian island in a school of all African American students. The school is in physical disrepair and many students are illiterate and lack even the most basic levels of knowledge. This new teacher uses creative teaching techniques to affect his students' lives. Conroy subsequently became a highly recognized novelist who wrote many novels, such as *The Prince of Tides* and *The Great Santini,* both of which were also made into films.

A Conversation with Rosa Parks
Type: Educational
Length: 21 m.
Date: 1997
Source: Edudex.com

This film portrays the life of Rosa Parks and her role in the civil rights movement.

The Court Martial of Jackie Robinson
Director: Larry Pearce
Stars: Andrew Braugher, Ruby Dee, and Daniel Stern
Type: Drama
Length: 94 m.
Date: 1990
Source: Turner

This made-for-TV story documents Jackie Robinson's wartime service and examines racism in the military.

Cousin Bobby
Director: Jonathan Demme
Stars: Jonathan Demme and Robert Castle
Type: Spiritual Biography
Length: 70 m.
Date: 1992
Source: Cinevista / Tesauro

Throughout his long career, Reverend Robert Castle diligently spread his radical message of civil rights and equality at the St. Mary's Episcopal Church in Harlem. Castle's cousin Jonathan Demme stars in the movie.

Crisis at Central High
Director: Lamont Johnson
Stars: William Russ, Regina Taylor, Joanne Woodward, and Charles Durning
Type: Drama
Length: 120 m.
Date: 1980
Source: Time-Life

This made-for-TV movie dramatizes the court-ordered integration of the Little Rock, Arkansas Central High School in 1957. As violence increased, it became necessary for the federal government to assign a military escort for the nine black teenagers who broke the color barriers.

Cry Freedom
Director: Richard Attenborough
Stars: Kevin Kline, Denzel Washington
Type: Drama
Length: 158 m.
Date: 1987
Source: Universal/MCA-U Video

This movie chronicles the story of a white journalist in South Africa who established a friendship with Stephen Biko (Denzel Washington), an outspoken black civil rights leader who was murdered by government troops in 1977. Kevin Kline, who plays the journalist, is determined to tell the truth about Biko. Washington received an Academy Award nomination for his performance as Biko.

Dangerous Minds
Director: John N. Smith
Stars: Michelle Pfeiffer, George Dzundza, Courtney Vance, Robin Bartlett, and Bruklin Harris
Type: Drama/Biography
Length: 99 m.
Date: 1995

Source: Buena Vista

Lou Anne Johnson (Michelle Pfeiffer), a nine-year veteran of the Marine Corps with a degree in education, begins a new job as a teacher at an urban California school filled with students who have severe problems and no interest in learning. Although her African American and Latino students initially dismiss her, she develops unique instructional techniques to motivate her students. *Dangerous Minds* was adapted from a memoir entitled *My Posse Don't Do Homework,* written by Lou Anne Johnson.

The Deadly Deception
Type: Documentary
Length: 60 m.
Date: 1993
Source: Nova, WGBH Educational Foundation, Films for the Humanities and Sciences

This video documents the infamous Tuskegee experiment in which the U.S. Department of Public Health left many African Americans untreated for syphilis. The movie interviews some survivors of the how human subjects were mistreated.

The Defiant Ones
Director: Stanley Kramer
Stars: Sidney Poitier, Tony Curtis
Type: Drama, Action
Length: 96 m.
Date: 1958
Source: UA/MGM-UA

A black convict (Sidney Poitier) escapes from a chain gang with a white convict (Tony Curtis). The men, who despise those of other races, are shackled together and must learn to work together to survive. As they flee the authorities, they develop a friendship. Both the script and the photography won Academy Awards. In 1986, the movie was remade for TV.

The Defiant Ones
Director: David Lowell Rich
Stars: William Sanderson, Thalmus Rasulala, Laurie O'Brien, and Carl Weathers
Type: Drama, Action

Length: 100 m.
Date: 1986
Source: MGM / UA TV

This film is a remake of the classic movie of the same name.

Do the Right Thing
Director: Spike Lee
Stars: Danny Aiello, Spike Lee, and Joie Lee
Type: Drama/Tragedy
Length: 120 m.
Date: 1989
Source: Universal

Director Spike Lee examines the racial and social tensions that occur in one block in Brooklyn, New York, on the hottest day of the year. The movie focuses on three of the block's businesses: a storefront radio station that employs a deejay (Samuel L. Jackson), a convenience store owned by a Korean couple, and Sal's Famous Pizzeria, the only white-operated business in the neighborhood. Tensions between African Americans and Italians increase after the pizza shop is burned.

A Dry White Season
Director: Euzhan Palcy
Stars: Donald Sutherland, Susan Sarandon, and Marlon Brando
Type: Drama
Length: 107 m.
Date: 1989
Source: MGM-UA, UAC

A white South African learns the truth about apartheid in his nation. However, his preconceived notions are challenged when his black gardener's son is arrested and beaten after a protest. After a subsequent arrest, the boy never returns, and the main character learns that the boy was murdered simply to gratify a local policeman. As he explores the boy's disappearance, he learns more about the subjective and violent nature of his nation's segregated system and eventually tries to prosecute the murderer.

Edge of the City
Director: Martin Ritt
Stars: Sidney Poitier, John Cassavetes

Type: Drama
Length: 85 m.
Date: 1957
Source: MGM

Edge of the City examines racial tensions and violence in the New York City railyards and recounts the story of a railroad worker (John Cassavetes) who establishes a relationship with his African American coworker played by Sydney Poitier. Their lives are made difficult by the presence of their mob-appointed supervisor who despises blacks. The supervisor kills Poitier and makes it appear to be an accident. Although the white worker knows the truth behind the murder, he is intimidated and scared into silence. However, the black worker's widow encourages his white coworker to challenge the supervisor.

Flaming Star
Director: Don Siegel
Stars: Elvis Presley, Dolores Del Rio
Type: Action, Western
Length: 92 m.
Date: 1960
Source: 20th/CBS-Fox

In this movie based on a novel by Clair Huffaker, Elvis Presley plays Pacer Burton, a biracial man in the West who was born to a white father and Indian mother. A series of Indian raids and the ensuing reprisals by white settlers divide his family and present Pacer with significant challenges.

Flirting
Director: John Duigan
Stars: Noah Taylor, Thandie Newton, Nicole Kidman
Type: Comedy/Drama/Romance
Length: 99 m.
Date: 1993
Source: Ind/Vidmark

Flirting is set in Australia in the 1960s and details the romantic relationship between an Australian boy and a girl from Uganda who lives in an Australian boarding school. The two youths explore how to express themselves in this biracial relationship, while their friends and schoolmates often challenge their relationship. One interesting character is a classmate played by Nicole Kidman, who had not yet achieved stardom and was in one of her earliest movies.

For Queen and Country
Director: Martin Stellman
Stars: Denzel Washington, Dorian Healy
Type: Drama
Length: 105 m.
Date: 1988
Source: Atlantic/Paramount

This movie describes a black paratrooper's transition from nine years in the British army to his home in England. The veteran faces numerous racist challenges in his home outside of London. His neighbors have suffered from crime, poverty, and unemployment and are searching desperately for a way to contribute to society. His ultimate challenge comes when a law concerning foreign-born citizens is changed and he is no longer considered a British citizen.

For Us the Living
Director: Michael Schultz
Stars: Janet MacLachlan, Laurence Fishburne, Howard E. Rollins, Jr., and Dick Anthony Williams
Type: Drama/Biography
Length: 84 m.
Date: 1988
Source: Charles Fries Productions

This movie recounts the life of civil rights leader Medgar Evers, played by Howard E. Rollins, Jr. The film concentrates primarily on the last years of Evers's life. Evers's hometown of Jackson, Mississippi, was one of the most prominent sites of the civil rights movement. In spite of threats to both him and his family, Evers diligently continued his work until June 1963 when he was assassinated in front of his home at the age of thirty-seven. *For Us the Living* was adapted from a book coauthored by Myrlie Evers, Ossie Davis, and J. Kenneth Rotcop, and was first telecast 22 March 1963, on PBS American Playhouse.

Four Little Girls
Director: Spike Lee

Stars: Chris McNair, Maxine McNair, Helen Pegues, Queen Nunn, Arthur Hanes, Jr., and Bill Baxley
Type: Documentary
Length: 102 m.
Date: 1997
Source: 40 Acres and a Mule Filmworks / HBO

This is the first feature-length documentary Spike Lee directed. It recounts the story of the 1963 bombing of an African American church in Birmingham, Alabama, that killed four young girls. The film examines the decades-long struggle to prosecute the offenders and also provides detailed pictures of the lives of the four girls.

Frederick Douglass: When the Lion Wrote History
Type: Educational
Length: 90 m.
Date: 1994
Source: Edudex.com

This PBS documentary chronicles the life of one of our nation's most famous African Americans. Douglass, born a slave, was taught to read as a young boy by a slave owner's wife. He was an extremely motivated student who continued his education on his own as he grew older. As a free black during the antebellum abolitionist movement and the Civil War, Douglass spoke out against slavery and also served as a consultant to President Lincoln. During Reconstruction and post-Reconstruction, Douglass continued to be a prominent advocate for the recently freed African Americans. In addition, he was one of the early supporters of the women's movement, especially suffrage for women. Douglass, an articulate and highly persuasive speaker, was perhaps the most influential nineteenth-century civil rights activist.

George Washington Carver
Type: Educational
Length: 30 m.
Date: 1998
Source: Edudex.com

This video explores the life of George Washington Carver, who was born into slavery and raised during Reconstruction.

Get on the Bus
Director: Spike Lee
Stars: Richard Belzer and De'Aundre Bonds
Type: Drama
Length: 122 m.
Date: 1996
Source: Columbia Tristar

Directed by Spike Lee, *Get on the Bus* analyzes the lives of men from Los Angeles as they journey to the Million Man March in Washington, D.C., in which many African American men marched to promote racial reconciliation. Financed by a private group of fifteen black American men (among them Will Smith and Wesley Snipes), the film was released one year after the 1995 March and promotes the importance of setting aside differences to work for the common good.

Ghosts of Mississippi
Director: Rob Reiner
Stars: Alec Baldwin and Whoopi Goldberg
Type: Drama
Length: 123 m.
Date: 1996
Source: Columbia

This movie, which received an Oscar nomination, examines the June 1963 assassination of Medgar Evers (James Pickens, Jr.) and the eventual conviction of his killer more than thirty years later. Medgar Evers, an African American civil rights leader from Jackson, Mississippi, was killed in front of his home. Despite persuasive evidence that Byron De La Beckwith was Evers's killer, the all-white juries hearing the initial case refused to convict him. Alec Baldwin plays a young lawyer who, assisted by Evers's widow Myrlie (Whoopie Goldberg), gathers sufficient new evidence to retry Beckwith.

Glory
Director: Edward Zwick
Stars: Matthew Broderick, Denzel Washington, Cary Elwes, Morgan Freeman, Cliff De Young, and Jihmi Kennedy
Type: Historical/War
Length: 122 m.
Date: 1989

Source: Columbia-Tristar

Glory was nominated for nine Academy Awards and won six, including an Oscar for best supporting actor Denzel Washington, best cinematography, and best sound recording. The film is based on Lincoln Kirstein's *Lay This Laurel* and Peter Bruchard's *One Gallant Rush,* and tells the story of the all-black members of the 54th Regiment of the Massachusetts Volunteer Infantry during the Civil War. *Glory* celebrates the Regiment's little-known act of courage at Fort Wagner, South Carolina, during the Civil War, which had been largely ignored because of the heroes' race. Although the Civil War was being fought on their behalf, African American soldiers were often denied adequate provisioning and support, and were frequently assigned to demeaning tasks. Morgan Freeman and fugitive slave Denzel Washington are the leaders of the Regiment, and Matthew Broderick plays the son of an influential abolitionist.

Go for Broke
Director: Robert Pirosh
Stars: Van Johnson, Lane Nakano
Type: Drama
Length: 93 m.
Date: 1951
Source: MGM

This World War II film commemorates the 442nd Regimental Combat Team, a unit composed of Japanese Americans who fought bravely during World War II and challenged the beliefs of their bigoted comrades. Many of the actual veterans of the combat unit acted in the film.

A Good Man in Africa
Director: Bruce Beresford
Stars: Sean Connery, Colin Friels
Type: Drama
Length: 93 m.
Date: 1994
Source: Gramercy-U/MCA-U

This film is based on a novel by William Boyd (who also wrote the film's screenplay) and is about a newly formed African country. One primary theme is that of blacks trying to overcome oppression by whites, and another theme is how the new nation struggles to overcome corruption and moral decadence. Alex Murray, played by Sean Connery, is an important character. He is a Scottish doctor who has lived in Africa for twenty-three years and is one of the few people who has established relationships with both the native peoples and the British colonials.

Grand Canyon
Director: Lawrence Kasdan
Stars: Danny Glover, Kevin Kline, Steve Martin, and Mary McDonnell
Type: Drama
Length: 134 m.
Date: 1991
Source: 20th/Fox

The title "Grand Canyon" is a symbolic title that refers to the racial and economic gaps that typically separate the lives of the main characters. In this film the canyon is bridged by a series of unlikely events when Kevin Kline, who plays an immigration attorney, experiences automobile trouble in a dangerous part of Los Angeles. Danny Glover, who plays a tow truck worker, rescues Kline from being a victim of a gang. Kline expresses his gratefulness to Glover by assisting him and his family in a series of ways.

Guess Who's Coming to Dinner?
Director: Stanley Kramer
Stars: Spencer Tracy, Sidney Poitier, Katharine Hepburn, Katharine Houghton, Cecil Kellaway, and Roy E. Glenn, Sr.
Type: Comedy/ Drama
Length: 108 m.
Date: 1967
Source: Columbia

Joey, a daughter of liberal parents, shocks them when she brings home an African American fiancé, John, a doctor played by Sidney Poitier. Many of the new couple's parents and supporters oppose the interracial marriage. Joey is determined to go ahead with the wedding in spite of peoples' disapproval, but John needs everyone's support before he marries. The film was nominated for ten Academy Awards, including best picture, and won two awards.

Half Slave, Half Free
Director: Gordon Parks
Stars: John Saxon, Petronia Paley, Joe Seneca, and Michael Tolan
Type: Drama
Length: 113 m.
Date: 1985
Source: Sony Video

Half Slave, Half Free was originally telecast on PBS in 1984 as *Solomon Northrup's Odyssey.* This film is based on the autobiography *Twelve Years a Slave,* and recounts the life of Solomon Northrup, a black freedman who was kidnapped in Washington, D.C., and sold into slavery in 1841. Avery Brooks stars as Northrup, who spent a dozen years in servitude in Louisiana before escaping.

Hart's War
Director: Gregory Hoblit
Stars: Bruce Willis, Colin Farrell, Terrence Howard, Cole Hauser, Marcel Iures, and Linus Roache
Type: Drama/War
Length: 125 m.
Date: 2002
Source: MGM/UM

Based on a novel by John Katzenbach, this film examines the racial tensions at a German POW camp in World War II. Lt. Tommy Hart (Colin Farrell) is the son of a wealthy and influential senator who served in a command center but finds it much more difficult in the camp when he is assigned the difficult job of defending two African American Air Force officers.

Heart of Dixie
Director: Martin Davidson
Stars: Ally Sheedy, Virginia Madsen
Type: Drama/Romance
Length: 105 m.
Date: 1989
Source: Orion

In a southern college during the 1950s, students reevaluate their worldview in light of the growing civil rights movement.

Heat Wave
Director: Kevin Hooks
Stars: Blair Underwood, Cicely Tyson, James Earl Jones, Sally Kirkland, and Margaret Avery
Type: Drama/Historical
Length: 92 m.
Date: 1990
Source: Propaganda Films / The Avnet-Kemer Company

Set during the Watts riots of the mid-1960s, this made-for-TV movie tells the story of *Los Angeles Times* reporter Robert Richardson (Blair Underwood), who was the only journalist on staff able to cover the story, because white reporters had difficulty entering the area and interviewing the rioters.

How Stella Got Her Groove Back
Director: Kevin Rodney Sullivan
Stars: Angela Bassett, Whoopi Goldberg, Taye Diggs, Regina King, Suzzanne Douglas, Michael J. Pagan
Type: Romance, Drama
Length: 121 m.
Date: 1998
Source: 20th Century Fox

Stella (Angela Bassett) is a highly successful, middle-aged San Francisco stockbroker who is also a divorced mother. Her intriguing friend Delilah (Whoopi Goldberg) from New York persuades Stella to vacation in Jamaica, where she meets a young, handsome Winston Shakespeare (Taye Diggs). Shakespeare initiates a romance with Stella, who is compelled to reevaluate her life and try to balance her desire for romance with her responsibilities of motherhood and work.

The Hurricane
Director: Norman Jewison
Stars: Denzel Washington, Vicellous Shannon, Deborah Kara Unger, Liev Schreiber, John Hannah
Type: Drama/Biography/Sports
Length: 125 m.
Date: 1999
Source: Universal

This movie examines the life of Rubin "Hurricane" Carter, a top-ranked middleweight boxer in the 1960s who was unjustly convicted for a triple murder in Patterson, New Jersey. Carter proclaimed his innocence throughout his trial and subsequent trials. The movie was nominated for three Golden Globes and one Academy Award, winning a Golden Globe for best actor.

I Passed for a White
Director: Fred Wilcox
Stars: Sonya Wilde, James Franciscus
Type: Drama
Length: 92 m.
Date: 1960
Source: Allied

A light-skinned young black woman moves to New York hoping to pass for a white person. She quickly marries a white wealthy man, but does not tell him the truth about her being black. Eventually the pressures caused by her deception cause her to breakdown.

In the Heat of the Night
Director: Norman Jewison
Stars: Rod Steiger, Sidney Poitier
Type: Drama, Action
Length: 109 m.
Date: 1967
Source: UA/MGM-U

In the Heat of the Night won the 1967 Academy Award for Best Picture in addition to four other Oscars. The movie is set in a small Mississippi town where an unusual murder has been committed, and the town's racist sheriff arrests Sidney Poitier, an African American from the North, for the murder. Eventually Poitier, who is also a law enforcement officer, and the sheriff work together to solve the murder. This film was based on the John Ball's novel of the same name. Two sequels of the movie were made, both starring Poitier. In 1987, a TV series version of *In the Heat of the Night* appeared, with Carroll O'Connor playing the sheriff.

Jungle Fever
Director: Spike Lee
Stars: Wesley Snipes, Annabella Sciorra, John Turturro, Samuel Jackson, Ruby Dee, Spike Lee, Ossie Davis, and Samuel L. Jackson

Type: Drama
Length: 132 m.
Date: 1991
Source: U/MCA

Spike Lee defines "jungle fever" as sexual attraction between members of two races. In this film, he examines the implications of a romantic relationship between an African American architect and an Italian woman. Wesley Snipes is Flipper, the happily married architect, and Annabella Sciorra is Angie, his romantic interest who is engaged to Italian American Paulie Carbonne. The two quickly become romantically involved when Angie takes a job as a temporary worker in Flipper's office. Their relationship generates extensive tension in both families.

Just Cause
Director: Arne Glimcher
Stars: Sean Connery, Laurence Fishburne
Type: Mystery/Drama
Length: 105 m.
Date: 1995
Source: Warner Brothers

A young African American is improperly convicted of raping and murdering a little black girl. Sean Connery, who plays a white law professor, tries to find the real killer many years later in an unexpectedly complicated case.

King
Director: Abby Mann
Stars: Paul Winfield, Cicely Tyson
Type: Drama
Length: 272 m.
Date: 1978
Source: NBC

This movie documents the life of Martin Luther King, Jr., and focuses on his rise to prominence during the 1950s. Cicely Tyson stars as King's widow, Coretta.

King: A Filmed Record . . . Montgomery to Memphis
Director: Sidney Lumet and Joseph L. Mankiewicz
Stars: Sidney Poitier, Paul Newman, Paul Winfield, Joanne Woodward, Harry Belafonte, Burt Lancaster, James Earl Jones

Type: Documentary
Length: 103 m.
Date: 1970
Source: Commonwealth United

This film documents the life of Martin Luther King, Jr., from the 1955 bus boycott in Montgomery, Alabama, to his 1968 assassination in Memphis, Tennessee. The film uses both historical footage from his life and interviews with prominent people who admired King, such as Paul Newman, Joanne Woodward, and James Earl Jones.

The Klansman
Director: Terence Young
Stars: Lee Marvin, Richard Burton, and Linda Evans
Type: Action/Drama
Length: 112 m.
Date: 1974
Source: Paramount

A southern sheriff challenges the local Ku Klux Klan. The town's underlying racial tension quickly explodes when the town's mayor rapes a woman. The mayor, who is also the head of the local chapter of the Ku Klux Klan, blames the rape on an innocent black man.

The Landlord
Director: Hal Ashby
Stars: Beau Bridges, Lee Grant, and Susan Anspach
Type: Satire, Comedy Drama
Length: 110 m.
Date: 1970
Source: UA

A rich, young white man buys an apartment in an area of Brooklyn that is predominantly African American. His parents look upon his decision unfavorably, and the family friction heightens when he becomes romantically involved with an African American woman.

The Life of a Black Cop
Type: Educational
Length: 22 m.
Date: 2000

Source: Films for the Humanities and Sciences

ABC News correspondent David Turecamo reports on the case of black officers who spoke out against police brutality.

Lincoln
Type: Educational
Length: 56 m.
Date: 1992
Source: Edudex.com

This film presents the story of the Civil War and Abraham Lincoln, told largely in his own words.

The Long Walk Home
Director: Richard Pearce
Stars: Sissy Spacek, Whoopi Goldberg, Dwight Schultz, Ving Rhames, Dylan Baker, Erika Alexander
Type: Drama/Historical
Length: 97 m.
Date: 1991
Source: Miramax

This film takes place during the Bus Boycott in Birmingham, Alabama, in 1955 and examines the racial tensions generated by the boycott, which began when an African American woman was arrested for refusing to relinquish her bus seat to a white man. The main character is Miriam Thompson (Sissy Spacek), a wealthy white woman from a privileged family. Because of the boycotts, Thompson must now drive to the African American part of town to pick up her maid, Odessa Cotter, played by Whoopi Goldberg. Thompson, who grew up in a relatively sheltered life, quickly realizes how large the economic and social gaps are between the two families. During the course of the film, Thompson is persuaded by Martin Luther King, Jr.'s, message of nonviolent resistance to injustice in his efforts to desegregate the Birmingham transportation system. Her husband, who is outraged by her behavior, joins a Klan-like organization.

Lost Boundaries
Director: Alfred Werker
Stars: Mel Ferrer, Beatrice Pearson
Type: Drama

Length: 105 m.
Date: 1949
Source: Ind

Lost Boundaries is a tale about a light-skinned African American whose family passes as white in an all-white New England community. When the truth is revealed, the family must respond to the horrified reactions of town members and friends. This 1949 movie was one of the first to start drawing attention to racial themes.

Malcolm X
Director: Spike Lee
Stars: Denzel Washington, Angela Bassett
Type: Drama
Length: 201 m.
Date: 1992
Source: Warner Brothers

Spike Lee's movie recounts the life of Malcolm X (Denzel Washington), the controversial black militant. The film begins with Malcolm's childhood, which included the murder of his father by the Ku Klux Klan and the institutionalization of his mother for insanity. Early in his life Malcolm turns to crime and is eventually convicted and earns a prison sentence. During his prison term, an inmate introduces him to the teachings of the Nation of Islam. Malcolm converts to Islam and becomes a disciple of the Honorable Elijah Mohammed. Malcolm becomes an incendiary speaker by preaching a doctrine of hate against white people and marries Betty Shabazz (Angela Bassett). The film documents the dissolution in his relationship with the Nation and ends with Malcolm's assassination.

The McMasters
Director: Alf Kjellin
Stars: Brock Peters, Burl Ives, and David Carradine
Type: Drama
Length: 90 m.
Date: 1969
Source: Ind/Xenon

A young African American Union soldier returns to his home in the South after the Civil War. After his return, he learns that very little has changed, and he struggles to rebuild his life.

Mississippi, America
Type: Educational
Length: 60 m.
Date: 1995
Source: Edudex.com

This documentary recounts the 1964 Freedom Summer, when a coalition of civil rights activists used voter registration drives to encourage many African Americans in Mississippi to vote. The film includes interviews with key figures of that period and some original footage of events. It concludes by analyzing Mississippi's contemporary crisis of poverty and lack of educational opportunities.

Mississippi Burning
Director: Alan Parker
Stars: Gene Hackman, Brad Dourif, Frances McDormand, Willem Dafoe, and R. Lee Ermey
Type: Drama
Length: 127 m.
Date: 1988
Source: Tri-Star/RCA-Col

This movie examines the Ku Klux Klan's murders of three civil rights workers in 1964. Two FBI agents (Gene Hackman and Willem Dafoe) and a local Mississippi sheriff investigate the disappearance of the three workers. The law enforcement officers solve the case through the testimony of a woman who seeks revenge for the beatings inflicted upon her by her Klan-connected husband. The film received ten Academy Award nominations and won one.

Mississippi Masala
Director: Mira Nair
Stars: Denzel Washington, Sarita Choudhury, Roshan Seth, Sharmila Tagore, Charles S. Dutton
Type: Drama
Length: 118 m.
Date: 1991
Source: Cinecom Entertainment Group

This film is set in the 1970s and tells the story of Indian Jay, a Ugandan resident who with his family fled the rule of Idi Amin and moved to Mississippi. Indian Jay loathes blacks and faces new challenges in the United States when his daughter falls in love with an African American (Denzel Washington). The movie examines how people involved with the couple try to overcome their prejudices.

Mixed Company
Director: Melville Shavelson
Stars: Joseph Bologna, Barbara Harris
Type: Comedy/Drama/Family
Length: 109 m.
Date: 1974
Source: UA

A couple with three children adopts three more children—one Vietnamese, one African American, and one Native American. The film recounts the life of this multicultural family and how it resolves various conflicts.

Murder in Mississippi
Director: Roger M. Young
Stars: Tom Hulce, Blair Underwood, Jennifer Grey, Josh Charles, and C. C. H. Pounder
Type: Drama
Length: 96 m.
Date: 1990
Source: David L. Wolper Productions

This made-for-TV movie addresses the same general topic as the film *Mississippi Burning*—the murders by the Ku Klux Klan of three civil rights workers in 1964. However, rather than focusing on the FBI investigation, this film explores the life of one of the white murder victims, Mickey Schwerner, a northerner who traveled to Mississippi to struggle alongside African American civil rights leaders.

Native Son
Director: Pierre Chenal
Stars: Richard Wright, Jean Wallace, Nicholas Joy, Gloria Madison, Charles Cane, Jean Michael
Type: Drama/Tragedy
Length: 91 m.
Date: 1951
Source: Argentina Sono Film

This is the film version of playwright Richard Wright's 1940 novel *Native Son.* Richard Wright stars as Bigger Thomas, a young African American from Chicago during the 1930s who works as the chauffeur for a wealthy family. Thomas accidentally kills the family's daughter and hides the body because he fears he might be lynched.

Native Son
Director: Jerrold Freedman
Stars: Carroll Baker, Akosua Busia, Matt Dillon, Art Evans, John Karlen, Victor Love, Elizabeth McGovern, and Oprah Winfrey
Type: Drama/Tragedy
Length: 112 m.
Date: 1986
Source: American Playhouse-Cinecom

This film is based on Richard Wright's novel by the same name and is a remake of the classic 1951 film. During the trial of Bigger Thomas, Oprah Winfrey makes a cameo appearance as Bigger's mother.

No Way Out
Director: Joseph L. Mankiewicz
Stars: Sidney Poitier, Richard Widmark, Linda Darnell, Horace (Stephen) McNally, and Mildred Joanne Smith
Type: Drama
Length: 110 m.
Date: 1950
Source: 20th Century Fox

Sidney Poitier makes his film debut as an African American doctor assigned to take care of a wounded criminal who loathes blacks. When the criminal's brother dies in the hospital, the criminal holds Poitier responsible for his death. The criminal eventually plans to kill Poitier and breaks out of the hospital with the doctor as a hostage.

Nothing But a Man
Director: Michael Roamer
Stars: Ivan Dixon, Abbey Lincoln
Type: Drama
Length: 95 m.
Date: 1964

Source: Ind/Touchstone

This movie explores the life of a working-class African American man who has difficulty holding a job and maintaining personal responsibilities. When he becomes romantically involved with a preacher's daughter in his small town, the minister tells him to straighten out his personal life. His father's death challenges him to reevaluate his life.

Pinky
Director: Elia Kazan
Stars: Jeanne Crain, Ethel Waters, and Ethel Barrymore
Type: Drama
Length: 102 m.
Date: 1949
Source: 20th/Fox

Patricia "Pinky" Johnson is a light-skinned black woman who tries to pass herself off as white while studying nursing at a New England medical institute. A white doctor falls in love with Patricia and wants to marry her, but Patricia refuses his proposal. Patricia believes their interracial marriage would not succeed and that Thomas would be unable to endure the attacks people would impose on their marriage. Patricia leaves New England to return to her childhood home in the South, where her family faces new problems.

Posse
Director: Mario Van Peebles
Stars: Mario Van Peebles, Blair Underwood, and Stephen Baldwin
Type: Western
Length: 113 m.
Date: 1993
Source: Polygram

This Western tells the story of racial hostilities between black and white cowboys. During the Spanish-American War, a group of black soldiers is assigned a dangerous mission behind enemy lines in Cuba to recover treasure. Believing that they will be killed when they relinquish the treasure, they flee for their homes instead of delivering the treasure to the colonel. *Los Locos,* filmed four years later in 1997, was a sequel to the Posse.

The Power of One
Director: John G. Avildsen
Stars: Stephen Dorff, Morgan Freeman, and John Osborne
Type: Drama
Length: 126 m.
Date: 1992
Source: Warner Bros

This story is set during World War II in South Africa and is based on Bryce Courtenay's novel. It follows the development of a young boy who takes boxing lessons from an African American boxer (Morgan Freeman); he becomes a boxing champion and antiapartheid leader.

Q & A
Director: Sidney Lumet
Stars: Nick Nolte, Timothy Hutton, and Armand Assante
Type: Drama
Length: 132 m.
Date: 1990
Source: Orion

Q&A was based on the novel by Edwin Torres, a New York State Supreme Court judge whose two other novels were later adapted into the film *Carlito's Way.* In *Q&A,* a New York City police officer shoots an unarmed Hispanic drug dealer, plants a gun on the dead man's body, and creates eyewitnesses to cover up his crime. However, after questioning the officer, the assistant district attorney believes that the officer is guilty. The assistant district attorney exhibits perseverance and creativity in an attempt to solve a complicated case.

Racial Profiling and Law Enforcement: America in Black and White
Type: Educational
Length: 44 m.
Date: 2000
Source: Films for the Humanities and Sciences

ABC News anchor Ted Koppel and correspondent Michel McQueen investigate racial profiling from the points of view of both victims and police.

Ragtime
Director: Milos Forman
Stars: Debbie Allen, James Cagney, Jeff Daniels, Brad Dourif, Fran Drescher, Moses Gunn, Elizabeth McGovern, Kenneth McMillan, Pat O'Brien, Donald O'Connor, and Howard E. Rollins, Jr.
Type: Drama
Length: 155 m.
Date: 1981
Source: Paramount

This film is based on E. L. Doctorow's novel *Ragtime,* a fictional account of the United States in the early twentieth century. The film concentrates on three story lines from the novel: an immigrant artist who becomes a movie director, a playboy who murders an architect for a woman, and an African American man who seeks justice when his car is destroyed by a racist fire chief.

Raisin in the Sun
Director: Daniel Petrie
Stars: Sidney Poitier, Ruby Dee, Claudia McNeil, and Ivan Dixon
Type: Drama
Length: 128 m.
Date: 1961
Source: Col/RCA

This film about a middle-class African American family is adapted from Lorraine Hansberry's award-winning play. After the father of the family dies, the family is torn about how to use the life insurance payment, and the film describes their challenges as they move from the inner city to the Chicago suburbs.

Red Ball Express
Director: Budd Boetticher
Stars: Sidney Poitier, Jeff Chandler, Alex Nicol, Charlie Drake, Judith Braun, and Hugh O'Brian
Type: Drama
Length: 83 m.
Date: 1952
Source: Universal

This World War II film documents the activities of the U.S. Army Transportation Corps, in which many of the outstanding drivers were African Americans denied other types of combat duty. Although beset by some internal differences, those differences are set aside as the corps is called upon to provide ammunition for the Allied offense to retake Paris in 1944.

Remember the Titans
Director: Boaz Yakin
Stars: Denzel Washington, Will Patton, Nicole Ari Parker, and Hayden Panettiere
Type: Drama/Sports
Length: 113 m.
Date: 2000
Source: Walt Disney

This movie is based on real-life events following the 1971 court order that forced three high schools in Virginia to integrate. Immediate controversy ensues when Coach Boone, an African American, is offered the position as head football coach ahead of the highly successful and experienced coach from the white high school who is offered a job as an assistant. The story recounts the town's racial hostility, the attempts among some townspeople to remove Coach Boone from his position, and the manner in which Boone galvanizes his racially integrated team to lead them to the state championship game.

In Remembrance of Martin
Type: Educational
Length: 60 m.
Date: 1996
Source: Edudex.com

This PBS documentary examines Martin Luther King, Jr.'s, leadership in the civil rights movement. Biographical information about King is drawn from many who knew and respected him. The film includes segments from Martin's widow, Coretta Scott King, Ralph Abernathy, Julian Bond, Bishop Desmond Tutu, and former President Jimmy Carter.

Roots
Director: Marvin J. Chomsky and David Greene (Vol. 1) and John Erman (Vol. 2)
Stars: Burl Ives, O. J. Simpson, Moses Gunn, Lorne Greene, Ben Vereen, Madge Sinclair, Cicely Tyson, Thalmus Ramsula,

Edward Asner, Ralph Waite, Ji-Tu Cumbuka, and Maya Angelou
Type: Drama/Historical
Length: 89 m.
Date: 1977
Source: ABC, Warner Home

Roots, based on Alex Haley's best-selling book of the same name, is one of the most successful and highly acclaimed TV miniseries of all time. The film traces Haley's family history from the birth of his great-great-great-grandfather, Kunta Kinte, in 1750 in Gambia through his family's service in bondage in the United States, and its eventual freedom after the Civil War. The miniseries ended its eight-day run as the most-watched drama in television history, with over 100 million viewers watching the final episode.

Rosewood
Director: John Singleton
Stars: Jon Voight, Ving Rhames, Don Cheadle, Bruce McGill, Loren Dean, Esther Rolle
Type: Action, Drama
Length: 140 m.
Date: 1997
Source: Warner Bros.

The movie is based in 1923 in the Florida town of Rosewood, a relatively affluent African American town next to a poor and predominantly white town. A series of events leads a number of whites to form a lynch mob to avenge the honor of a young woman who alleges that a black man assaulted her.

Ruby Bridges
Director: Euzhan Palcy
Stars: Chaz Monet, Penelope Ann Miller, and Kevin Pollack
Type: Drama
Length: 89 m.
Date: 1999
Source: Disney

This movie is based on the true story of Ruby Bridges, a six-year-old African-American girl who scores very well on early scholastics tests and is chosen by the New Orleans school district to be the first African American to integrate that city's public school system.

Sapphire
Director: Basil Dearden
Stars: Nigel Patrick, Michael Craig, and Yvonne Mitchell
Type: Mystery/Drama
Length: 92 m.
Date: 1959
Source: Rank

In London in the 1950s, Scotland Yard inspectors investigate the murder of a black female music student who had been portraying herself as white.

Sarafina!
Director: James Roodt
Stars: Leleti Khumalo, Whoopi Goldberg
Type: Drama
Length: 116 m.
Date: 1992
Source: Touchstone

Sarafina! is an antiapartheid film about a young girl from Soweto, South Africa, who experiences a political awakening. Her teacher (Whoopi Goldberg) encourages the girl to not blindly follow the apartheid system and challenges her to reconsider her views about race-related issues.

Save the Last Dance
Director: Thomas Carter
Stars: Julia Stiles, Sean Patrick Thomas, Kerry Washington, Fredro Starr, Terry Kinney, and Bianca Lawson
Type: Drama
Length: 112 m.
Date: 2001
Source: Paramount

After the unexpected death of her mother, white girl Sarah Johnson moves to Chicago to live with her father. Sarah initially has difficulty adjusting to her new school, but soon befriends Derek, an African American. The two share an interest in dance—although Sarah's love for ballet differs from Derek's enjoyment of hip-hop. As their relationship deepens, Sarah and Derek learn how to face additional pressures from those who disapprove of their relationship.

School Daze
Director: Spike Lee
Stars: Laurence Fishburne, Spike Lee
Type: Comedy, Drama
Length: 120 m.
Date: 1988
Source: Col/RCA

This Spike Lee–directed film examines life at an African American college and is based on Lee's student experience at Morehouse College. Even at an all-black institution, there are differences between the light- and dark-skinned African Americans. Laurence Fishburne plays the main character, and Spike Lee plays a first-year student in a significant supporting role.

Separate But Equal
Director: George Stevens, Jr.
Stars: Sidney Poitier, Burt Lancaster, Cleavon Little
Type: Drama
Length: 194 m.
Date: 1991
Source: ABC/Republic

This movie is based on the landmark trial *Brown v. Board of Education of Topeka, Kansas,* the 1954 U.S. Supreme Court decision that required schools to be racially integrated by overturning the "separate but equal" doctrine established in *Plessy v. Ferguson* (1896). Sidney Poitier plays Thurgood Marshall, the lead plaintiff's attorney, who became the first African American Supreme Court justice.

Shaft
Director: John Singleton
Stars: Samuel L. Jackson, Vanessa L. Williams, Jeffrey Wright, Christian Bale, Busta Rhymes, and Dan Hedaya
Type: Action
Length: 98 m.
Date: 2000
Source: Paramount

John Shaft, a police officer played by Samuel L. Jackson, is assigned with his partner to investigate a racially motivated murder that involved the killing of an African American college student by the son of a wealthy New York couple. Shaft tries to bring the murderer to justice and persuade a key witness to testify.

She's Gotta Have It
Director: Spike Lee
Stars: Tracy Camila Johns, Tommy Redmond Hicks, and Spike Lee
Type: Comedy/Drama
Length: 84 m.
Date: 1986
Source:

Spike Lee directs and acts in this film that examines modern black sexuality. The main character is Nola Darling, a young African American woman from Brooklyn who has ongoing sexual relationships with three men and cannot choose one of them.

Sidney Poitier: One Bright Light
Director: Lee Grant
Type: History/ Biography
Length: 60 m.
Date: 1999
Source: Fox Lorber CentreStage

This PBS film documents the life of Sydney Poitier from his humble beginnings in the Bahamas. Poitier both acted in and directed many of the most critically acclaimed films and broke many color barriers in the film industry. He was the first African American to win a best actor Oscar.

The Skin Game
Director: Paul Bogart
Stars: James Garner, Louis Gossett, Jr., and Susan Clark
Type: Comedy/Drama
Length: 102 m.
Date: 1971
Source: Warner Bros

James Garner and Louis Gossett, Jr., play con men who take advantage of people in the antebellum West. Their scam involves the white Garner selling the black Gossett into slavery for a high price and then liberating him, a scam they repeatedly employ. However, they eventually get into trouble and are assisted by a female pickpocket.

Skinheads USA: The Pathology of Hate
Type: Educational
Length: 54 m.
Date: 2000
Source: Films for the Humanities and Sciences

This educational program provides an extended inside look at the growth of white supremacy groups.

Slavery in America
Type: Educational
Length: 20 m.
Date: 1999
Source: Edudex.com

This film examines the history of slavery from 1619 through the time of the abolitionists.

Soldier's Story
Director: Norman Jewison
Stars: Howard E. Rollins, Jr., Adolph Caesar, Art Evans, David Alan Grier, David Harris, and Dennis Lipscomb
Type: Mystery
Length: 101 m.
Date: 1984
Source: Columbia

Nominated for three Academy Awards (best picture, best supporting actor, and best adapted screenplay), this film was inspired by the Herman Melville novel *Billy Budd.* It is set at a military base in Louisiana in the 1940s where an African American sergeant is murdered. Captain Davenport (Howard E. Rollins, Jr.), who is invited to the base to investigate the murder, believes that two white men were responsible for Waters's death, but his investigation shows that many people of all races had motive to kill the sergeant.

Soul Man
Director: Steve Miner
Stars: C. Thomas Howell, Rae Down Chong, and Arye Gross
Type: Comedy/Satire
Length: 101 m.
Date: 1986
Source: New World

To increase his chances of being accepted to and receive financial aid from law schools, a wealthy white student dyes his skin black. After claiming to be African American, he wins a large scholarship to Harvard. The film portrays the unexpected challenges he faces in trying to obtain a law degree as someone perceived to be an African American.

Sounder
Director: Martin Ritt
Stars: Cicely Tyson, Paul Winfield, Kevin Hooks, Carmen Mathews, Taj Mahal, and James Best
Type: Drama
Length: 105 m.
Date: 1972
Source: Fox

This adaptation of William Armstrong's novel was nominated for four Academy Awards. Set during the 1930s, this movie recounts the lives of African American sharecroppers struggling to survive the Great Depression. After enduring poverty, the family's father steals to provide for his family. The film depicts the struggles the family faces after the father is sent to prison.

As Summers Die
Director: Jean Claude Tramont
Stars: Scott Glenn, Jamie Lee Curtis, and Penny Fuller
Type: Drama
Length: 100 m.
Date: 1986
Source: Ind/Cinergi

Set in the segregationist South of the 1950s, the film portrays the wealthy but decadent members of a landed-gentry white family attempting to defraud a feisty old black woman, on whose property oil has been discovered. An idealistic attorney tries to protect the woman's interests and finds himself with two unsuspected allies, two members of the white family who are seeking to obtain the oil-rich land. This movie was produced as an "HBO Premiere" attraction.

Tick, Tick, Tick . . .
Director: Ralph Nelson
Stars: Jim Brown, George Kennedy

Type: Suspense, Drama
Length: 100 m.
Date: 1969
Source: MGM

Racial hostilities are triggered in a small southern town during the 1960s when the town has its first African American sheriff and a murder occurs. The new officer must prove himself to the townspeople by resolving the crime justly.

A Time to Kill
Director: Joel Schumacher
Stars: Matthew McConaughey, Samuel L. Jackson, Carl Lee Hailey, Sandra Bullock, Kevin Spacey, Brenda Fricker, Ethel Twitty, Oliver Platt
Type: Drama
Length: 150 m.
Date: 1996
Source: Regency Enterprise/Warner Bros

This film, based on John Grisham's first novel, is set in the South during the 1950s or 1960s and opens with a young African American child being brutally assaulted and raped by white men. Concerned that the men will not be adequately punished, the story's star, Carl Lee Hailey (Samuel L. Jackson), shoots his daughter's assailants. Carl Lee's trial triggers extensive protests and rioting and revives the local chapter of the Ku Klux Klan. Carl Lee generates more controversy when he turns down the NAACP's offer to defend him and instead chooses a young white attorney, Jake Brigance (Matthew McConaughey), for his counsel.

Uncle Tom's Cabin
Director: Stan Lathan
Stars: Avery Brooks, Endyia Kinney, Jenny Lewis, Samuel L. Jackson, and Edward Woodward
Type: Drama
Length: 110 m.
Date: 1987
Source: Showtime

This is a movie adaptation of Harriet Beecher Stowe's novel *Uncle Tom's Cabin,* which characterizes Uncle Tom as an intelligent non-submissive slave.

Understanding the Civil Rights Movement
Type: Educational
Length: 47 m.
Date: 2000
Source: Edudex.com

This film examines the events that led to the civil rights movements of the 1960s.

Understanding Race
Type: Educational
Length: 52 m.
Date: 2000
Source: Films for the Humanities and Sciences

This program examines the history and power of the conception of "race," viewing it within historical, scientific, and cultural contexts.

Waiting to Exhale
Director: Forest Whitaker
Stars: Whitney Houston, Angela Bassett, Loretta Devine, Lela Rochon, and Gregory Hines, and Dennis Haysbert
Type: Comedy/Drama
Length: 127 minutes
Date: 1995
Source: 20th Century Fox

Forest Whitaker adopts Terry McMillan's best-selling novel. The central characters are four African American women who are trying to deal with men, careers, and their families.

Walk a Mile in My Shoes: The 90-Year History of the NAACP
Type: Educational
Length: 48 m.
Date: 2000
Source: Edudex.com

The film is hosted by NAACP chairman Julian Bond and documents the role of the NAACP in the United States during the twentieth century.

The Well
Director: Russell Rouse and Leo Popkin

Stars: Richard Rober, Henry Morgan
Type: Drama
Length: 85 m.
Date: 1951
Source: Ind/VCI

This film examines a racially segregated town and how it unites to rescue an African American girl who fell down a well.

The Wilby Conspiracy
Director: Ralph Nelson
Stars: Sidney Poitier, Michael Caine, and Nicole Williamson
Type: Action
Length: 105 m.
Date: 1975
Source: UAC

This film was set in South Africa during apartheid and depicts the story of a white miner who assists a black revolutionary get to safety. This film is based on a novel by Peter Driscoll.

A World Apart
Director: Chris Menges
Stars: Barbara Hershey, Johdi May
Type: Drama
Length: 110 m.
Date: 1987
Source: Atlantic-Paramount

This film tells the story of a teenage girl who grows up in South Africa in the 1960s during apartheid. The film was inspired by South African journalist Ruth First and her daughter Shawn Slovo (who wrote the film's screenplay). In the film, the young girl's mother is imprisoned for her antiapartheid stances. The movie examines how the mother and daughter's relationship is strained and how they try to resolve things.

Websites

Hopwood v. Texas homepage is http://www.law.utexas.edu/hopwood/hopwood.htm.

This page is operated by the Tarlton Law Library at the University of Texas and contains a very thorough archive of materials regarding *Hopwood v. Texas.* All petitions, motions and briefs involving the case can be downloaded. The site also contains many reactions and commentary about the case.

University of Michigan Court Cases on the Use of Racial Preferences in Admissions.
http://www.umich.edu/~urel/admissions/

This website provides updates on the ongoing lawsuits (*Grutter v. Bollinger* and *Gratz v. Bollinger*) filed against the University of Michigan for using race as a factor in admissions decisions at its undergraduate college and law school.

Index

About the Author

David B. Mustard is an assistant professor of economics at Terry College, University of Georgia, in Athens, Georgia.